Protest by the Poor

The New York City-Rand Institute

The New York City-Rand Institute is a nonprofit research institution formed primarily to conduct programs of scientific research and study, and provide reports and recommendations relevant to the operations, planning, or administration of the City of New York. The Institute was established in 1969 as a joint venture by the City of New York and The Rand Corporation as a center for the continuing application of scientific and analytic techniques to problems of urban life and local government. Its trustees are appointed jointly by the City and Rand. Its program includes work on health planning, policy, and delivery; drug abuse; housing; fire protection; criminal justice; welfare; economic development; water resources; and other city problems.

Protest by the Poor

The Welfare Rights
Movement in New
York City

Larry R. Jackson

William A. Johnson

Lexington Books
D.C. Heath and Company
Lexington, Massachusetts
Toronto   London

Library of Congress Cataloging in Publication Data

Jackson, Larry R.
  Protest by the poor: the welfare rights movement in New York City.

  Bibliography: p.
  1. Welfare Rights Movement—New York (City) 2. Public welfare—New York (City) I. Johnson, William Arthur, 1936-   joint author. II. Title.

HV99.N59J25   322.4'4   74-581
ISBN 0-669-93062-8

Published simultaneously in Canada.

Printed in the United States of America.

International Standard Book Number: 9-669-93062-8

Library of Congress Catalog Card Number: 74-581

To Cheryl and Margie

Contents

List of Figures

List of Tables

Preface

This study is concerned with two broad issues. First, it analyzes the origins, growth, and tactics of protest groups involved with welfare in New York City. Second, it examines whether these groups have been responsible, in part, for the recent increase in New York City's Aid to Families with Dependent Children (AFDC) rolls. At the same time, the study considers other factors such as rising grant levels and liberalized acceptances thought to have influenced the city's caseload.

The authors focus on one welfare jurisdiction—New York City. This was done, in part, because both authors were affiliated with The New York City-Rand Institute at the time the study was conceived and executed. Moreover, other studies of protest activity, and especially the caseload increase, have attempted to draw generalizations across welfare jurisdiction boundaries. This has often led to erroneous results.

A study of New York City's caseload increase has general interest. One out of ten of the nation's welfare recipients lives in New York City. Given that one must examine protest activity and the reasons for rising caseloads in the nation as a whole by examining specific welfare jurisdictions, the obvious place to start is New York. In addition, protest activity has occurred in other welfare jurisdictions. There is much of a general nature that can be learned from the experience of this city. Given the availability of suitable data, such as the publicly available information used in this study, there is no reason why the methodology used here cannot be used elsewhere.

This is one of several studies by The New York City-Rand Institute about public assistance in the city. Unlike others, it has been financed entirely from the Institute's own resources in an effort to contribute to knowledge of the welfare rights movement at both the local and national levels.

Acknowledgments

The first part of this study was written under the direction of the late Wallace Sayre and Charles Hamilton of Columbia University. We are deeply indebted to both men for their many comments and suggestions. We are also indebted to Richard A. Cloward of the Columbia School of Social Work who has read and commented on an earlier draft. Joan Wohlstetter of The New York City-Rand Institute provided invaluable research assistance at the beginning of the project, especially in estimating the population at risk discussed in Appendix B. Several pages of Appendix B were originally drafted by Joan Wohlstetter. Elizabeth Durbin of New York University assisted us in a number of ways to understand the operation of New York's welfare system. Susanna Purnell of The Rand Corporation also provided research assistance, while Irving N. Fisher, formerly of Rand, made many useful suggestions about the statistical analysis contained in Chapters 13 through 18. Parts of the draft have been read and commented on by Robert Levine and Peter Rydell of The New York City-Rand Institute.

Our understanding of the welfare rights movement was enhanced by numerous interviews with individuals who participated in welfare rights activities in New York City. Hulbert James, a staff organizer and leading strategist of the New York City welfare rights movement, was especially helpful in providing information and a deeper insight into the dynamics of this urban political movement. Other individuals interviewed were Joyce Berson, Ezra Birnbaum, Grace Cade, Richard Cloward, Cheryl Covian, Father William Duncan, Marty Eisman, Frank Espada, Dave Gilman, James Graham, Mamie Hall, Gloria Joyner, Barbara Laurence, Rhoda Linton, Barbara Lounds, Charlotte Lyons, Sydelle Moore, Carmen Olivia, Stephanie Oursler, Beulah Sanders, and Jeanette Washington.

Finally, we are especially indebted to the National Welfare Rights Organization, the City-Wide Coordinating Committee of Welfare Groups, the Citizens Welfare Action Group, the Poverty Rights Action Center, Mobilization for Youth, and the Brooklyn Welfare Action Council for their permission to have access to their files, memoranda, and other related documents under their control.

Summary

Welfare rights activities were the product of three developments during the 1960s: the civil rights movement, the War on Poverty, and the evolution of social welfare thought. In New York City, the welfare rights movement received initial impetus from Mobilization for Youth. However, it soon developed grass-roots support in the ghetto communities, particularly in Brooklyn and on the Lower East Side, and by 1967 was operating very largely on its own initiative and with its own resources. In 1968 the movement reached its peak. By that time, the movement was able to organize mass demonstrations at city welfare offices to disrupt operations and to extract from the welfare system substantial benefits for its members.

Several generalizations can be made about the growth of New York City's welfare rights movement. First, welfare rights organizations are recipient-oriented; they are primarily concerned with the interests of the welfare population. For this reason, they have tended to stress benefit levels, treatment by caseworkers, and other matters of immediate concern to welfare families. One of the first organized efforts in New York City was the winter clothing campaign. The purpose of this campaign was to increase the amount of winter clothing allowances. This was followed by the minimum standards campaign through which the movement sought to assure to members the full benefits to which they were entitled under law.

The grant level was not the only concern of welfare rights organizations in the city. More dignified treatment by caseworkers, less inconvenience in dealing with welfare officials, and greater protection against termination or the threat of termination of a case, have also been important group objectives. In each instance, however, the groups' objectives have been recipient-oriented; they have sought to improve the position of existing welfare families and not the poverty population as a whole.

We stress this because oftentimes welfare rights organizations are represented as having urged eligible nonrecipients to apply for assistance or having pressed welfare officials to accept a larger number of applicants. In fact, these have not been major activities of the movement. Being recipient-oriented, local welfare rights groups, at least, have not been primarily concerned with getting nonrecipients on to the welfare rolls.

This does not mean, however, that welfare rights organizations have had no influence on openings. Rather, this influence, if it has existed, has been more a by-product of their efforts to obtain higher benefit levels and other concessions for the membership. Welfare rights groups have publicized the availability of welfare by word of mouth and demonstrations at various city offices. They have also helped to reduce the stigma attached to welfare dependency and to increase the self-confidence and even militancy of the poverty population, perhaps emboldening some segments of this population to apply for public assistance. Finally, to the extent that welfare rights activites have influenced the grant level, they have increased incentives for nonrecipients to apply and for recipients to stay on welfare and, in this way, also have affected applications and closings.

A second major point that should be stressed is that welfare rights groups have also been member-oriented, particularly at the local level. The local groups consist primarily of mothers banded together to advance their own immediate interests. Membership gave these mothers an advantage over other welfare recipients in receiving special or supplemental grants, once available under New York State's welfare law, as well as other benefits from the welfare administration. It provided them with knowledge of what they were entitled to and how they could obtain it, as well as some organizational backing in getting it. This, in turn, contributed to the rapid growth of the welfare rights movement in New York City.

Again, this does not mean that welfare rights organizations were exclusive groups or that they denied information and support to nonmembers. Rather, members were simply in a better position to obtain and use the information and support provided by these organizations. Through word of mouth and neighborly contact, nonmembers probably benefited from welfare rights activities. However, they almost certainly benefited much less than did members.

Finally, there have been important changes in welfare rights tactics over time. There were from the start demonstrations at welfare centers and other city office buildings. There were also city-wide conferences and protest meetings. However, prior to 1968, as the welfare rights organizations were building their strength in the city, much of their activity was conducted at the local level. Groups held meetings at which the members were informed about what they were entitled to under law and were urged to demand their rights from their caseworkers. Checklists of items that could be obtained through special grants were circulated to the membership. In this way, the welfare rights movement provided a service to members that the welfare administration should have provided; it interpreted and explained the law to the members to ensure that they obtained all to which they were entitled.

In May 1968, there was a major change in welfare rights tactics. The movement began an intensive city-wide campaign of demonstrations at the various welfare centers and other city offices. There were several reasons for this change in tactics. First, there was growing militancy in the ranks of the welfare rights movement. There was also growing strength. The movement had the manpower or, more properly, the womanpower to undertake daily demonstrations in all parts of the city. Perhaps most important, the state legislature had become aware of the influence of the welfare rights movement and, in particular, its ability to take advantage of the special grants, and was about to end most of these grants. The demonstrations were a conscious effort by the welfare rights leadership to build popular support for the movement and for retention of the special grant.

This change in tactics also affected how the welfare rights organizations influenced grant levels and the caseload. The demonstrations served to publicize both the availability of special grants and of welfare in general to the poverty population as a whole. Nonmembers and members alike received this information. For this reason, the benefits of welfare rights activities ceased to be a private good and became much more a public good.

To talk meaningfully about the impact of welfare rights activities in New York City, it is useful to express the change in the caseload as a function of three decision variables—the acceptance rate, the applications rate, and the closings rate. The determinants of each of these variables can then be examined separately. In doing this, we concentrate on Aid to Families with Dependent Children (AFDC), the most controversial and rapidly growing category of assistance. We also focus on the first eight months of 1968, the period in which the city's welfare rights movement attained its greatest strength and the city's AFDC caseload grew most rapidly.

When we estimate the individual and cumulative effects of changes in the three decision variables, increased applications and (to a lesser extent) the lower closings rate were clearly most responsible for growth in the city's AFDC caseload during the latter half of the 1960s. Acceptance rates have been less important. This finding calls into question the frequent assertion that liberal policies and lax administration by the city have been major contributors to the unprecedented growth in the city's caseload in recent years.

During the first eight months of 1968, welfare rights organizations influenced the overall grant level in their efforts to obtain higher special grants for their members. Moreover, the nature of their influence varied over time with changes in their tactics. Although the measured impact of welfare rights groups on the average grant level was small, the impact on the grant received by members appears to have been substantial. It is no surprise, therefore, that this was a period of rapid growth in the groups' membership.

The acceptance rate has risen since 1966. Although this increase has had a direct impact on the city's AFDC caseload, it has not had an indirect impact by encouraging applications or closings. Nor do our results support the frequent assertion that welfare rights activities have been a factor in recent increases in the city's acceptance rates.

The extraordinary increase in applications in 1968 was the result of at least two factors. First, applications rose with the grant level. More applicants were attracted to welfare assistance the more remunerative this assistance became. In other words, welfare applicants appear to have been economically rational.

Our analysis also indicates that welfare rights activities had a major influence on the level of applications in 1968. The impact of these activities was both direct and indirect. Welfare rights organizations encouraged applicants, first by the information and publicity resulting from their demonstrations, and second by their influence on the grant level which, in turn, encouraged applications. The indirect effect was stronger prior to the shift in tactics toward more militant confrontation with the welfare administration in May 1968. The direct effect was stronger after this shift.

Finally, local welfare rights groups do not appear to have influenced the level of closings, even though one of their important activities has been to demand fair hearings and otherwise protest termination of assistance to member families. However, closings have been affected by the grant level in a way consistent with the relationship between the grant level and applications. The higher the grant level in a district, the lower the percentage of AFDC cases closed. This, too, suggests economic rationality on the part of welfare recipients.

In short, welfare rights groups emerge from our study as highly effective organizations during the period which we have studied. They were able to provide their membership with higher grant levels. This was a major benefit to the membership that, while it lasted, helped to ensure its commitment to the movement. At the same time, these organizations helped to bring many eligible nonrecipients into the system by encouraging new applicants. This was, however, a by-product of their activities that did not benefit directly the membership. In other words, welfare rights activities provided a social good by assisting a larger percentage of families to obtain public assistance who were eligible for it under the law.

However, the foundation on which the movement was built in the city was fragile. It depended on the continuation of special grants, which in turn depended on the mood of the state legislature. The successful exploitation of special grants by the welfare rights movement was largely responsible for termination of these grants on September 1, 1968. From that moment, New York City's welfare rights movement has declined in strength.

It is not clear, however, that the long-run effects of this strategy have, on balance, been injurious to the welfare population. Although the average benefit level in New York City, in real dollars, has fallen since abandonment of the special grant, it is probable that the benefit level would have been reduced anyway as the economy worsened and, consequently, the state's budgetary problems intensified. At the least, welfare payments are now being distributed more equitably among welfare recipients than they were under the system of special grants.

Also it is not clear that the net effect of this strategy has been injurious to the welfare rights organizations themselves, as some critics both within and outside the movement have alleged. If there were no special grant, the movement in New York City might have been much weaker today than it now is. The special grant was, in a sense, a once-and-for-all opportunity for the movement, available at the right time and in the right place.

If, however, welfare rights organizations are to continue to grow, they will have to find some substitute possessing the essential attributes of the special grant, a substitute that provides a clearly private benefit to the membership. The movement could, perhaps, hit upon another means of attracting membership.

Some leaders of the movement have suggested, for example, working toward a closed shop with welfare rights groups acting as sole bargaining agents with the city. This, however, seems to be wishful thinking given the temper of times and the comparatively powerless position of the welfare poor.

Another significant finding of the study is that low-income families are economically rational. Actual and potential welfare recipients respond to changes in the grant level both in applying for, and in terminating, their welfare status. The evidence suggests, in other words, that welfare recipients are aware of what is in their own self-interest and act accordingly.

Although most economists have accepted this pattern of behavior since Adam Smith, others have not. There is a tendency to think that low-income families require close supervision because they do not act in ways consistent with their own self-interest. Low-income families may require some guidance in understanding the complex maze of welfare regulations that has been established by society, and some organizational backing to push their way through this maze. However, probably no one knows more about what is in a person's interest than the person himself.

Another finding is that the low-income population appears to respond rapidly to changes in incentives. Applicants typically respond to current, not past grant levels. They also respond to this month's and not last month's welfare rights activity. All things considered, this suggests surprisingly good communication within the low-income community.

Finally, our study suggests some measure of arbitrary behavior by local welfare centers. Prior to May 1968, different attitudes at different welfare centers seem to have been a factor in the distribution of special grants. The acceptance rate also varied substantially from one welfare center to another. This raises questions about whether standards are being applied equitably in determining need and eligibility and, if they are not, whether the existing system should be replaced by another that does not place a premium on the particular part of the city in which the recipient lives.

1 Introduction

The unprecedented growth in welfare dependency has been one of the most publicized yet least understood developments of the past decade. This growth has been especially great in New York City. In 1960, 4 percent of the people living in the city were on welfare; in 1970, 14 percent.[1] With over a million of its residents receiving public assistance at any one time, New York City is increasingly a city of dependents, a repository for the nation's poor and indigent population.

Welfare has also become far more controversial than it was a decade ago. The press reports one problem with welfare after another: deplorable housing conditions for welfare recipients; crime rings in New York City to obtain and cash fraudulent or stolen welfare checks; failure of the system to provide welfare allotments equivalent to minimum poverty standards; alleged misapplication of funds by welfare officials; the housing of a welfare family in the Waldorf Astoria. On a request by several New York State Congressmen, the federal government has subjected the city's welfare system to special study.[2] The persistent increase in caseloads has also been a major cause of New York City's disintegrating fiscal position. It has led a liberal mayor to assert that the city can no longer maintain state welfare standards and to initiate court action to free it from legal requirements to do so. In short, by the end of the decade, New York City was faced with a crisis in welfare that, along with the city's other problems, has lent awesome credibility to the frequent assertion that it is ungovernable.

Some have argued that it is unjust to single out New York City. The recent growth in welfare dependency and inadequacies of public assistance have been a national phenomenon. This may be true. However, for the entire nation the number of welfare recipients went from nearly 4 percent to only 6 percent of the population during the decade.[3] Although there are other cities in which welfare incidence and the caseload increase have been greater, New York City is close to the lead. A study focusing on the city's caseload increase is justified in its own right. It is also a beginning toward a much needed, larger study of the caseload increase for the nation as a whole.

We stress the word "beginning." So much that has been written and said about public assistance seems to be little more than speculation. Although the nation's welfare system generates large quantities of data, there has been surprisingly little solid analysis of these data. Yet there are many views about the role of welfare rights organizations and explanations for the recent increase in welfare caseloads. Some observers have pointed to the growing militancy of the poverty population as the primary reason for the caseload increase; others to changing attitudes toward family stability; still others to liberalization of welfare eligibility standards and a breakdown in these standards at the local, welfare center level. Hopefully, our study will provide some analytical rigor to a rather confused, yet critically important issue in America today.

The study deliberately concentrates on New York City. Given the availability of suitable data, however, there is no reason why a similar study might not be undertaken for other welfare jurisdictions as well.

It also concentrates, for the most part, on one category of assistance—Aid to Families with Dependent Children (AFDC). This is the largest and most controversial category in both the nation and the city. In New York City, it accounts for about one-half of the caseload and over two-thirds of the welfare population, and has grown more rapidly than any other type of assistance during the past five years.[4] AFDC consists almost entirely of families without a male head of the household. Illegitimacy and desertion are the two most important reasons for the absence of the man. More than any other category, AFDC contradicts the traditional ethical standards of the nation toward marriage and family stability. For this reason, this category has been the object of criticism by Congress, the state legislature, and the public. In the popular view, AFDC is *the* welfare problem.

There are other categories of assistance. For example, in 1961 Congress established Aid to Families of Dependent Children with an Unemployed Parent (AFDC-U) to allow assistance, in those states choosing to participate, to impoverished families where both the father and mother are present and able-bodied, but unemployed and without employment compensation. The purpose of AFDC-U is to lessen incentives created by AFDC for the father to desert his family to ensure its eligibility for welfare assistance. In New York City, AFDC-U was called Temporary Aid to Dependent Children (TADC) during the period covered by this study. It is also treated as a separate category of assistance. Therefore, when we talk about AFDC, we do not include AFDC-U families as is often done in other welfare jurisdictions. AFDC-U covers a small number of recipients, has not grown in recent years, and has been relatively noncontroversial.[a]

There are, in addition, three other federally supported categories of assistance that require some form of physical disability on the part of the recipient—Aid to the Disabled, Aid to the Blind, and Old Age Assistance. Together, these categories account for about 12 percent of New York City's welfare population. On paper, the three have grown rapidly since 1965. This is primarily because of reassignments from other categories. The disability categories have also been relatively noncontroversial.

These five programs are federally supported. In addition, there is in most

---

[a]In 1970, AFDC-U served less than 4 percent of New York City's welfare population. Moreover, between 1965 and 1970 the AFDC-U caseload remained virtually constant.

states a sixth program that is entirely state or locally supported. This is usually called General Assistance; in New York State it is called Home Relief (HR). The major difference between HR and the other categories is the absence of federal support. For some reason, the recipient is eligible for assistance under state law, but not under the more restrictive federal law. There are two general types of HR cases in New York. One is the single woman too well to receive Aid to the Disabled or the Blind, too young to receive Old Age Assistance, and without dependent children making her eligible for AFDC. The other is the male-headed family where the father is employed, but at a wage income that falls below the state's income support level. HR is, next to AFDC, the most controversial category of assistance in the city. However, it accounts for less than 20 percent of the city's welfare cases.[b]

Finally, the study concentrates, for the most part, on welfare rights groups, militant organizations of welfare recipients banded together to advance their individual and common interests vis-à-vis the welfare system. The welfare rights movement began almost spontaneously in a number of areas of the nation during the early and middle 1960s. In the mid-1960s, these organizations had, by the best count, only a few hundred members in the entire country. By 1967, there were in New York City alone over 2500 dues-paying members of the National Welfare Rights Organization; by 1968, nearly 6000. Most were black AFDC mothers. Between 1965 and 1968 the movement took hold and became a significant force for advancement of the interests of the city's welfare population.

There were two basic reasons for the rapid growth of welfare rights groups. First, the movement developed an organization at the local, city, and national levels that made it an effective advocate of welfare recipients' interests. By 1967, the City-Wide Coordinating Committee of Welfare Groups (hereafter referred to as "City-Wide") and the National Welfare Rights Organization had been established. These groups helped to direct, focus, and provide leadership to what had previously been a rather disparate movement. Equally important has been the proliferation of neighborhood groups. By 1968, there were nearly seventy local organizations in New York City affiliated with the National Welfare Rights Organization (NWRO) and at least twenty others involved one way or another in welfare activities. These local groups have served as a bridge between welfare families and the national and City-Wide organizations. They have also been the primary instrument for applying pressures on local welfare center officials to obtain, among other things, a more generous distribution of grants and better treatment by the welfare administration.

In the remainder of this study we discuss at length the origins and activities of

[b]Data on the number of welfare cases and recipients are published each month in the *Monthly Statistical Report*. Some confusion may be caused by our use of the word "case." Throughout, we treat it as synonymous with the word "family." We also treat single recipients as cases, even though, for categories of assistance involving some disability, they are not considered "cases" by the welfare administration.

the welfare rights movement, and examine the effect of the movement, as well as other factors, on New York City's AFDC caseload and grant level.

2
Theories of Protest and Organizational Activity

Protest activity is one way dissident groups are able to influence American political life. Although this type of activity has increasingly been identified with minority groups, it has not been restricted to these groups. Most segments of the American public have, at one time or another, used protest as a method of either demonstrating alienation, seeking redress of grievances, or demanding greater rewards and services from society.[1]

The civil rights movement has sought, not without considerable difficulty, to use protest on behalf of blacks and other low-income people. Community action and other groups affiliated with War on Poverty programs have encouraged protest tactics in their attempts to mobilize the poor, especially the urban poor. As a result, protest politics has become a permanent part of the urban American political landscape. Tenant groups, high school and university students, welfare mothers, public employees, militant feminists, and a powerful, broadly based movement directed against American foreign policy in Asia have all embraced, with differing degrees of success, protest politics and tactics. Accordingly, there is revived interest in protest among academics of several disciplines. In this chapter we consider some of the theoretical discussion of protest behavior that is particularly relevant to our own discussion of the welfare rights movement.

The Literature about Protest Activity

Sidney Verba has suggested the existence of a "crisis in participation" in contemporary America.[2] Verba notes three dimensions to participation: the participant, the issue, and modes of participation. A "crisis" occurs because all three dimensions change simultaneously. New people from different strata of society desire to participate, participating around new issues, and most important, introducing new modes of participation. Society has experienced changes in each of the dimensions, but this has rarely occurred simultaneously.

Verba's description of the "crisis in participation" is particularly appropriate in a discussion of the welfare rights movement. The movement involves a group that, in the past, had not participated extensively in the formulation of welfare policy or, for that matter, in the nation's political process. The group is concerned with an issue that by and large had been ignored by the nation and had become the preserve of a relatively small group of social welfare professionals and others involved in the administration of welfare programs. Finally, the movement has used techniques of persuasion that are novel to the welfare system and in many ways far more controversial than those used by other segments of society.[3] Welfare rights groups have resorted to conventional acts of participation such as voting, political campaigning, writing letters to government officials, attending meetings, submitting petitions, supporting pressure groups, and advertising in the press. However, they have also used newer, more controversial modes of participation such as sit-ins, wade-ins, pray-ins, freedom rides, marches, and the "liberation" of buildings.

The gains from protest activity have grown because the government has grown and now affects many aspects of life previously left to the private sector. An increasing number of interests are seeking larger shares of federal, state, and local resources. As a result, control over governmental decisions has grown in importance for most segments of society.

Samuel Lubell suggests that the battle over the allocation of governmental expenditures is creating a "society of claimants," warring and feuding with one another and, in the process, tearing apart traditional party alignments.[4] Consideration of the newer modes of participation is critical to understanding whether and how protest activity has secured a larger share of the nation's resources for the welfare population. For example, Amitai Etzioni has concluded that demonstrations "are a particularly effective mode of political expression in an age of television, for underpriviledged groups, and for prodding stalemated bureaucracies into taking necessary action. Indeed, demonstrations are becoming part of the daily routine of our democracy and its most distinctive mark."[5] Defining demonstrations as "public acts designed to call attention to or express a position,"[6] Etzioni likens demonstrations for the citizen to strikes for the worker. Etzioni also argues that demonstrations cannot be viewed as a tool of particular dissident groups such as blacks and students because numerous middle-class and professional groups have also used some form of this mode of participation.[7] The seemingly widening use of demonstrations is giving legitimacy to this mode of participation and is forcing social scientists to redefine what constitutes participation in a democratic society.

Protest associated with the civil rights movement has produced an extensive body of literature. The participation of black students in the movement[8] and black political leadership in both northern and southern communities are particularly well documented. Several studies have also examined interracial attempts to achieve racial harmony in southern communities.[9] Perhaps most important, however, have been studies seeking to test the efficacy of black political participation[10] and socialization, or resocialization of blacks.[11]

There is also an extensive literature on voting as a means of advancing minority interests. Gunnar Myrdal argued that the vote is an effective political instrument, primarily for securing civil service employment and greater justice for minority communities.[12] However, much of the recent work on black participation suggests that the ballot may not be as valuable a tool for political advancement as democratic theory and values would suggest.[13] Studies of political behavior in Durham, Tuskegee, and Philadelphia have also concluded that the vote has been a weak political instrument.[14]

Although protest activity has produced a large body of literature, until recently it has suffered from a notable lack of theoretical discussion. Much of the literature on welfare and black protest is unsystematic and offers few theoretical concepts that might aid in constructing viable theories describing the relationship between recent welfare rights activity and the political process. A body of literature is growing, however, that examines the theoretical basis for other types of protest.[15] Hopefully, this literature will contribute to a more systematic analysis of protest by welfare rights groups.

To this end, this study is an attempt to analyze the political behavior of lower-class, relatively powerless groups, and their impact upon public policy. It utilizes as a case study organizations of welfare mothers in New York City. In seeking to explain the political behavior of these protest groups, we have drawn upon two academic disciplines—political science and economics. We are concerned primarily with welfare rights organizations as political protest groups, as aggregates of individuals who have opted to join together to make substantive demands and seek certain rewards from the political system. We attempt to measure the impact that these groups have had both on the welfare system and on the larger political process.

The affirmation of a national commitment to eradicate poverty and the subsequent declaration of a war on poverty focused attention less on the racial basis and more on the class basis of inequality in American society. The United States has experienced tenant strikes in public housing, demonstrations by groups funded by the Office of Economic Opportunity (OEO), a poor people's campaign, a march on Washington, and militant welfare demonstrations involving march-ins, sit-ins, wade-ins, and pray-ins.

In this study, we hope to answer some questions about protest, particularly by low-income and low-status groups possessing few political resources. How did the welfare rights movement begin and why has it grown? How are its members recruited? Under what conditions has the movement been successful? How has it been able to influence public policy? What has it accomplished for its members? As a basis for our own analysis, we draw most heavily on five discussions of protest and organizational activity: James Q. Wilson's classic theoretical article on protest;[16] Wallace Sayre's and Herbert Kaufman's analysis of New York City government;[17] David Truman's examination of the governmental process;[18] Michael Lipsky's new theory of the reformulation of urban protest;[19] and Mancur Olson's theory of organizational behavior.[20] With a slight modification, we accept Sayre's and Kaufman's notion of a political process consisting of actors who work within a patterned set of rules of the game to strive for certain rewards and to obtain or maintain certain benefits. From Wilson, we incorporate the idea that protest activity can be conceptualized as a form of bargaining, in which most low-income persons possess few resources with which to bargain and are essentially powerless.[21] From Olson, we draw the observation that groups, if they are to survive, must provide at least some private goods, benefits to individuals that cannot be obtained without membership. While many groups pursue public goods—that is, benefits for members and nonmembers alike—these are frequently "by-products" of group activity.

Sayre and Kaufman view protest political activity such as direct-action tactics and strikes by public employees and civil rights activists as intended to force city officials to intervene on their behalf by dramatizing their claims. While they recognize that these tactics are not new, they do not see their becoming accepted strategies of political action in New York. Rather, the tactics will continue to be extraordinary ways of exerting influence in the city.

Sayre and Kaufman also believe that these kinds of tactics will have a high negative cost for their practitioners. The recent experience of welfare rights organizations in New York City suggests that in the long run Sayre and Kaufman may be correct, but that in the short run protest activity has had a high positive rate of return for welfare rights members. This activity substantially increased the average grant level (see Chapter 15). However, it also encouraged legislative action that has been harmful to the interests of the city's welfare recipients.

Models of Protest Activity

There are at least four basic models or theoretical approaches to a study of protest activity: The first is essentially descriptive. It tells how protest activity does or does not work. The remaining three models are prescriptive. They indicate how protest activity can be made to work.

The Bargaining Model

Wilson's discussion of protest concentrates on bargaining. It defines *bargaining* as "any situation in which two or more parties seek conflicting ends through the exchange of compensations."[22] Because poor people have few resources with which to bargain, their major problem is to assemble resources. Moreover, protest requires mass action which, in turn, depends upon negative inducements. Mass action can take four forms: verbal, physical, economic, and political. In addition to mass action, protest has two other requisites. First there ought to exist general goals behind which mass action can be mobilized. These goals can be specific or general, defensive or assertive, welfare or status. They are directly related to mass action. Second, there should be specific targets of protest activity capable of granting desired rewards. The targets must be able to respond, and there must be a fair chance that they will respond to demands by those protesting.

Wilson argues that "the prospects of vigorous, extensive, and organized Negro protests in large northern cities are poor."[23] He advances five reasons for this conclusion:

1. Protest ends are general, assertive, and have a status orientation.
2. Protest targets have become ambiguous.
3. Goals being sought are least applicable to those blacks most suited to protest.
4. For some specific goals where protest could occur, the situation places a negative value on protest.
5. Blacks are not organized on a continuing basis for protest activity. Voluntary associations are led by the middle-class and lack a mass base.

Wilson's analysis is limited in scope because it concentrates on protest as a means of explaining black civic action and allows use of negative inducements only. In addition, Banfield and Wilson argue that it is unrealistic to expect significant political activity to come from the black lower classes, and that middle-class leadership must account for any political activity that has occurred.[24]

Many of these assumptions concerning lower-class political behavior can be tested, and for a broader segment of the population than the black lower classes. One of the purposes of this study is to examine the validity of this model for New York City's welfare recipients. Suffice it to say here, all five of the reasons advanced by Wilson have to a greater or lesser degree not been constraints on welfare rights activity in the city, at least prior to 1968. As we will note in subsequent sections, the welfare rights organizations' ends were specific and oriented toward economic as well as status goals. Their targets were also specific—the caseworker and welfare center. Moreover, the movement was able to draw upon the welfare population, not only for many of its followers, but also its leaders. Because of this, welfare protest activity became a continuing lower-class movement. Our discussion of the remaining three models indicates some of the reasons why the welfare rights movement has not fitted into Wilson's model.

The Third Party Model

The third party model represents the most systematic attempt to provide a theoretical perspective for the study of protest as a political resource.[25] It focuses on protest by relatively powerless groups and how it can be made to work. Protest is defined as a "mode of political action oriented toward objection to one or more policies or conditions, characterized by showmanship or display of an unconventional nature, and undertaken to obtain rewards from political or economic systems while working within the systems."[26] Protest activity is successful when the public reacts so that target groups respond favorably to the protestors. However, protest is a difficult strategy because the protest leaders must manage four constituencies simultaneously:

1. Protest leaders must nurture and sustain an organization comprised of people with whom they may or may not share common values.
2. They must articulate goals and choose strategies so as to maximize their public exposure through the communications media.
3. They must have an impact on third parties in the political conflict.
4. Finally, they must maximize chances of success among those target groups capable of granting their goals.

This model provides a useful approach to analyzing how relatively powerless groups, who possess few if any political resources, can succeed in protest activity. The key lies in the ability of protest leaders to manage effectively each of these constituencies. It lies, therefore, in their ability to play one off against the other in the interests of the group.

The Democratic Participation Model

Supporters of the democratic participation model[27] assume that in democratic societies there are some groups that can only be incorporated through direct action tactics. How do movements originate for these groups and under what conditions can they be successful? Unincorporated groups lack the numbers and organization to force change alone.

Two prerequisites are thought necessary for successful direct action in a democratic society.[28] First, a dilemma must exist; there must be a direct conflict between reality and the generally professed goals and values of society. The unincorporated group seeks allies and, where a dilemma exists, attentive publics are seen by adherents of this model as sympathetically awaiting mobilization. However, the existence of a dilemma is by itself not sufficient. Not enough people may feel strongly enough about the dilemma. Some amount of disorder is necessary to coerce those opposed and to mobilize those favoring the groups' goals. To create disorder, protest groups need members. Tactics have to be developed that establish for the movement a popular base or, barring this, some other means of recruitment.

One tactic would be to focus on targets that yield easy victories. If protest activity can attract a sufficient number of members to succeed in drawing concessions from the political system, a natural growth process may occur. The movement demonstrates success and attracts more members, including those who were committed to routine means, but who are now willing to shift to nonroutine means as their effectiveness is demonstrated and legitimized. Appropriate tactics would allow a protest movement simultaneously to create disorder and to focus attention on a dilemma. Success, in other words, would allow a protest movement to achieve its ends despite its own internal weaknesses and the powerlessness of the group.[a]

The Theory of Public Goods and Group Behavior

Finally, in discussing the welfare rights movement, one must consider the economics of group behavior, whether in protest or in some other activity intended to achieve benefits for the welfare population. Olson, drawing on the theory of public goods, argues that organizations are generally expected to further the common interests of their members: "Purely personal or individual interests can be advanced, and usually advanced more efficiently, by individual, unorganized action."[29] Olson equates many group objectives with collective or public goods, goods which can be enjoyed by a number of persons simultaneously.[b] However, because nonmembers may benefit from group activity, some individuals may be discouraged from joining, particularly if there is a cost associated with membership. For example, if unions secure benefits for an industry's work force as a whole, some workers may conclude that by not joining the union they can still enjoy the benefits without paying union dues or incurring retaliation by management. In other words, the obligations of group membership are likely to fall on a relatively few individuals. Which individuals assume these obligations will depend, among other things, on the size of the group, its composition, and its objectives.

Despite the fact that an individual may enjoy some of the benefits of group activity without being a member, there are a number of groups in our society that are concerned with social objectives. Moreover, many of these groups have been successful. Olson offers several reasons for this paradox. Some groups may appeal to the noneconomic motives of individuals, such as patriotism or class loyalty. Others may rely on compulsion or the threat of imprisonment. Olson also offers another explanation. The collective goods that groups secure may be "by-products" of more basic activities directed toward clearly private ends—that is, benefits that individual members can realize only if they belong to the group. Good examples of such groups have been New York City's welfare rights organizations.

---

[a]Those who have advanced the Democratic participation model cite the effort to desegregate public accommodations in Maryland between 1960 and 1964. This study should serve as a useful comparison with our own work on welfare rights activity in New York City.

[b]A classic example of a public good is public health. The eradication of malaria benefits the community as a whole, i.e., it can be enjoyed by all individuals simultaneously. By contrast, an apple, a private good, is eaten and enjoyed by only one person at a time.

One can clearly identify public goods among the objectives of welfare rights activities. Legal action may result in court decisions that benefit all welfare recipients. Successful lobbying before a state legislature or the Congress may result in an increase in basic grant levels that also benefits all recipients. However, a major strength of the welfare rights organizations, in New York City especially, is that they have provided their members with benefits that could be obtained through membership only. Probably the most important of these benefits was the information and support that welfare rights organizations gave members seeking special grants before the system of special grants was abandoned in 1968. The system of special grants was so complex and information about these grants so limited that, while the system lasted, it offered welfare rights organizations an opportunity to offer their membership something that could not be obtained elsewhere. The welfare rights organizations provided a service in many ways similar to that provided the more affluent by tax consultants.

To examine welfare rights organizations in the context of the economics of group behavior, one must determine whether the benefits from welfare rights activity affect all recipients or whether they are, more purely, returns to the membership only. One must consider, in other words, whether the results of political participation in welfare rights activities are public or private goods or some combination of the two. The answer has considerable bearing on whether welfare rights organizations are likely to be viable proponents of the interests of the poor.

Conclusions

One can conceive of conditions under which effective protest activity can be launched by low-income, relatively powerless segments of society. Much depends on how successfully the leaders of protest groups provide appropriate incentives to the various constituencies involved. Among these incentives are positive, private rewards to the membership to ensure its commitment; inducements to the media to publicize protest activity; the enlistment of support by influential members of the community; and finally, because of all these, maximization of pressures on the targets of protest activity which, in the case of the welfare rights movement, have been the caseworkers, the welfare centers, the state legislatures, and the Congress. With this discussion as background, we now turn to an analysis of the origins and activities of the welfare rights movement in New York City.

3 The Origins of Welfare Protest Activity in America

On September 19, 1967, at hearings before the Senate's Committee on Finance, Beulah Sanders declared:

I do not believe that we should be forced to work. I do not believe that we should be forced to take training if it is not meaningful. If you are going to give us something that we can hope for and advance in, possibilities to go on to higher salaries, then I would agree to do it.

This is why we have had the disturbance in New York City and across the country. We, the welfare recipients, have tried to keep down the disturbance among our people, but the unrest is steadily growing. The welfare recipients are tired. They are tired of people dictating to them telling them how they must live.[1]

On June 12, 1968, at another congressional hearing, Beulah Sanders said:

The departments have made welfare clients for the past thirty years feel that, you know, they are dirt and they have no voice at all. What we have given our people is the right to really speak out, the right to dignity, to let the department know that just because they are on welfare, they have to have the same respect as any other American citizen.[2]

These statements indicate the attitudes, philosophy, and militancy that, by 1968, had come to characterize the nation's welfare rights movement.

By 1968, the National Welfare Rights Organization (NWRO) had emerged as one of several successors to the civil rights movement. Demonstrations in city after city, widespread efforts to organize and protect the rights of welfare recipients, and continuous political action and lobbying intended to influence local, state, and national public welfare policy on behalf of the recipient have been the principal activities of the NWRO since its inception.

The NWRO represents the first significant attempt since the 1930s by recipients of public welfare to organize and influence the nation's welfare system. During the depression, unemployment councils were established in many industrial areas. These councils were first organized by the National Unemployment Council of the United States, which had ties with the Communist party.[3] Later, in 1935, a non-Communist national organization of the unemployed and relief recipients was established, called the Workers Alliance of America.[4] Other organizations were formed during the depression to work on behalf of specific segments of the relief population. The best known of these organizations was the

Townsend Movement which acted on behalf of the aged.[5] Demonstrations, hunger marches, highly vocal and sometimes violent protest, arrests and jail sentences often resulted from these groups' activities.

The NWRO, unlike its predecessors of the depression era, has emerged as a coherent, functioning national organization during a period of general economic prosperity. However, this prosperity does not extend to all segments of the population, particularly to minority and dependent groups. Hence, unlike its predecessors, which were composed primarily of unemployed white men, the NWRO has had as its principal constituency black women, almost all of them recipients of AFDC.

This is an important distinction between the two groups of relief recipients. The groups formed during the depression consisted for the most part of temporarily unemployed workers who could return to the ranks of the employed after the depression; the welfare rights organizations consist of dependent families who, for a complex set of reasons, have relatively little prospect for future entry into the job market, at least at more than poverty-level wages. For this reason, the NWRO's constituency is more likely to depend permanently on public assistance. Both movements, however, were successful in utilizing mass protest tactics to gain public aid for families faced with serious economic difficulties.[6]

The welfare rights movement had its origins in three relatively recent occurrences: the civil rights movement, the War on Poverty, and changes in public welfare philosophy.

The Civil Rights Movement

The civil rights movement grew out of the distinctive, segregated black subculture of the South. Within this relatively limited context, it possessed certain organizational and normative advantages. The civil rights era was characterized by the prominence of the clergy as leaders of the movement, the role of the church as a community institution, the mobilization of the long-suffering black people to seek some elemental share of modern life, and their demand for basic political and social rights long denied in the South.

The strategy of nonviolence was successful because the movement's roots were firmly planted in the black subculture of the region and, more important, many of its grievances were clearly supported by the values of the larger political community. The civil rights movement established and maintained an unprecedented alliance with many trade unions, religious groups, and factions of both major national parties. It was able to manipulate the highly visible tactics of public disorder to wrest concessions from established institutions. Through the media, many small, rural southern towns and their officials became national household words. As a result, a mass black movement emerged in the 1960s that, despite all of its contradictions and internal antagonisms, was a well-organized and functioning political force on behalf of black Americans.

The movement's successes were considerable. Focusing on the goal of an integrated society, the movement and its allies were influential in enacting voting rights, public accommodations, fair housing, and poverty legislation. Blacks were appointed to high government positions, including the Cabinet, the Supreme Court, and important governmental agencies. Administrative sanctions were leveled against discrimination on carriers operating in interstate commerce. Segregation in public education in the South was challenged and, in many communities, ended. With the enactment of the Manpower Development and Training Act in 1962 and the Economic Opportunity Act in 1964, the federal government committed itself to improving the economic position of the nation's minority groups. Finally, through the Civil Rights Act of 1964, it shattered the legal foundations of economic discrimination altogether. Thus, by the mid-1960s the federal government, under the constant prodding of the civil rights movement on issues accorded wide legitimacy by the general populace, had made a major contribution in helping to redress the economic imbalance between blacks and whites.

However, viewed historically, perhaps the greatest success of the civil rights movement has been the political socialization of the black American.[7] The movement mobilized large numbers of blacks who heretofore had been outside the dominant political culture in a tightly defined and highly restrictive ethnic subculture.[8] It created an awareness of the operations of local, state, and national politics among important segments of the black community. Blacks increasingly organized for the promotion of group interests and became more optimistic about the possibility of achieving change within the political system.

During the early 1960s, groups with middle-class leadership and oriented toward middle-class or lower middle-class constituencies provided the basis of the effort to improve the position of blacks within the dominant political system in America. The National Association for the Advancement of Colored People (NAACP) and the Urban League, although supported by the Southern Christian Leadership Conference (SCLC), the Congress of Racial Equality (CORE), and the Student Nonviolent Coordinating Committee (SNCC), were foremost in the drive for black economic equality.

But if the civil rights movement's success in obtaining status goals, primarily in the South, was substantial, its success in achieving welfare-oriented goals in the North was relatively negligible. Its initial objectives were thought legitimate by much of the general populace in the North and by influential segments of the nonsouthern political establishment. The political dynamics and recruitment needs of the civil rights movement required immediate, highly visible successes. Such successes could be found in the quest for such generally accepted status goals as public accommodations and voting rights legislation. Later, when the movement expanded its interests to include welfare-oriented gains such as conpensatory hiring, improved education, and increased employment opportunities in the construction trades, it was quickly discovered that these welfare-oriented goals often were not accorded the legitimacy given the status goals.[9] Indeed, many segments of society were openly hostile to the specific welfare demands of the civil rights movement. Thus Martin Luther King's drive in Chicago in 1966 for improved economic opportunities for blacks produced meager results. In addition, the civil rights movement sought the more widespread acceptance of the legitimacy of black culture, which to many nonblacks represented the "culture of poverty" and the antithesis of what American society either was or should be. Thus the movement's pursuit of less widely accepted goals after 1965 helped to dissolve the conditions necessary for successful nonviolent protest.[10]

The civil rights movement resulted in soaring expectations among blacks of all economic strata. These expectations were strengthened by the progress of black peoples elsewhere, particularly in Africa. However, because they were less fully satisfied when the movement shifted from status to welfare goals, this change was to create and exacerbate frustrations, particularly among younger civil rights and social activists. Nowhere was this disillusion greater than among elements of the lower-class black community in the northern cities. Members of this community increasingly recognized that the overwhelming majority of the black populace in the northern metropolitan areas had achieved only symbolic rewards from the decade of disorder in southern rural areas. Not only were their rewards from the civil rights movement few, their demands for welfare-oriented goals were not likely to be met by a movement that concentrated upon status goals and whose alliance with the white community would inevitably be strained by advocacy of many welfare-oriented goals.

The urban riots of the mid-sixties resulted from the failure of the movement to keep pace with the demands that it had inspired. The riots proved explosive for the old political order, an order consisting of the then-established civil rights groups, their various friends and allies, and, most important, tactics and strategies stressing interaction and cooperation with the established institutions and political forces of the larger society.

The fate of SNCC is particularly illustrative of the decline of the civil rights movement.[11] SNCC was organized in 1960 by young lower-middle and middle-class, highly mobile students as an outgrowth of the sit-in movement. It rapidly advanced to the forefront of the civil rights movement by mobilizing predominantly rural black communities to seek equal political rights. From 1960 through the summer of 1964, SNCC continued to seek this objective within the framework of integrated society. During this period, SNCC sought and successfully established a political base in the rural south, where it contributed to the heightened political consciousness of the black populace that until then had lacked the opportunity for genuine political and civic participation. It supported establishment of the Mississippi Freedom Democratic Party (MFDP), aided in the election of Julian Bond in Georgia, and sparked early political organization among the blacks in Loundes and Macon Counties, Alabama, the precursors of expanding black control of many local political units in the South.

By the summer of 1964, after reprisals by the southern establishment and the absence of promised support from the Justice Department, SNCC began to distrust liberal intentions and to question the value of integration. The failure of the Freedom Summer Project in 1964 through compromise of the MFDP's efforts at the Democratic Convention destroyed SNCC's last commitment to liberal values and integration and created dissensions from which the civil rights movement still has not been able to recover. During the latter half of the 1960s, even while its leading spokesmen were introducing the concept of black power, SNCC suffered a visible organizational decline. SNCC was lured from its natural constituency in the rural South by the presumed political potential of urban riots and rebellion in the North, yet failed to develop a coherent urban strategy. Still, many of its programmatic and ideological concepts remain influential. SNCC's disenchantment with liberalism and integration, its subsequent attempt to shift its program to the North, and its organizational decline reflect broader issues that have colored the debate over the course of the black movement which SNCC sparked.

Emerging from within the institutional framework created by the older, primarily middle-class groups, younger activists now began to explore alternative strategies and to seek, often in highly erratic ways, to develop new concepts through which they could reanalyze and redefine their total cultural, social, economic, and political response to the continued subordinate status of the black American. Often, although not always, this search veered in the direction of greater ethnic assertiveness. References to a separate "nationality" were inserted in the black agenda, juxtaposed with the competing objective of integration. Other political forces emerged which continued to utilize the tactics of mass public disorder. However, these tactics were now designed to achieve welfare-oriented goals and to develop new organizations, skills, and political roles among urban lower-class communities. The welfare rights movement was one outgrowth of this change in focus.

Two other developments were occurring simultaneously that would have a profound impact upon the course of the black movement and public welfare policy. These factors were the nation's renewed interest in eradicating poverty and growing criticism of the nation's welfare system by economists, political scientists, and members of the social welfare profession.

The War on Poverty

The Kennedy era was a period of experimentation and change. Poverty was rediscovered. Michael Harrington pointed to "socially invisible" pockets of poverty and sparked a widespread debate from which has emerged a substantial literature on poverty in America.[12] Within the government, Mollie Orshansky almost single-handedly pioneered the development of a poverty index and profile of poverty, while others have studied low-income lifestyles and what it means to grow up poor.[13] Simultaneously, black writers using an autobiographical literary form were publishing highly personalized accounts of the grim and harsh world of the black poor.[14]

Economists also distinguished the old and new faces of poverty.[15] The former was a more generalized condition. The old poor provided the basis for the political machines and the trade union movement. The immigrant working class, which constituted much of the old poor, was mobilized by political organizations in areas where they lived and by labor unions where they worked. On this basis, a new political coalition was forged by Franklin D. Roosevelt that helped transform the lives of a large segment of the old poor.[16] By contrast, the new poor were characterized as having "missed the political and social gains of the thirties."[17] They were the invisible poor. Being members of minority groups, they were largely ignored by the political system.[18] Harrington declares:

In a sense, one might define the contemporary poor in the United States as those who, for reasons beyond their control, cannot help themselves. All the most decisive factors making for opportunity and advance are against them. They are born going downward, and most of them stay down. They are victims whose lives are endlessly blown round and round the other America.[19]

The new poor, possessing no substantial economic leverage as workers, and having few if any organizational resources with which to pressure governments, often were the hapless and powerless clients of welfare state bureaucracies.

The willingness of the Kennedy administration to experiment with new ideas and programs coincided with several private initiatives that were already in progress. Out of this experimentation eventually emerged the Economic Opportunity Act of 1964 and President Johnson's declaration of a War on Poverty.[20] Several separate experiments with community action type programs led eventually to the community action component of the War on Poverty. The Ford Foundation, the President's Committee on Juvenile Delinquency, and the National Institute of Mental Health were all instrumental in developing and funding a new, community action approach toward social welfare and the increasingly difficult problems of decaying cities.

The Ford Foundation, reversing its earlier interest in metropolitan government and urban renewal as possible solutions to city problems, began in 1957, through its Public Affairs Department, to search for new and innovative approaches to the ills of the central cities. In March 1960, it made a grant of $1.25 million to seven urban school systems and, proving successful, extended this grant to include three more cities a year later. These grants were considered interim measures in the evolution of a more comprehensive program for combating urban poverty. Paul Ylvisakar, director of the Public Affairs Department, noted that the grants were regarded as a "stepping stone" to larger grants that would generate more coherent, community-based programs for attacking problems in poor areas.[21]

The foundation found itself in the unusual position of seeking to develop a comprehensive program and an appropriate institutional form to establish and operate this program. The foundation recognized early that a school system, voluntary agencies, or municipal authority centered in a city hall would be too narrow in scope for what it envisioned—a program that would combine the efforts of both public and private institutions with the broadest possible latitude in their activities.

One year later, on December 28, 1961, the Oakland, California Inter-Agency Project was awarded a grant of $2 million. In 1962, grants of varying sizes were given to Community Progress Incorporated in New Haven, the Council of Community Advancement in Philadelphia, and the Action for Boston Community Development in Boston. In 1963, $7 million was granted to create a state-wide North Carolina Fund to stimulate community action programs at the county level, and a grant of $2 million was awarded to Mobilization for Youth (MFY), a community action group on New York City's Lower East Side. Finally, in 1963, a planning grant was awarded to Washington's United Planning Organization. These grants comprised the Ford Foundation's grey areas projects, all of which, with the exception of the Washington planning grant, were to establish and maintain actual programs and training operations in the selected communities.[22]

Through its grey areas program, the foundation hoped to stimulate the creation of a new local institutional form to reverse the trend toward physical and human decay in the central cities.[23] Innovative programs, it was hoped, would stimulate fresh ideas and approaches that would energize the poor and end the waste of human resources now trapped in the culture of poverty in American cities. Finally, this new institutional form, it was thought, would be a potential means of coordinating the numerous and diverse programs that dealt with the problems of the urban poor.

The President's Committee on Juvenile Delinquency was also instrumental in developing new approaches to the problems of poverty in the central cities.[24] Unlike the Ford Foundation's grey areas projects, which began at the time of a conservative administration and a divided Congress, with neither willing to endorse major domestic reforms, the President's Committee was established by a liberal administration, eager to experiment with new ideas, and influenced considerably by both the growing civil rights movement and the inclusion of large numbers of black voters in its electoral constituency. The President's Committee was strategically placed. Established by executive order on May 11, 1961, it was technically supervised by the secretaries of labor; health, education and welfare; and the attorney general. However, real influence was exerted by Robert Kennedy, who in turn delegated his authority to an assistant, David Hackett, the committee's executive director.

The President's Committee, although originally charged with studying juvenile delinquency, actually studied much more. It successfully negotiated a delinquency bill through Congress, a bill that had been stalled for six years. Then the committee moved to exert its control over the newly established Office of Juvenile Delinquency and Youth Development in HEW (OJD). Lloyd Ohlin, one of the "young Turks" involved in the challenge to established social welfare practices and a former consultant to both the Ford Foundation and the committee, was appointed to head the new agency.

Thus the OJD and the President's Committee were staffed by reform-minded individuals with similar attitudes, many of whom had also worked or consulted for the Ford Foundation. Hackett was heavily influenced by new social welfare theories among members of the welfare profession and, in a memorandum to Attorney General Robert Kennedy on November 6, 1963, declared that we must have an approach to solving the problem of juvenile delinquency that is broadly based and concentrates on the family, school, local labor market, and other parts of the environment:

This comprehensive approach precludes the use of traditional concepts and plans which call for dealing merely with the delinquent in uncoordinated programs. It requires the development of new opportunities for disadvantaged youth and change in the institutions which affect them. To create this kind of program, the President's Committee has encouraged local planning leading to a coordination of resources for a total attack on the problems of disadvantaged youth.[25]

Rather than treat the effects of poverty, the Juvenile Delinquency Program tried to combat poverty by emphasizing access to opportunity.

Both the President's Committee and the Ford Foundation shared a common focus: programs emphasizing changes in the environment rather than simply the correction of the individual; coordination of programs concerned with poverty; and the creation of local constituencies, including not only community leaders, but also the ordinary residents of the poverty areas themselves.[26] Four of the Ford Foundation's grey areas projects and New York's MFY received support from the President's Committee. Both the Ford Foundation and the Committee sought to stimulate change by making use of the demonstration project. To this end, they concentrated their resources in a few highly selective projects emphasizing new approaches to education, vocational training, employment services, legal aid, and neighborhood service centers.

By 1964, the Ford Foundation had awarded nearly $20 million in support of experimental community action programs. The growth of these programs involved a "continued broadening of interests and refinement of strategy." Over time, additional problems were brought into the purview of the programs, and as the programs broadened, more institutions and communities became involved.[27]

By 1964, there were seventeen community action demonstration projects. These projects were to become the operating models for similar community action agencies under Title II of the Economic Opportunity Act of 1964. Hackett anticipated as much in a memorandum to Walter Heller on November 6, 1963, in which he urged that the projects develop a "dramatic approach" in order to launch a comprehensive attack on poverty.[28] With the passage of the Economic Opportunity Act in 1964, and the declaration of the War on Poverty, a new era appeared to be developing in American politics, an era which, according to Moynihan, would see "a new kind of American government, the inner-city community action agency."[29]

The Community Action Program (CAP) was to be the principal means of focusing all available resources upon the goal of attaining for low-income segments of the population the skills, knowledge, motivation, and opportunities for becoming fully self-sufficient. In each community, action agencies were to be the focal point of a united effort to combat poverty and to provide communications links between federal programs and the poor. By June 1968, there were 1012 community action agencies. Of these, 978 were private agencies and 34 public.[30] A review of economic opportunity programs concluded that these agencies

have generally been successful in initiating or expanding and continuing a variety of programs and activities which have brought new or additional services and benefits to the poor that previously were unavailable or available only on a limited basis. Certain of these services are, by their nature and intent, calculated to gradually bring about changes in community and social standards and institutional practices whereby such services will become generally available from existing or newly created institutions. There is evidence that some changes have already begun.[31]

The operational arm of the CAP program is the neighborhood center, the link between the community action agency and the poor. It is the initial contact point; it provides services to the poor, either directly or by referral. Finally, it is responsible for continuing communication with the poor.

Neighborhood centers have had three basic tasks:

1. To make the services of other local and private agencies more easily available to neighborhood residents
2. To organize and sustain the participation of local residents in the program
3. To mobilize the resources of other local agencies in a concerted and unified effort to combat poverty.[32]

These service centers ostensibly use several techniques to increase the awareness of the poor about the agencies and resources that are available. First, they identify the poor in their communities, determine their needs (often through house-to-house canvassing), suggest various programs available to the poor, and, finally, encourage the poor to make use of the local neighborhood centers. Outreach is followed by intake and referral. After identifying the needs of the poor, the centers direct local residents to the agencies and programs from which assistance is most likely to be available. Finally, follow-up is used to assess the agency's or program's performance and to see if additional needs exist.

From OEO's inception through FY 1968, federal funding for neighborhood centers totaled $333.2 million (see Table 3-1). By 1968, roughly 15 percent of all CAP expenditures were spread among 870 primary and 1810 satellite neighborhood action centers in operation throughout the country.[33] Studies by OEO allege that, in about two-thirds of the communities that have CAPs, they have exercised a significant influence in one or more areas such as public or private welfare, education, and unemployment.[34] The assistance provided by the neighborhood centers includes employment counseling and job placement, aid in obtaining welfare and better housing, consumer education, and health and legal aid services.

The results of OEO's efforts have been especially dramatic and controversial in the area of legal rights for the poor. Between 1965 and 1968, the Legal Services Program spent approximately $86.5 million, and by FY 1968 had 267 projects, 850 neighborhood law offices, and 1600 full-time lawyers representing the needs of the poor throughout the country.[35] Through the efforts of the Legal Services Program and similar private agencies, a number of eligibility rules long used by welfare administrations to keep the poor off the assistance rolls collapsed under litigation and pressures by organized community groups. Similar gains were made in employment, housing, and other services.

Table 3-1
OEO Funding for CAP Agencies and Neighborhood Action Centers (Millions of Dollars)

Year	CAP Funds	Neighborhood Action Center Funds	NAC as a Percentage of Total CAP Funds
1965	236.5	24.3	10.3
1966	627.9	77.0	12.3
1967	804.2	99.5	12.4
1968	866.8	132.4	15.3
Total	2,535.4	333.2	13.1

Source: Comptroller-General of the United States, *Review of Economic Opportunity Programs*, Report to the Congress of the United States, 91st Cong., 1st sess., 1969, pp. 172-73; also see Sar Levitan, *The Great Society's Poor Law: A New Approach to Poverty*, Johns Hopkins Press, Baltimore, Maryland, 1969, p. 123. Data from the two sources differ slightly.

A good example of this new type of legal organization was the San Francisco Neighborhood Legal Assistance Foundation, a community-controlled, federally financed legal service agency for the poor in operation since October 1966.[36] By 1969, the foundation had 120 paid staff members, including 50 full-time lawyers and 30 part-time law students. This staff was complemented by volunteer social workers, law students, and private attorneys. The staff attorneys were generally young and attended the leading law schools.[a] Only one-fourth came from minority groups. Budgeted at well over $1 million per year, the foundation's funding came almost entirely from OEO and was channeled through the Economic Opportunity Council of San Francisco.

Thousands of clients have been served each month by the five neighborhood offices of the foundation. Most of these clients were seeing a lawyer for the first time. The overwhelming majority had incomes below the poverty line and most were on welfare. Thirty percent of the clients sought aid in a family problem, followed closely by disputes with various administrative agencies involving welfare, social security, unemployment insurance, and the draft. Among other achievements, the foundation has delayed a major urban renewal project that would have demolished 4500 units of low-income housing, displacing 10,000 persons.

The foundation's accomplishments have been most notable in the area of welfare. Several legal actions successfully challenged the restrictive administration of the state's welfare system. One led to the invalidation of the California residency requirement, making an additional 60,000 persons eligible for welfare benefits. Two thousand San Francisco recipients of general assistance were kept on the rolls despite a planned cutoff for reasons of economy. San Francisco and Alameda counties were ordered by the court to raise AFDC rent allotments to levels reflecting the state's minimum sanitation and safety standards. Finally, the courts have invalidated a California statute which placed a ceiling on AFDC grants below the state's own minimum subsistence standards. The foundation estimates that the payments received by welfare recipients will increase by between $50 and $100 million if these court decisions are enforced. Simultaneously, the foundation has aided in the formation of an active city-wide welfare rights organization and has supported the organization's attempts to influence administrative and legislative decisionmakers.

Besides the Legal Services Program, sponsored directly by OEO, various private agencies and law schools have also become involved with legal services. The National Legal Aid and Defenders Association (NLADA) has begun to participate in various legal issues affecting the poverty population. In 1966, NLADA reported that it had 252 affiliated legal aid offices, 125 voluntary committees of state and local legal associations, and nearly 200 local public defender associations, all engaged in offering some form of legal assistance to the poor in civil and criminal matters. Other legal groups have followed NLADA's

[a]One-third graduated from Harvard, Columbia, or Yale.

example. The Scholarship, Education and Defense Fund for Racial Equality, The American Civil Liberties Union, the Law Students Civil Rights Research Council, and the National Organization for the Rights of the Indigent have all become involved in the legal rights movement. Many law schools have also responded to the new climate, assisted by OEO's Legal Services Program, by altering traditional law school curricula.[37] They have also established research centers and institutes on welfare, race, and poverty, the best known being at the state universities of Wisconsin, Illinois, New York, Michigan, and California. From this development has come a succession of litigation, poverty information reviews, and law review articles concerning the rights of the poor.

It is difficult to measure the overall impact on welfare of the very substantial amount of legal activity that has taken place since the mid-1960s. For example, Levitan declares that of the 1968 Legal Services Program caseload, only 7000 cases out of 282,000, or approximately 3 percent, were concerned with state and local welfare issues.[38] However, these figures may be misleading because poverty lawyers have tended to emphasize strategic issues that aid the maximum number of persons. In San Francisco, the association's coordinator stated that his agency's mission was "to find leverage points in the system to bring about a redistribution of power and income more favorable to the poor."[39] Two general approaches were used: strategic advocacy and economic development. The former had its greatest gains in the welfare area. At first, litigation—with emphasis on class suits—and various administrative and legislative actions were the principal tools used. However, to be effective these measures had to have political support from the middle class as well as the poor. Many arbitrary restrictions and administrative practices were successfully challenged in the courts. Because of this, the Legal Services Program has had considerable impact on the welfare caseload.

The Evolution of Public Welfare Philosophy

Finally, the traditional methods and goals of the public welfare profession have come under attack by the "young Turks" within the profession. The "young Turks" and the theories upon which they have based this attack have been influential in the development of both public policy and professional attitudes towards the problems of poverty in America.

The program of both the Ford Foundation and the President's Committee on Juvenile Delinquency shared a common conceptual framework in their desire to stimulate innovative policies for alleviating poverty. Both were also influenced by the theories of Richard Cloward and Lloyd Ohlin, who were deeply involved in the emergence of the community action program as academic theorists and government policymakers. Both Cloward and Ohlin participated in the initial development of MFY.[40] Ohlin, in particular, was in an influential position, serving at one time or another as consultant to the National Institute of Mental Health, the Youth Program of the Ford Foundation, the President's Committee on Juvenile Delinquency, and, finally, as the director of the Department of Health, Education, and Welfare's Office of Juvenile Delinquency. All were sources of funding for experimental community action programs. Cloward also served as the first director of research for Mobilization for Youth.

Cloward's and Ohlin's approach to the prevention of juvenile delinquency was a modification and extension of a general conceptual analysis originally advanced by Robert Merton.[41] Merton suggested an analysis of social behavior which stressed the relationship between the social structure in which an individual lived and the individual's personality development. He compared the widespread belief that American society offered equal opportunity for all with the position of the lower-class individual, more often than not confronted with cumulative forms of inequality of opportunity. Merton saw such an individual as having several options: He could conform and lower his aspirations; he could accept great risks in seeking to elevate himself; he could fall into mental disorder; he could band together with others like himself to move forcibly into a higher position in the social structure, or, at the extreme, he could try to create a new social structure. Applying Merton's concepts to the question of juvenile delinquency, Cloward and Ohlin saw the problem as one of members of a subculture, with legitimate opportunites restricted, engaging in illicit opportunities to gain status. From that they concluded that such behavior could be altered only through changing the larger social structure, rather than changing the individual.

We hope that we have at least made it clear that extending services to delinquent individuals or groups cannot prevent the rise of delinquency in others. For delinquency is not, in the final analysis, a property of individuals or even of sub-cultures; it is a property of the social systems in which these individuals and groups are enmeshed. The pressures that produce delinquency originate in these structures, as do the forces that shape the content of specialized sub-cultural adaptations. The target for preventive action, then, should be defined, not as the individual or group that exhibits the delinquent patterns, but as the social setting that gives rise to delinquency.[42]

Traditional social casework methods stressed the individual defects of those engaged in antisocial behavior. Cloward's and Ohlin's break with this view addressed itself to equality of opportunity and placed the problem of juvenile delinquency within this framework. Since there are, obviously, differences in opportunities in our society, their views suggested a drastic reordering of the nation's "opportunity structure."

Moreover, evidence has increasingly been proffered that has challenged some of the basic assumptions of the social casework approach. One study has assessed the impact of intensive social casework assistance on fifty multiproblem families.[43] These families were given intensive service by caseworkers who possessed the Master of Social Work degree, had previous field experience, and carried half the normal caseload. A control group of fifty similar families received normal assistance and case aid. After an intensive treatment phase of thirty-one months, the authors of the study declared:

The essential finding was that, while the demonstration group attained a slightly better degree of family functioning, its margin of progress over the control group was not significant in the statistical sense. That is, the demonstration group's greater advance could be attributed to chance alone.[44]

While some studies conclude that social work is not effective, others find that it is effective to a limited degree.[45] The challenge to the traditional social casework philosophy is now well advanced.

Not only has the social work-settlement house approach to resolving the welfare problems of the poor come under attack from government officials and social scientists, it has also come under attack from its major clientele—the northern black communities. Silberman has aptly termed this divorce the "revolt against welfare colonialism."[46] Recipients have increasingly begun to challenge the view that existing social welfare programs and their methods of operation are a solution to their problems. Indeed, many have come to view these programs as an attempt to dampen the anger and disaffection of the welfare community before it can erupt into social protest that might upset the status quo. Concepts of the "underdeveloped nation" and "colonial rule" were borrowed from writings about the third world and applied to the situation of northern black communities. White control of black communities has become a controversial political and social issue, typified by the ubiquitous presence of the alien businessman and social worker, and it is the latter who is, perhaps, the more disliked of the two.

In the eyes of many recipients, welfare officials are nonmembers of the community who serve, primarily, an investigatory or police function rather than providing for the needs of the indigent. According to Silberman, "the failure of the enormous American social welfare effort stems from . . . the social worker's preoccupation with doing for people instead of doing with them, a preoccupation that destroys the dignity and arouses the hostility of the people who are supposed to be helped."[47] The relationship between municipal welfare departments and their clientele, according to Silberman, is a "more or less perpetual state of war."[48] One view of the social welfare establishment was expressed by the editor of the *Amsterdam News*:

I'm fed up with social workers in Harlem because the average social worker in Harlem prostitutes the misery of the community and spends three quarters of his time trying to convert that misery into dollars and cents to put in his own pocket. . . .
So the folks downtown say in unison to the Harlem "expert": "What can we

do for these people to prevent this?" This is what our expert has been waiting for.

"I don't have all the answers gentlemen," he says. "But I think I'm on the right track toward a solution to the problem. With about $250,000 I could pull together a research team of eminent social workers, psychologists, psychiatrists, anthropologists—the whole bit—and these men will come up with the answer for you in 18 months."

"In other words," say the City Fathers, "you need $250,000 to get started, is that right?"

And so the Harlem expert, whom you don't even know, and who doesn't even know you, hops on the "A" train with a quarter of a million dollars of your money and mine to spend studying you.[49]

Another Harlem resident declared:

Well, man, you know what I think about it, like I mentioned before, with the politicians in Harlem, I think the welfare could help if they really knew the problems that existed and didn't take such an objective view as they have, you know like, what I mean is they will send people a check, a family, you know, a check for a certain amount of money, and say if someone, a friend perhaps, who is doing a little better than that family wants to give the family something, say like a kitchen set, you know, like maybe they bought something new and they are getting rid of this and it's better than what the family has so they give them the old kitchen set . . . well, when the investigator comes in, man, she puts these people through charges, you know, about where did you get this and you know. They want to know too many things which I think they should be glad to have people to assist these people other than themselves.[50]

In short, the 1960s were a time of testing and challenge for the traditional social casework approach and the concepts that were its foundation. Whether this approach has survived the test, only time can tell.

Conclusion

The welfare rights organizations arose from the civil rights movement, the War on Poverty, and changes in social welfare philosophy. The civil rights movement waned after the passage of the 1965 Voting Rights Act. Having concentrated on undermining the legal foundations of segregation, the movement ran into increasing opposition when it began to seek welfare-oriented goals. Such goals did not receive the legitimacy that had been accorded to the movement's quest for equal status in the South. As long as the movement concentrated on ensuring to blacks the opportunity to compete for accepted societal rewards such as buying a home, voting, or attending school the movement enjoyed success. As Moynihan points out, "the [black] demand for equality of opportunity has been generally perceived by White Americans as a demand for liberty."[51] Liberty requires only that blacks be able to start the race, or to have a go at a competitive struggle with the understanding that an equal opportunity to compete may not guarantee equal income. However, Bayard Rustin argues that the problems of black America cannot be resolved by granting liberty alone because basic socioeconomic conditions, rather than legal inequalities, constitute the fundamental problem facing blacks.[52] Rustin calls for radical change and vast new programs in housing, education, income redistribution, and health. These new programs, according to Rustin, are attainable only through a radical coalition of blacks, trade unions, churches, and other white liberal groups.

The southern civil rights movement, aside from legitimizing public disorder as a protest strategy, has also spawned social and political activists who are well trained in implementing this strategy to induce change. Many of these activists, as well as the tactics of the civil rights movement, reemerged in the newly created OEO structures that have given low-income communities much of their institutional base. Others found their way into private ventures that shared similar goals with the movement and the War on Poverty. The shift of former civil rights activists to the pursuit of goals having an economic content was made complete by the various Great Society programs.

The War on Poverty not only mobilized some of the poor, it also identified target populations within poverty areas, isolated their primary needs, and sought to direct these poor to public agencies capable of providing assistance. Often these were public welfare agencies. Thousands of people were able to obtain assistance from Legal Services Program lawyers, Community Action Program (CAP) personnel, and VISTA volunteers.

A 1967 report on the impact of OEO programs in a selected area of East Baltimore is illustrative.[53] Several community action programs were initiated following the 1960 election. In a target area in East Baltimore, between September 1965 and September 1966, the AFDC caseload increased by 36.6 percent in contrast with a city-wide increase during the same period of only 8.6 percent. The growth in the AFDC caseload in the community action target area was four times the growth for Baltimore as a whole.

This, of course, can mean many things. It is possible, for example, that the community action program focused on the areas of the city where the need was greatest. It also suggests, however, that the program successfully located and identified families with children who were eligible for, but not receiving, welfare. The report concluded:

It cannot be doubted that all of this dedicated and highly publicized activity has brought awareness of the variety of public and private social welfare services to those living in poverty to a degree never before experienced. When poor people are everywhere encouraged to make use of these resources—by publicity, by action workers on their own block, by teachers of their children in schools, by their doctors and by any social agency they may happen to have contact with, a surge of response must be expected. It is the contention of this report that the increase of the AFDC caseload reflects this response to the anti-poverty effort, and that the poor families of this State through a combination of some changes in their alternative forms of maintenance and perhaps for the major part encouraged by the national effort to do something about poverty have responded to the use of public services, including welfare, in numbers heretofore unequalled.[54]

In short, the War on Poverty identified a target population, isolated its primary need as being additional sources of income maintenance, and then made use of the most convenient public agency, the public welfare system, to achieve it.

Finally, a contradiction exists within the social welfare system itself, a direct conflict between the reality of the system and its professed goals and values. The administration of the welfare system is admittedly deficient. For example, a 1970 HEW report found that the welfare programs of thirty-nine states failed to meet federal standards completely.[55] While some violations, the report concluded, were minor, others involved major instances of noncompliance with congressional provisions and recent Supreme Court decisions enlarging the rights of public assistance recipients. Eight states had failed to satisfy requirements for implementing a 1969 court decision abolishing minimum residency requirements for eligibility. Fifteen states had failed to implement a 1968 ruling striking down the so-called man-in-the-house limitation on children's aid. Ten states had no federally approved regulations for implementing the 1967 Social Security amendments with regard to work incentives and the computation of welfare benefits. Nine states faced a possible loss of aid for failure to provide fair hearings as required by statute. Only eleven states were found to meet fully federal welfare requirements.

In this, then, we have the necessary and sufficient conditions under which the National Welfare Rights Organization was to develop: a crisis in the social welfare profession, the realignment of national politics, a reemergence of reform, an identified and sympathetic inner-city population needing and wanting additional income, a growing cadre of activists trained in the strategy and tactics of protest and, finally, through the Great Society, institutions and structures that afforded an opportunity for this unlikely combination of circumstances to result in a movement seeking change on behalf of the urban lower class.

The shift of focus toward welfare-oriented goals has had two consequences. Minority groups, and especially blacks, now demand not only the possibility of equality but the fact of equality. Or, as Glazer puts it, they are demanding "equality of economic results."[56] This has resulted in a political crisis. The attempt by rising ethnic groups to obtain recognition, opportunity, and a share of power is a common theme in American political history. However, the demand for more equal disposable incomes has created greater than usual conflict between white and black interests. By pursuing this goal, the black movement is competing directly with other segments of society for services and resources. It has also divided white sympathizers. Black demands, as Wilson points out, have now made a major issue out of the choice between liberty and equality of opportunity. White liberals tend to be more concerned with equality of opportunity; white radicals with equality of economic results.[57] For these reasons, this change in focus by the black movement severely strained the foundation of alliances on which the movement rested.[58]

4 The National Welfare Rights Organization

The Growth of a National Welfare Rights Movement

Since the early 1960s many local groups of welfare recipients had been formed to obtain redress of particular grievances against local welfare administrations. Although the beginnings of most of these welfare rights organizations (WROs) are obscure, several early instances of welfare rights activity have been well documented.

In 1962 a WRO was organized in Alameda County, California, with recipients being assisted by Bay Area students and civil rights groups.[1] The experience of a 38-year-old AFDC mother with seven children led to the formation of the Alameda WRO. The roof of her house had been destroyed by fire, and when this was reported to the welfare department, her check was delayed because she was "living in unfit housing." The woman tried to move but could not without assistance. A social-work student at the University of California took up the AFDC mother's cause and began to question the welfare department about the legal basis for its action. There was none, and the check was released.[2] The Alameda WRO then challenged a welfare department vocational training program that required recipients to pick strawberries in exchange for welfare grants. The organization's principal tactic was a sit-in at the welfare department.

WRO activity spread to other low-income communities in California, to Long Beach, Los Angeles, and Monterey and Contra Costa Counties. In each instance, the stimulus for organization was different—inadequate housing, employment policies, or a reaction to practices by the administration that violated or, at least, stretched the law. The result, however, was the same—the beginning of an organized welfare rights movement among the recipient population.

The movement spread. In Colorado, a National Association of Social Workers chapter helped AFDC mothers to form social action groups to protect their legal rights.[3] WROs emerged simultaneously in such major cities as New York, Cleveland, Boston, Oakland, and Los Angeles.[4] Aside from recipients, others influential in establishing WROs were civil rights workers, social workers and social-work students, clergymen, the Northern Student Movement, the Students for a Democratic Society (SDS), and, most important, neighborhood community action workers affiliated with the War on Poverty.

Thus, by the mid-sixties determined assistance recipients in various parts of the country began to form groups and demand benefits prescribed by welfare law. These groups concentrated on local issues and developed policies in response to local problems, with local leaders to guide them. Little if any communication or coordination existed between these highly disparate groups, and national organizers were almost nonexistent.

Into this breach in the growing welfare rights movement stepped George Wiley armed with a widely publicized action strategy developed by Richard Cloward and Frances Fox Piven. In late 1965, Cloward and Piven circulated a draft paper detailing an action strategy for mobilizing the poor.[5] This strategy evolved from their experiences at MFY and in working with low-income communities in New York City. Cloward and Piven describe their central thesis:

[This strategy] called upon those who were working with welfare recipients, as well as other activists, to form a movement with the express purpose of getting thousands of families onto the relief rolls, for we had by then conducted sufficient research to establish that only half of the eligible poor were on the rolls. We also reasoned that campaigns to double and triple the relief rolls would produce significant pressure for national reforms in the relief system, perhaps along the lines of a national guaranteed minimum income. Rapidly rising rolls would mean procedural turmoil in the cumbersome welfare bureaucracies, fiscal turmoil in the localities where existing sources of tax revenue were already overburdened, and political turmoil as an alerted electorate divided on the question of how to overcome this disruption in local government. To deal with these problems . . . mayors and governors would call upon the federal government with increasing insistency to establish a federally financed minimum income.[6]

In short, what the Cloward-Piven strategy advocated was no less than a national revolt against the administration of public assistance, a revolt to be characterized by the poor themselves demanding receipt of legally mandated services and resources. The system would be used in its own destruction.

George Wiley was an associate director of the Congress of Racial Equality (CORE) under James Farmer. He had previously been a professor of chemistry at Syracuse University. The resignation of Farmer in 1966 and the emergence of Floyd McKissick as the new CORE leader led to a new emphasis on programs aimed at the northern black ghettos. Wiley subsequently resigned from CORE.

Prior to his resignation, Wiley had been impressed by the developing welfare rights movement and the potential provided by welfare issues as organizing tools. He was also impressed by the views espoused by Cloward, with whom he sat on a CORE advisory group. From February to May 1966, Wiley worked with the Citizens Crusade Against Poverty lobbying for the passage of a broadly based minimum wage bill. In this way, he built up a network of contacts in the welfare and poverty area. Sensing that a new organizational structure was needed, Wiley sought to interest the Citizens Crusade Against Poverty in an organization based on the Cloward and Piven strategy. Failing to persuade the Citizens Crusade, in May 1966 Wiley founded a private, independent action group, the Poverty

Rights Action Center (PRAC). PRAC was to provide communications, coordination, and related services to civil rights and grass-roots antipoverty activists scattered across the nation in order to promote concerted action on selected major issues.[7]

PRAC was rooted in a belief in the efficacy of political activism as a means of producing change. The founders of PRAC emphasized that without a level of activism like that during the height of the civil rights movement, which led to the involvement of large numbers of people and produced many benefits for blacks, the prospects for changes in the welfare system would be slight.

The decline in the civil rights movement lessened the ability of activists to mount effective campaigns toward common objectives. The movement, which had earlier provided a unifying purpose and direction, was now divided and beset with financial problems and a lack of agreement on both short- and long-term goals. Most important, activists upon leaving the civil rights movement were dispersing across the country and involving themselves in a wide range of local problems and political initiatives. Because of this, the lines of communication that had connected local activists were becoming more tenuous. Simultaneously, a new and increasingly militant leadership was emerging as a potential successor to the civil rights movement. This was particularly true of organizations in the low-income communities of northern cities.

PRAC recognized that involvement with community action and poverty programs provided an opportunity for a new configuration of forces to promote social change in the United States. What was missing was a vehicle for channeling these forces into concerted action. PRAC determined to serve this function with the following set of objectives.[8]

1. To develop nationwide support for major antipoverty and civil rights measures
2. To develop nationwide support for significant local antipoverty and civil rights movements
3. To provide surveillance and pressures on federal agencies handling programs designed to help the poor
4. To provide advice and assistance to local groups coming to Washington to lobby for support of their programs before federal agencies.

On May 23, 1966, PRAC opened its national headquarters in Washington with a staff of four. Its intent was to develop a system of rapid communication, to prepare "how-to-do-it" information guides for major action strategies, to identify key targets for pressure, and to develop a surveillance program for selected federal agencies. The development of a national welfare rights movement became the first major task of PRAC. To this end, contacts were developed with WROs throughout the country, with the local WROs encouraged to put greater pressures on local welfare departments.

By May 1966, Wiley's attempt to organize the WROs began to receive national attention. Concerned groups in Ohio, united under the Ohio Committee for Adequate Welfare, decided to stage a 155-mile walk to the state capitol in Columbus to present a petition of grievances and to dramatize their demands for a decent welfare allowance.[9] Prominent among their grievances was the inadequacy of monthly allowances relative to the state's own minimum standards.[10] The Ohio Committee for Adequate Welfare wanted an additional $30 million in AFDC grants to attain these standards. The march began in Cleveland. On June 20, 1966, under the leadership of the Rev. Paul Younger and Edith Doering, 40 marchers began the walk to Columbus. By June 30, 1966, when the marchers reached Columbus, their ranks had swollen by well over 2,000 recipients and supporters from all over the state.[11] Through the efforts of PRAC, simultaneous WRO demonstrations were held in fifteen other cities.[12]

On August 6 and 7, PRAC brought together 136 recipients representing more than 100 welfare rights organizations in twenty-four cities and eleven states for the first national meeting of the welfare rights movement.[13] This body formed the National Coordinating Committee of Welfare Rights Groups (NCC), composed of 11 representatives from each major state attending the meeting.[a] NCC was meant to be a temporary instrument to shape the new movement's policy and to launch a three-month, nationwide organizing campaign in September. This campaign centered around demands for benefits illegally denied to recipients, the right to represent recipients before welfare administrations and at hearings, and the power to organize and bargain collectively on their behalf. It used such tactics as picketing, sit-ins, and school boycotts.[14]

In December, the NCC was expanded to include representatives from new organizations affiliating with the NWRO. In February 1967, a second national organization meeting was held in Washington, D.C., attracting more than 350 recipients from nearly 200 WROs in seventy cities and twenty-six states. Delegates participated in training workshops on welfare law and organizational techniques. The conference also developed and presented to Congress and HEW its first national legislative program.[15] In April, the NCC adopted a membership rule that would prove critical for the future development of the NWRO—the payment of dues. This rule was designed to strengthen both national and local grass-roots organizations and to build a committed membership base. Following this, negotiating sessions were held with the Department of Agriculture and HEW over changes in the food stamp and welfare programs. In June, a campaign designed to secure minimal family needs, backed up by requests for fair hearings, resulted in improved benefits for 5,000 recipients in forty cities. By the summer of 1967, the NWRO had become a coherent, functioning national organization, with its principal objective expressed in its slogan, "More Money Now."

PRAC's intensive organizing activity during the two-year period was rewarded

[a]Massachusetts, New York, New Jersey, Maryland, the District of Columbia, Pennsylvania, Ohio, Michigan, Illinois, Missouri, and California.

on August 25, 1967, when the first National Welfare Rights Convention was convened in Washington, D.C. At this convention, 178 locally elected delegates and alternates represented approximately seventy-five WROs in forty-five cities and twenty-one states. A constitution was written and adopted, national officers elected, a platform of goals drawn up, and the first national relief organization since the 1930s born.

The Organization of the NWRO

The NWRO is a nationwide federation of local welfare rights organizations. Each local WRO is a fully independent and autonomous unit, determining its own program, hiring and paying its own staff, making its own decisions, and raising its own funds. NWRO links all of these groups into a nationwide organization (see Figure 4-1).

Individuals may not join the NWRO directly, but can affiliate only by belonging to a local group in their community. The NWRO permits the following to become members: any welfare recipient; anyone who has been a welfare recipient during the past five years; or anyone who is poor, defined roughly by using $4400 per year for a family of four as base level poverty line.[16] However, many local WROs have stricter requirements for membership. Some permit only actual welfare recipients to join.

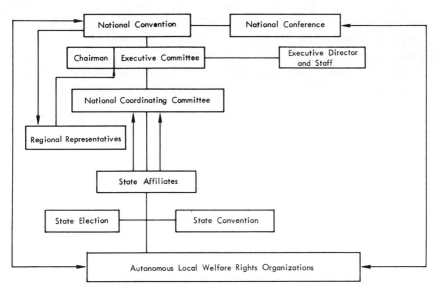

Figure 4-1. National Welfare Rights Organization Organizational Chart

Local groups can affiliate with the NWRO when they have at least twenty-five members who have paid NWRO dues, $1 per year. To stimulate the development of new groups, the NWRO allows new groups to begin to affiliate when ten welfare recipients sign up and pay dues.

By affiliating with the NWRO, local groups gain access to resources and services that could not be obtained were they on their own. Affiliation brings to the local organizations NWRO's national newsletter, use of a nationwide communications network, research and informational assistance, legal aid, programmatic materials, and fund-raising assistance. The NWRO's headquarters are run by an executive director and his staff and serve as a communications center and source of financial and material support for the local WROs.

The highest policy-making body in the NWRO is the National Convention, which is held every two years. Here, broad policy is formulated and national officers elected by the representatives of local groups. During the years in which a convention is not held, there is a National Conference to formulate policy. All city and state WRO officers must be designated as delegates of local WROs to have a vote at national policy-making meetings. Local WROs are entitled to send delegates and alternates based on the number of members the local WROs have previously registered with the NWRO.[17] Local WROs are responsible for the financial support of their representatives at national policy meetings.

Between national meetings, two bodies make NWRO policy: the Executive Committee and the National Coordinating Committee (NCC). The more important policy-making instrument is the Executive Committee, which meets eight times each year and is composed of the nine nationally elected officers.[b] Second in importance is the NCC. This consists of the officers plus one representative and one alternate from each state with affiliated local WROs.[c] The NCC meets four times a year in different parts of the country. Normally, cities may not be directly represented on the NCC. However, exceptions are made for cities with extraordinarily large numbers of NWRO members and local WROs who, because of geography or other special problems, cannot be effectively represented by a state organization.[d]

Finally, the national executive director and his staff play a critical role in keeping NWRO functioning. By serving as a communications center and a national hub of activity, they service and coordinate the activities of a large number of local groups. George Wiley, NWRO's first executive director, was the most influential figure in the national welfare rights movement.

---

[b]These nine officers are the chairman, the first, second, and third vice-chairmen; treasurer; corresponding, recording, and financial secretaries; and the sergeant-at-arms.

[c]The NWRO requires that all affiliated groups in a state have a voice in selecting their NCC representative and alternate.

[d]New York City is a good example. There has been vigorous welfare rights activity in the city and little in most other parts of the state.

**The Goals and Accomplishments of
the NWRO**

The NWRO's list of goals is prefaced by its organizational slogan: "Jobs or Income Now—Decent Jobs with Adequate Pay for Those Who Can Work and Adequate Income for Those Who Cannot." Its specific goals are:[18]

1. Adequate Income: A system that guarantees enough money for all Americans to live dignified lives above the level of poverty.
2. Dignity: A system that guarantees recipients the full freedoms, rights, and respect as all American citizens.
3. Justice: A fair and open system that guarantees recipients the full protection of the Constitution.
4. Democracy: A system that guarantees recipients direct participation in the decisions under which they must live.

These goals are illustrative of the developments that have occurred in welfare recipients' efforts to end their subordinate status in American society.

The NWRO focuses solely upon public assistance. Within the area of public assistance, its concentration is even more narrowly oriented. As a rule, it has ignored and even rejected some related issues raised at one time or another by nonclient groups. Good examples are such goals as increasing the number of social caseworkers relative to the caseload and augmenting social and psychological services, which are often stressed by the social-work establishment as the best ways of reforming the welfare system. Instead, the NWRO has had only two basic objectives: to ameliorate and, if possible, eliminate the complex set of restrictive eligibility conditions and rules that confront the recipient; and, more important, to increase the amount of income support that the system provides.

The NWRO has compiled a list of practices by welfare departments across the nation that it considers illegal.[19]

1. Midnight raids.
2. Racial discrimination.
3. Illegal termination of recipients.
4. Illegal rejection of applicants.
5. Discrimination against large families.
6. Threatening, scaring or intimidating recipients.
7. Searches and seizures without warrants.
8. Not giving recipients special grants for clothing, household furnishings, etc., which the law requires.
9. Giving recipients smaller grants than the law says they should receive.
10. Discriminating against families with illegitimate children.

11. Forcing recipients to accept other social services in order to keep their welfare grants.
12. Counting against recipients income that they do not have or did not receive.
13. Making friends or nonlegally responsible relatives pay child support.
14. Not giving fair hearings within the time limits set by law.
15. Forcing mothers with young children to take jobs or job training.
16. Forcing recipients to live in segregated or substandard housing.
17. Not informing recipients of their rights of appeal.

To emphasize its determination to eliminate what it considers illegal, oppressive, and burdensome eligibility conditions, the NWRO also advocates the principle of welfare as a right, legally mandated by the Congress and state legislatures. In order to strengthen this view, NWRO has drawn up a *Welfare Bill of Rights* consisting of thirteen points:

1. The right to be a member of a welfare rights organization.
2. The right to fair and equal treatment, free from discrimination based on race or color.
3. The right to apply for any welfare program and to have that application put in writing.
4. The right to have the welfare department make a decision promptly after application for aid.
5. The right to be told in writing the specific reason for denial of aid.
6. The right to appeal a decision thought to be wrong, including denials and reduction of assistance, and to be given a fair hearing before an impartial referee.
7. The right to get welfare payments without being forced to spend the money as the welfare department wants.
8. The right to be treated with respect.
9. The right to be treated in a way that does not invade your privacy.
10. The right to receive welfare aid without having the welfare department ask you questions about who your social friends are, such as who you are going with.
11. The right to have the same constitutional protections all other citizens have.
12. The right to be told and informed by the welfare department of all your rights, including the ways you can best make sure that you can get your welfare money.
13. The right to have, to get, and to give advice during all contacts with the welfare department, including when applying, when being investigated, and during fair hearings.

Finally, in perhaps its most concerted national lobbying effort yet, the NWRO has advanced an income plan of its own to compete with the Nixon administration's family assistance plan. The NWRO's income plan calls for a guaranteed annual income of $6,500 per annum for a family of four, instead of $2,400 which was considered by Congress. The NWRO campaign on behalf of its own plan has attempted simultaneously to stimulate and encourage pressure from below through its organizational affiliates and their local allies, while also seeking to mobilize support from above through both conventional and unconventional lobbying tactics.

In short, the NWRO has sought to implement its goals by means of mass political protest, strategic advocacy, court tests, and lobbying. By and large, the goals of the NWRO are of a type for which mass action can and has been most readily mobilized. These goals are specific, assertive, and oriented toward tangible benefits for welfare recipients. Moreover, not only would achievement of these goals result in tangible benefits for the NWRO's clientele, there also exists a reasonable probability that many of these goals will be at least partially achieved. The primary reason for this is that many of the NWRO's demands have already been legally mandated by Congress and the state legislatures. For this reason, the NWRO has enjoyed some notable successes, particularly in its initial activities.

The NWRO is now one of the best-known protest organizations serving the low-income population of the nation. It is composed principally of black mothers who are recipients of AFDC. Its activities have been widely publicized, particularly in the ghettos of northern cities. There, local WROs have staged hundreds of demonstrations involving thousands of welfare mothers and their sympathizers, including social workers, lawyers, Catholic priests, and Protestant ministers. In 1967, a sit-in at the Boston welfare department, protesting summary terminations of recipients without hearings, led to conflict with the police followed by three days of rioting. In New York City, welfare centers have been badly damaged, mounted police have charged recipient demonstrators, and thousands of clients and their sympathizers have been jailed. WRO activity in New York City was particularly intense between 1966 and 1968. The experience gained from activity in New York City has set a pattern for WROs elsewhere and subsequent nationwide campaigns.

The NWRO was a major participant in the ill-fated Poor People's Campaign in Washington, D.C. in 1968. The largest single demonstration in that campaign was the Mother's Day march by more than 7,000 recipients, led by Coretta King and George Wiley, through riot-scarred black sections of Washington.[20] National guardsmen armed with fixed bayonets and riot guns were called out in Madison, Wisconsin after more than 200 recipients and students seized the state legislature protesting welfare appropriation cuts. The *Welfare Fighter*, NWRO's newsletter, describes what happened:

An insistent and determined crowd of welfare mothers seized the chambers of the Wisconsin State Assembly the day before, September 29. The occupation of the state capitol came at the end of a week long 90-mile march from Milwaukee to Madison by welfare mothers and supporters. . . .

Completing the final leg of the march . . . about 2,000 people stormed through the front door and forcibly entered the empty chambers of the state assembly, packing it to the walls.[21]

This incident received nationwide attention in the national communications media.

An excellent illustration of how the NWRO operates with respect to local WROs, its ability to form alliances and to operate through the courts, and its success in applying pressure on state and federal welfare bureaucracies was the Nevada campaign during the winter and spring of 1971.[22] In the winter, the director of the Nevada State Welfare Department terminated summarily 3,000 recipients and simultaneously reduced the grants of another 4,500 recipients. A few months later, as a result of the NWRO's "Operation Nevada," that same director announced that he was in a "life and death struggle" with Nevada's WRO.[23] What the director meant was that he had initiated a policy that stirred into action a surprising coalition of forces. Welfare rights lawyers immediately challenged his actions as arbitrary, capricious, and illegal. Subsequently, the state was ordered by the court to reinstate, retroactive to the original termination date, all recipients summarily dropped from the rolls. On April 8, 1971, another court decision led to the restoration of full grants to the 4,500 recipients whose checks had been reduced and, in an unusual action, the federal court established a watchdog system to monitor future attempts by state authorities to violate welfare laws.

Instead of submitting to the director's action, a small band of WRO members in Nevada determined to resist the termination. They invited the NWRO to join them in their fight, which it did by providing staff and legal assistance. Other groups were also mobilized. The League of Women Voters produced and distributed literature about the state's action. The Franciscan Center also allied itself with the Clark County WRO. While litigation proceeded, the NWRO demonstrated on the Las Vegas Strip and at the state capitol at Carson City. In the end, the NWRO won a complete victory. In describing the lessons learned from this episode, the chairwoman of the Clark County WRO declared:

We have demonstrated that when poor people stand up for their rights, speak up for their rights, march for their rights, go to jail for their rights, and organize for their rights, they can win their rights. Now we intend to demonstrate that organized poor people not only can win their rights but can protect them after they are won.[24]

As a direct result of NWRO's efforts, several new local WROs were organized in Nevada. Subsequently, HEW issued a report sustaining the NWRO's position: that Nevada acted illegally in terminating the dependency status and reducing the grants of welfare recipients and that the original levels were legally mandated by the state.

Welfare rights activity has typically taken two forms: organizing around individual grievances; and organizing large mass-based campaigns around legal entitlements which recipients either are not aware of, or, if aware, do not exercise.[25] By far the more difficult approach is to organize around individual grievances.[26] In attempting this approach, WRO organizers almost always begin by preparing a highly simplified version of local welfare regulations.[27] Oftentimes, handbooks of welfare regulations are based on documents obtained covertly from sympathizers within the welfare bureaucracy and during sit-ins or other disruptive activities at welfare centers. These handbooks are then given wide distribution and publicity through the ghetto's communication network of poverty programs, churches, storefronts, local WROs, community groups, and social clubs. Cloward and Piven argue that the handbooks have been especially important in initiating welfare rights activity by alerting people to the ways in which the system often rejects applicants or reduces benefits without any legal basis.[28] Perhaps the greatest single fear among recipients and the focus of much individual grievance work is the practice of arbitrary terminations without notice.

In contrast to protest activity organized around individual grievances have been campaigns for legal entitlements such as special grants for clothing, household furnishings, and other benefits. Utilizing a combination of numbers, good organization, coercion, and the widespread bureaucratic fear of an incident triggering violence, many mass-benefit campaigns have been waged successfully in various localities including New York City. However, the movement's initial gains have typically depended upon the strength and tenacity of the local WRO rather than upon the national organization.

For example, a number of WROs, particularly in Philadelphia and New York City, have been able to negotiate credit agreements with stores. The NWRO has also sought credit agreements with two major national corporations, Montgomery Ward and Sears. It had some success with the former, but little with the latter.[29] An agreement between the NWRO and Montgomery Ward calls for the extension of credit to 3,000 NWRO members in nine geographical areas.[e] Potential applicants are selected by the NWRO and introduced to Montgomery Ward, where they are screened according to regular credit procedures. Montgomery Ward informs the NWRO of all rejections and, if recipients give their assent, of delinquents also. Furthermore, Montgomery Ward agrees to assist the NWRO in its consumer education program by providing to 500 local WROs technical assistance, advance notice and information on sales, and catalogs.

Because of widespread publicity after its protest activities and its successes in achieving tangible benefits for its members, the NWRO grew rapidly. At the end of 1967 it had about 5,000 members; by the end of 1968, approximately 10,000. These members represented roughly 40,000 recipients in thirty-five states affiliated with over 200 local WROs. By the summer of 1969 the NWRO

[e]These areas are Baltimore, Washington, Chicago, Kansas City, Los Angeles, Detroit, Dallas, Fort Worth, and Oakland.

claimed 25,000 dues-paying members in forty-six states. Assuming that each member represented an average family of four, the NWRO had come to serve nearly 100,000 clients.[f]

By 1968, the NWRO's publicity network had become so extensive that its activities were covered in metropolitan dailies in New York, Boston, Chicago, Philadelphia, San Diego, Providence, Ann Arbor, Tucson, and Wilmington. More important, the NWRO's internal communications network had developed to the point that it now provided the local WROs a direct link with each other as well as the national organization.

In 1968, the federal government in effect recognized the NWRO as an agent of the nation's welfare mothers. This recognition was extended in the form of a $434,930 contract between the Department of Labor and the National Self-Help Corporation (NASHCO), a nonpolitical corporate instrument organized and controlled by the NWRO to accept grants and contracts. The contract called for NASHCO to provide information on the recently enacted 1967 Social Security Amendments, particularly the Work Incentive Program (WIN), and to train recipients to help ensure the success of that program.

The parties to the contract perceived their respective roles differently. The Department of Labor saw itself gaining WIN trainees from the contracts and some feedback about the program's operation for relatively small costs. Initially, the NWRO strenuously opposed the enactment of the 1967 amendments, calling WIN the "WIP" and characterizing it as a "slave labor act."[30] Indeed, delegates to an NWRO-sponsored convention in Washington, D.C. staged a brief sit-in at hearings before the Senate Finance Committee on the then proposed 1967 amendments. George Wiley also had a face-to-face confrontation with Wilbur Mills at the latter's home during an antiamendment demonstration.[31] For the NWRO, in other words, acceptance of the contract meant a significant break with its past policy. Despite internal opposition, George Wiley argued that, by accepting the contract, the NWRO was simply informing recipients of their rights and that, officially, the NWRO remained opposed to the amendments.[32] The value of the contract to the NWRO was clear. Cloward and Piven noted that it provided the NWRO "a sum roughly equivalent to the total amount raised from private sources after the organization was formed in early 1966.[33] The federal government was certainly aware that a substantial portion of the contract funds would be used to strengthen the organization of the NWRO. Subsequently, NASHCO sought a $300,000 contract with HEW to develop information systems to inform clients of benefits and services. However, this time, HEW rejected NASHCO's proposal.

By 1970, it was clear that the NWRO had grown into a coherent and functioning organization with a constitution, elected leadership, a national headquarters, and an effective communications network linking hundreds of autonomous and independent local WROs.[34] The movement has continued to

[f]In 1969 membership eligibility rules were changed to allow families of the working poor with incomes below $5,500 per annum to join the NWRO.

grow and spread rapidly since its inception in 1966. Its constituency of low-income residents located primarily in the large northern cities is, perhaps, unique on the contemporary political scene. The NWRO has also sought to establish and maintain links with similar organizations concerned with other social and economic issues (a good example is the National Tenants Organization). Because of the NWRO communications network, these other groups have been able to observe and share in the experience of the welfare rights movement.

The existence of a national headquarters gives local WROs added support and ability to call in a "concentrated package of support," as Operation Nevada so clearly illustrated. Besides the associated links and benefits derived from affiliation, the welfare rights movement has provided for the first time in recent American political history an opportunity for poor clients of the welfare system to engage welfare policymakers without the need for either appointed or elected surrogates. This process is critical, for, by recruiting, mobilizing, and engaging in significant political action, a substantial number of persons from the urban lower-class, welfare rights organizations have increased the social and political training of their members, with a consequent increase in their participation in the political process.

The movement has, in this way, helped to develop some of the latent leadership talents that exist within the welfare population. Welfare mothers participate in generating their own programs and strategies, while simultaneously mastering new political skills. New routes of social and political mobility have also been opened for the leadership. This is a most important accomplishment of the movement, for welfare rights activity has created a cadre of highly politicized and battle-tested women who, though they have focused on the welfare issue, are now involving themselves more deeply in other issues as well.

Because of local welfare rights activities, recipients and their sympathizers now have regular face-to-face meetings and negotiating sessions with welfare administrations. For example, on February 25, 1969, NWRO's Executive Committee met with then HEW Secretary Robert Finch to discuss matters of mutual concern. Countless other sessions like this have occurred at both the national and local level, with local WRO leaders gaining valuable political training and insight from these sessions.

Both the supporters and the opponents of the welfare rights movement have also discussed its impact on the welfare caseload and, in particular, its contribution to the substantial increase in welfare dependency during the past five years. Cloward and Piven, for example, suggest that welfare rights groups have mounted large-scale campaigns to obtain benefits to which many recipients are entitled but few receive.[35] In New York City, Cloward and Piven assert that these groups' campaigns have been responsible, directly or indirectly, for the following:

1. The monthly level of special grants was only $3 million in June 1967; it was $13 million in June 1968.

2. The average monthly special grant per recipient jumped from $40 in 1965 to $100 in 1968.
3. The welfare rights movement has influenced, to some extent, acceptances and closings and, in this way, has contributed to increased rolls.

Although the welfare rights organizations have primarily served persons already receiving assistance, their activities on behalf of recipients have had the side-effect, or "by-product" to use Olson's terminology, of making eligible nonrecipients more aware of their rights and less fearful of applying for assistance. In the latter parts of this study we examine at length some of the effects of welfare rights activity in New York City. In particular, we estimate the impact of this activity on the grant level and, both directly and indirectly, on applications, acceptances, and closings. Hopefully, this analysis will demonstrate more clearly what the welfare rights movement has accomplished.

The administration of welfare and, because of this, the activities of welfare rights organizations have been in large part local phenomena. Although the NWRO has had a general impact on the nation's caseload and grant levels, among other things because of its court actions, the operating unit of the welfare rights movement has been largely the local welfare rights organization. To understand better how the welfare rights movement has functioned and what it has accomplished, it is necessary, therefore, to examine the movement at the local level. For this reason, for the remainder of this study, we concentrate on the most important welfare jurisdiction in the country with the oldest and most active welfare rights movement—New York City.

5 The Emergence of Local Welfare Rights Activity in New York City

What were the origins of protest activity by New York City's welfare poor? What factors accounted for the emergence of active grass-roots welfare rights organizations in the city? The answers to these questions will, hopefully, provide an understanding of the political forces operating in the northern urban ghettos. They will also permit a better understanding of the motivations and attitudes of clients of the welfare system.

For the social scientist, militant political activity among the welfare poor is a particularly intriguing phenomenon. A well-established view in the profession is that low-status groups and lower-class persons in general tend to be politically apathetic and quiescent.[1] Seymour Lipset suggests that "low-status groups are also less apt to participate in formal organizations, read fewer magazines and books regularly, possess less information on public affairs, vote less, and in general take less interest in politics."[2] Lipset also notes that on the rare occasions when low-status persons are active, their "low education, low participation in political or voluntary organizations of any type, little reading, isolated occupations, economic insecurity, and authoritarian family patterns" all contribute to an authoritarian predisposition.[3] What, then, explains the emergence of coherent and sustained political activity by a segment of the urban poor in New York City, despite the fact that the city's political system has long been dominated by a liberal philosophy and has had a historic sensitivity toward the needs of the poor?

Living Conditions of the City's Welfare Recipients

During the past decade many concerned scholars, journalists, novelists, government officials, and ghetto residents have written accounts of the lifestyle of welfare recipients.[4] Several of these accounts have focused on the plight of welfare families living in New York City. In addition, there have been several surveys of New York City residents on welfare which tend to confirm the rather harsh portrait painted in the popular literature. A 1966 sample of welfare families is particularly useful in describing the lifestyle of welfare recipients in the city.[5]

Life on welfare is far from pleasurable. The mother is the sole adult in 70 percent of all welfare families. Relatively few welfare families have been able to get into public housing. Rats and hallway garbage are found in many of the buildings housing welfare recipients. One-third of the publicly assisted households average more than one and a half persons per room. Most welfare families lack certain basic amenities.[a]

School absenteeism is high among welfare children. More than one-half of the welfare mothers in the city have children in school. One-third of these mothers keep their school-age children at home on occasion to help in housework. About 30 percent also keep their children at home at times because they lack the means to purchase necessary shoes or clothing and 20 percent because of shame about the way their children are dressed.

Welfare families tend to be mobile within the city. About one-fourth of the families in the sample have lived in their neighborhoods for less than one year and half less than three years. However, this does not mean that most welfare families have migrated from outside the city. To the contrary, three-fourths of the mothers were either born in New York City or had lived there for over a decade, a fact tending to discredit the popular notion that the recent increase in welfare dependency in New York has been the result of an influx of the poor from other parts of the country.

A relatively large number of welfare mothers are unhappy with the neighborhoods in which they live. One in four rate their neighborhoods as bad or very bad, while one in five are afraid to walk in the neighborhood even in the daytime.

Welfare mothers are, as a rule, well-informed and recognize the need for education and employment. Four out of ten welfare mothers read newspapers daily. Half read magazines regularly, while 25 percent watch television four hours or more each day. Most mothers have attended high school. However, only one in six has graduated. Another one in six never got beyond the fourth grade. Most welfare mothers believe they did not get a fair chance to acquire the schooling they wanted. Most mothers have also had some work experience and 70 percent would prefer to be employed if adequate child care could be arranged.

Other studies tend to confirm this picture of the conditions and attitudes of the city's welfare families. Two aspects of life in the city—education and housing—are particularly well documented.

Education. Nearly one-third of all students in the city's public schools receive some form of assistance. Welfare students suffer disproportionately from the many problems besetting the city's school system.[6] Among the difficulties confronting welfare children are limited funds for transportation, clothing,

---

[a]For example, while nine out of ten families have a clock and a television set or a radio, only one-fourth have a telephone and three in ten have either a washing or sewing machine. Six in ten do not have a clinical thermometer. A fifth of the families lack a medicine cabinet and eight in ten a bathroom scale.

lunches, and participation in special educational and extracurricular activities. For example, welfare children are often unable to participate in class trips because of parental inability to provide the extra money these trips require. As a result, welfare children may suffer from psychological isolation and a loss of educational experience with a resulting impact on the child's performance in school. Often where welfare students are placed in classes with middle-income students, this may lead to rebellion and truancy or other forms of disruptive behavior which may not be understood by teachers and administrators. In one instance reported by McBarnette, in which poor black students were bussed to middle-income neighborhoods, the black students did not participate in extra-curricular programs. The black students were not deliberately excluded by white students, but by the hour and a half it took to get home, the black students simply did not have time to participate. McBarnette also reports instances of delays in granting free transportation passes and school lunches resulting in higher costs to welfare students.[7] In addition, the school lunch program causes some embarrassment to low-income pupils because required cards are often visible to nonwelfare pupils in the vicinity of the lunch counter.[8]

McBarnette concludes:

1. When welfare clothing allotment checks do not arrive in time for the beginning of school, students sometimes attend school in shabby attire. On occasion there are emotional and disciplinary problems because of this.
2. Requirements that parents appear at school to sign for student lunch passes result in loss of time and additional travel expenses.
3. Pupils forced to travel long distances via public transportation sometimes become truants rather than face the penalties of frequent lateness.
4. Additional expenditures for such items as gym sneakers and gymsuits are a handicap, especially when pupils face penalties for lack of equipment.
5. Pupils often feel stigmatized as welfare recipients when they are asked to stand in a free lunch line or are otherwise separated from other students in the school.
6. Identification of welfare status on school records also stigmatizes these pupils.[9]

Housing. Similar problems confront the welfare recipient in housing. In October 1969, Louis Harris and Associates conducted a survey of 431 New York City households in transition from white to nonwhite occupancy.[10] The housing conditions of welfare tenant families were found to be substantially worse than those of their self-supporting neighbors. A greater number of these families live in problem-ridden units in the worst buildings located in the fastest declining neighborhoods.[11] Relative to nonwelfare tenants, welfare tenants are more often exposed to the problems of drug addiction, crimes against the person, rat and roach infestation, poor maintenance and service, and below standard housing conditions. Fewer welfare households can point to recent repairs or improvements, although a higher percentage claim the need for such repairs. Disputes with the landlord over kitchen, bathroom, and plumbing-related problems are less often resolved satisfactorily for welfare tenants than for nonwelfare tenants. Most buildings housing welfare recipients lack a superintendent, a fact that probably accounts for the lower level of services provided.

The Sternlieb report on housing conditions in New York City has also found that welfare tenantry is concentrated in the city's oldest and poorest categories of housing.[12] Moreover, structures housing welfare recipients tend to have an extraordinary number of building code violations.

Not only is welfare housing typically of the poorest quality, in 1969 New York City paid $235 million in welfare rents without any efforts to exert control over the quality of housing provided. These welfare rent allowances supported approximately 15 percent of the city's rental housing stock.[13] In discussing welfare housing in New York, a New York City-Rand Institute study concluded:

About 60 percent of all welfare households occupy Old-Law or New-Law tenements, and those buildings containing welfare families are typically in worse condition than buildings without welfare tenants. Thus, welfare occupied buildings of each type have two or three times the average number of uncorrected housing code violations for all buildings of that type.

One striking feature of welfare housing is overcrowding. Even large welfare families tend to occupy small apartments, with households of five or more persons averaging less than one room per person. Another striking feature is instability of tenure; about a fourth of all welfare cases move each year.

It is fairly clear that welfare rent allowances do not secure well-maintained or even safe and sanitary housing for many welfare clients and that large welfare households are usually overcrowded.[14]

Public housing provides little relief to welfare recipients in New York City. Less than 10 percent of all New York City families in public housing were on welfare in 1968.[15] In early 1971, this occupancy rate was 27 percent.[16] Although small, the share of the welfare population in the city's public housing has been growing.

The condition of welfare housing in New York City reflects a national pattern. Relatively few welfare recipients are living in public housing (see Table 5-1). A recent study by the federal government estimates that welfare clients spend $1.1 billion on housing each year, but that this expenditure does not provide clients with the quality of housing enjoyed by most nonwelfare citizens. Nor does it insure adequate maintenance and upkeep.[17] The study concludes that "at least one-half of all assistance recipients live in housing which is deteriorating or dilapidated, unsafe, unsanitary, or overcrowded."[18] AFDC recipients, the report also notes, are far more likely to live in poor quality housing than recipients of other types of assistance.[19]

Table 5-1

Federally Aided Public Assistance Recipients Residing in Public Housing Units, by Type of Program, May 1968 (Thousands)

Type of Program	All Public Assistance Recipients		Recipients in Public Housing		Incidence (Percent of Total)
	Number	Percent	Number	Percent	
Total Programs	8,383	100.0	584	100.0	7.0
Adult Programs	2,770	33.0	72	12.3	2.6
AFDC Programs	5,615	67.0	512[a]	87.7	9.1

[a]Estimate based on an assumed average of 4.0 recipients per AFDC household in public housing.

Source: U.S. Government, Department of Health, Education, and Welfare, *The Role of Public Welfare in Housing*, Report to the House Committee on Ways and Means and the Senate Committee on Finance, U.S. Government Printing Office, Washington, D.C., January 1969, p. 82.

Other Conditions of the Welfare Poor. New York City Welfare mothers believe that both they and their children are less healthy than more affluent segments of society.[20] The poor in general, and the welfare poor in particular, also report far greater prevalence of illness than other groups. Yet at the same time, they have a lower rate of utilization of medical services.[21] Black and Puerto Rican recipients also tend to use medical clinics, while white recipients are more likely to be served by private physicians.

Another study has compared the health of two samples of black mothers, one publicly assisted, the other low-income nonassisted families residing in public housing.[22] The study concludes that respondents from the welfare sample were more likely than those from the low-income nonwelfare sample to assess their own health and that of their children negatively, to report greater sickness, and to worry about health problems.

David Caplovitz has examined the economic difficulties confronting low-income families in New York City, many of them on welfare. Caplovitz has found that one weapon used by merchants against welfare recipients is the threat of reporting credit purchases to the welfare department. Welfare families cannot be garnisheed and are legally mandated not to make credit purchases.[23] Cloward and Piven have also documented extensively various practices by welfare administrations such as variations in relief policies in differing parts of a state, the barring of relief to eligible nonrecipients, and underbudgeting of recipients.[24]

Finally, research on New York City poverty areas has constructed remarkably uniform accounts of the attitude of welfare recipients toward the welfare system and the services it provides.[25] Most important, the studies of the City University of New York (CUNY) have shown that black recipients tend to be the most distrustful of the welfare system, more certain about their political identification, and more likely to participate in the political process by registering and voting than white or Puerto Rican recipients (see Table 5-2). Further, blacks express a greater unmet need for money than other groups sampled, feel more strongly that the welfare department has no respect for them and does not trust them, and are more likely not to want to discuss personal problems with caseworkers.[26] In short, blacks tend, more than other segments of the welfare population, not to perceive the welfare department as a helping agency.

Not surprisingly, many welfare recipients, particularly black recipients, have assumed an adversary rather than a client relationship to the welfare administration. Recipients have begun legal action to obtain equal rights in such aspects of life as individual privacy, morals, housing, employment, and various criteria for eligibility.[27] Charles Reich has gone so far as to suggest the recognition of a new property right that would elevate the recipient to a position not unlike that of a business regulated by the government.[28]

Do the living conditions of welfare recipients explain the emergence in New York City of organized protest activity by part of the welfare population? To answer this question, a distinction must be drawn between the "poor" and the "welfare poor." The welfare poor are "service-users"; they are clients of a large government bureaucracy and, while they are surely among the urban poor, they are also not the poorest of the poor. As wards of society, they are assured a level of disposable income and financial well-being that the nonassisted poor do not have. They are also a subset of the poor that has been structured, organized, and made distinct from the total poverty population by the government's assistance program.

Many political scientists have noted that receptivity to revolution, protest, and radicalism is often greater among persons and groups suffering relative deprivation, rather than the stable poor.[b] Crane Brinton, reflecting this view in his classic on revolution, argues that revolutionary societies tend to have experienced economic advance prior to the revolution and that radical movements typically originate among people who feel restraint and annoyance rather than complete oppression.[29] Brinton declares:

Certainly these revolutions are not started by down-and-outers, by starving miserable people. These revolutionists are not worms turning, not children of despair. These revolutions are born of hope, and their philosophies are normally optimistic.[30]

Although deprivation may be a necessary condition for the emergence of political radicalism among the welfare poor, it is not a sufficient condition.

[b]This point has been made by, among others, Marx and DeTocqueville. Durkheim has argued that stable poverty, rather than producing radicalism and protest, most often leads to conservatism.

Table 5-2

Political Identification and 1964 Voting Behavior of Mothers on Welfare (Percentage of Total)

Characteristics	Total	Respondent Mothers		
		White	Black	Puerto Rican
Political Identification				
Democrat	67	57	73	60
Republican	8	10	8	9
Independent	2	3	2	2
No opinion	23	30	17	29
Total	100	100	100	100
1964 Voting Behavior				
Voted	25	30	34	12
Registered, did not vote	3	1	3	3
Not registered	63	62	52	77
Under age	8	7	10	7
No answer	1	1	1	1
Total	100	100	100	100
Number	(2,179)	(208)	(1,017)	(954)

Source: Lawrence Podell, *Families on Welfare in New York City*, p. 112.

The same is true of race. The welfare rights movement is a predominantly black movement. However, the successful emergence of political radicalism among a segment of the welfare poor cannot be satisfactorily explained solely by changes over time in the racial composition of the welfare population. In fact, the racial composition of New York City's AFDC rolls remained relatively stable throughout the 1960s (see Table 5-3).

The emergence of political radicalism among the welfare poor has paralleled other changes in the city's political life. John Lindsay, a liberal, reform-oriented politician, became mayor on January 1, 1966. Lindsay's first welfare commissioner was Mitchell Ginsberg, a professor at the Columbia University School of Social Work and an advocate of total overhaul of both the city's and the nation's public assistance programs.[31] In addition, President Johnson declared the War on Poverty, with New York City being a key area of experimentation for new community action programs.[c]

The mid-1960s also witnessed a dramatic upsurge in political activity among the city's black and, to a lesser degree, Puerto Rican communities. Sayre and Kaufman noted in 1965 that:

[c]HARYOU-ACT in Harlem and the MFY program on the Lower East Side were the largest and most influential community action programs in the city.

Table 5-3
The Racial Composition of AFDC Mothers in New York City, 1961, 1967, and 1968

Racial and Ethnic Group	1961		1967		1968		Percentage Increase 1961-67	Net Increase 1961-67		Percentage Increase 1967-68	Net Increase 1967-68	
	Number	%	Number	%	Number	%		Number	%		Number	%
White	6,447	12.6	14,905	11.4	22,776	13.0	131.2	8,458	10.6	52.8	7,871	17.6
Puerto Rican	19,060	37.3	48,552	37.2	70,321	40.1	154.7	29,492	37.1	44.8	21,769	48.6
Black	25,603	50.1	67,155	51.4	82,278	46.9	162.3	41,552	52.3	22.5	15,123	33.8
Total	51,110	100.0	130,612	100.0	175,375	100.0	155.5	79,502	100.0	34.3	44,763	100.0

Source: U.S. Government, Department of Health, Education, and Welfare, *Report of Findings of a Special Review of AFDC in New York City*, report to the House Ways and Means Committee (Washington, D.C.: U.S. Government Printing Office, 1969), p. 59.

Negro civil rights groups and their allies turned to direct action—sit-ins in the headquarters of the Board of Education and the Mayor's office, blockage of construction, obstruction of traffic, rent strikes, school boycotts—in order to dramatize their plight and to oblige city officials to modify public policies and intervene in the labor market on behalf of the victims of discrimination.[32]

Moreover, the goals of the black community veered sharply away from their past emphasis on status as new groups emerged to challenge the older, more traditional groups for community leadership.

One striking example of this divergence has occurred in the issue of education.[33] After the 1954 Supreme Court decision outlawing segregation in public school education, New York City experienced continuing controversy between civil rights groups and white neighborhood organizations over the scope, speed, and methods with which the Board of Education should seek a desegregated school system. On February 3 and March 16, 1964, blacks initiated, with impressive results, city-wide school boycotts designed to speed up the desegregation process. However, by the end of 1966, following the Intermediate School 201 controversy in East Harlem and the formation of a People's Board of Education, the movement's focus shifted away from desegregation and toward improvement in quality and local control.[34] In 1968, this shift within the black community on educational goals led to a protracted conflict between the teachers' union and a local school board in Brooklyn over the issue of community control of schools. This conflict ended only after several city-wide teachers' strikes laden with overtones of ethnic hostility.[35]

In short, by the mid-1960s the conditions were ripe for the emergence of a welfare rights movement in the city. Welfare recipients were poor, but not totally oppressed. They had grievances, but also had a receptive environment for correcting them. And, finally, they were becoming increasingly exposed to the tactic of protest as a means of resolving these grievances.

The Lower East Side Experience under the MFY Program

The earliest activity among the welfare poor in New York City was associated with the MFY programs on Manhattan's Lower East Side.[36] MFY developed out of a need for newer and more innovative approaches to the problems of inner-city youth. The concept of MFY originated at a board meeting of the Lower East Side Neighborhood Association (LENA) held at the Henry Street Settlement House in June 1957.[d] There, it was proposed that LENA and the settlement houses develop a coordinated program for dealing with community problems, especially the startling growth in juvenile delinquency in the neighborhood. This resulted in a planning group lasting four and a half years.

[d]LENA was a community based organization formed in 1955 and supported by a variety of community groups.

Frances Fox Piven has described the development of the MFY program as a problem of organizational coordination. The group at the Henry Street Settlement House drew up broad outlines of the program. Funds had to be obtained and coordination arranged between local agencies, the National Institute of Mental Health, the Columbia University School of Social Work, the Ford Foundation, the President's Committee on Juvenile Delinquency, and other agencies involved in the program.[37]

The preliminary planning for MFY was done by faculty members from the Columbia University School of Social Work (CUSSW) under a grant from the Taconic Foundation. At first, the Columbia group envisioned an umbrella agency drawing on different sources of funding and using new techniques for controlling juvenile delinquency. Their initial proposal suggested greater financial support for LENA and the settlement houses without in any way broadening control over social welfare policy. The proposal was submitted to the NIMH for funding. However, the NIMH rejected it with the suggestion that it could be resubmitted for a planning grant.

The CUSSW planners were now given considerable freedom in redrafting the plan. Piven states:

The requirements for mounting a program had forced the local practitioners to emerge on to the national social welfare scene of the foundation, the university, and government; a scene dominated by a more cosmopolitan professionalism, emphasizing values of science and rationalism.[38]

In 1959 NIMH awarded a planning grant of $404,667 covering a two-year period. The revised plan, prepared by Richard Cloward and Lloyd Ohlin, stressed "expanding opportunities" as a basis of direct community action. Because of the NIMH grant, by the end of 1961 MFY possessed a conceptual and organizational framework and was in an advanced stage of operational planning.[e]

The 1961 report submitted to the NIMH, the Ford Foundation, and the President's Committee on Juvenile Delinquency (PCJD) fully adopted the "opportunity structure" theories of Cloward and Ohlin and proposed changing the existing system as the method of combating juvenile delinquency. Simultaneously, the report called for the mobilization of the total community in an effort to alter the institutions that define the opportunity structure.[39]

By 1961 MFY ceased to be a program designed primarily to combat gang conflict, drug use, and juvenile delinquency and became, instead, the intended instrument of far-reaching social change. To this end it emphasized increasing the ability of local citizens to participate in and influence events in their communities. It dramatized community needs and began activities to satisfy these needs. It also improved communication between the disadvantaged and various community institutions and trained local leaders.[40]

[e]This organizational framework included a 33-member board of directors. Eleven members of the board were from the CUSSW faculty.

MFY began its service operations in 1962 with a staff of 300 and a research division[f] and four program divisions.[g] In 1964, a Legal Services Division was added. The MFY program was costly. From 1962 to 1965 MFY received $1.8 million from the Ford Foundation, $5.3 million from the NIMH, $1.9 million from the PCJD, $9.0 million from the Department of Labor, and $4.2 million from the city of New York.[41]

MFY discovered early that its target population did not participate in the various government programs available to it. By developing a new casework approach and a strong emphasis on providing concrete, immediate services to its clientele, the MFY planners, through the Program of Services to Individuals and Families (SIF), set about to make low-income persons more aware of existing opportunities and to induce them to take advantage of these opportunities. In this way, the planners hoped that the target population would "overcome the self-defeating adaptation that prevented people from taking advantage of what was available to change their lives."[42] The need to provide tangible services to the poor was explained by MFY:

In work with families from extremely deprived economic groups, concrete social services will be strongly emphasized. There are a number of reasons for this emphasis. Groups cannot be helped if they cannot be reached. It is generally conceded that lower-class persons are drawn to agencies which have concrete services to offer. Their social and economic problems are both concrete and overwhelming, and they are quite naturally in search of equally concrete ways of solving these problems.[43]

The MFY proposed a strategy employing social services and community resources generally as instruments of social change. Central to the planners' conception of a new casework approach was the delivery system. There had to be a new, informal, decentralized system, in contrast to the conspicuously large and impersonal bureaucracies with which most of the urban poor have had to deal. Thus was born the idea of the neighborhood service center, which one writer dubbed "helping stations."

The term helping station connotes a locally based, visible, available place to which people, particularly newcomers to a neighborhood, can go with their service needs or for information. And once there, if the place is friendly and warm, low income persons, especially newcomers and those with language difficulties, usually feel able to request immediate, direct service and obtain information about many of their daily problems such as housing, education, public welfare, certain legal problems, consumer problems, and the like. Sometimes the requests are for small emergency financial grants such as money

---

[f]The first director of the research division was Prof. Richard Cloward of the CUSSW.

[g]The four program divisions were: Educational Services, Employment Services, Services to Individuals and Families, and Community Development. The program divisions were combined into an Action Division headed by George Braeger.

for a new shirt to take a new job; for a few hours of baby sitting; or for just a cup of coffee; a chance to rest from the heat or to have a letter interpreted.[44]

The operative arms of the SIF program were four neighborhood centers offering the target population a wide variety of services. Social workers, aided by a corps of experts, performed the centers' activities. Together, they constituted an "under-the-roof" staff of baby-sitters, escorts, and visiting homemakers that provided for some of the immediate needs of the clientele. They also offered an inquiry service through which the client could obtain information on housing, education, welfare, and various consumer and legal problems. A social planning service provided additional benefits for those in need of extensive social casework aid. Finally, a liaison resource service operated in and out of the various municipal agencies to aid clients in time of emergency and to reduce the need for the client to run the gauntlet of municipal agencies in search of a solution to his or her problem.

The first Neighborhood Service Center (NSC) opened on the Lower East Side on November 13, 1962. By early 1963 it was clear that far more people were using the center than had been originally anticipated, with much of the center's resources being spent on the client's behalf for basic survival needs such as food, clothing, and housing. It was also clear that many of the clients who required survival assistance were either receiving or eligible to receive assistance from public or private agencies.[45]

Over time, NSC officials catalogued a wide range of grievances against the welfare administration by the client population.

1. The welfare administration is quick to terminate welfare families and slow to put them back on the rolls.
2. The administration is not receptive to clients' opinions and complaints.
3. The administration is cold and distant and does not care for the individual welfare family.
4. Yet, in its need to investigate welfare families, the administration pries too deeply into the private affairs of these families.
5. The administration does not inform recipients of what is rightfully theirs under law.
6. The administration does not pay enough to welfare clients, but pays too much to administration personnel.
7. The welfare administration does not provide sufficient incentives for clients to enroll in training programs and, in this way, free themselves from dependence on public assistance.
8. The system does not ensure decent housing and living conditions to recipients.[46]

By 1964, NSC workers had clearly become clients' advocates on the Lower East Side. Advocacy has been defined in this context as:

the willingness to intervene with a government agency on behalf of a low-income person. It does not mean helping the poor man to help himself or enabling him to better manage his transactions with the government department. It means filling in the power deficit on his side of the transaction by providing him with a defender who has specialized knowledge of the rules and regulations of the system.[47]

By 1964, the primary institutional target of the NSC program had also become the welfare department, with NSC workers trying to promote change in its methods and operations by a variety of advocacy tactics. Cloward and Elman describe the operation of a neighborhood service center on Stanton Street:

An advocate in this context is one who intervenes on behalf of a client with a public agency to secure an entitlement or right which has been obscured or denied. To act effectively, the advocate must accept his client's definition of the injustice, but he must also have sufficient knowledge of the law and of government's administrative procedures to discern remediable issues or disputable questions of fact in the emotional testimony of the client, and then seek a solution in harmony with the client's interests. In practice, the Stanton Street advocates often found that they had to instruct the representatives of agencies such as Welfare in what was the law and how it should be interpreted. Beyond their ability to interpret a client's account without losing his confidence, the advocate's most demanding task was to serve notice on his opposite number in the Welfare Department that he was prepared to move a notch further up the hierarchy if justice was not tendered on the present level.

Thus the advocates listened to endless tales of woe; they totaled up scores of welfare budgets to detect underbudgeting; they placed telephone calls to a bewildering number of functionaries and sometimes accompanied clients when they went to see these people in person. They argued and they cajoled. They framed rebuttals to cases put forward by Welfare, and they also attacked when necessary. When, for example, a Stanton Street woman was charged with child neglect, the alert worker was able to show that she had been consistently underbudgeted for more than a year, which made here child-rearing efforts virtually futile. When another client was evicted for nonpayment of rent, the worker forced Welfare to make such a payment by showing that the Department had failed in its legal obligation to do so. Whether the workers' threats were made politely or in anger, as a technique of careful manipulation or with blustering disregard for the sensibilities of their opposite numbers, they served notice on the low-level Welfare employee that he would be held responsible for his actions to his supervisor—and so on up the line. Thus advocacy on behalf of the clients was the bludgeon by which this city agency was made more responsive to a portion of its Lower East Side constituency. At 199 Stanton Street the workers came to serve as surrogates for their clients with the bureaucratically arranged world outside the welfare ghetto.[48]

The Program of Services to Individuals and Families (SIF) maintained an up-to-date welfare bulletin to keep NSC workers informed about the minutiae of ever-changing welfare policy. Indeed, SIF often kept its own workers better informed than the Welfare Department staff. When advocacy tactics failed to thwart bureaucratic injustices, the MFY Legal Services Unit challenged the department's decisions. The unit, under the direction of Edward Sparer, developed the basic philosophy that the legal needs of the poor arose largely from their uneven relationship with government-sponsored social welfare programs and the bureaucracies that administered them, and that these needs were not adequately served by the legal profession.[49] Sparer argued for the need to develop legal representation for welfare recipients. He also argued that welfare benefits were a right and that the rule of law had to be applied to the administration of social welfare programs. By 1964, Sparer's legal doctrines had become official MFY policy.[50]

In 1965 MFY veered away from its support of advocacy and toward the organization of client groups functioning on their own behalf. By 1965 it had become clear that MFY's efforts had not been successful in prodding New York City's Welfare Department to initiate departmental reforms. Indeed, with four centers in operation on the Lower East Side, there was instead increasing antagonism between MFY workers and departmental personnel.[51] MFY's legal activities especially angered the city's welfare commissioner. Lower-echelon welfare personnel also felt harassed by MFY workers. As Cloward and Elman point out, caseworkers began to react by exhibiting "hostility and impatience towards their clients who by now had transferred some of their previous dependency on welfare to the storefront on Stanton Street.[52] Welfare clients were also becoming active:

The Program heads . . . began to wonder whether, if the clients were given support and encouragement, they could begin to take over some of the burden of dealing with Welfare. If fifty clients all needed the same items of clothing, they reasoned, it might be more effective to make one request on behalf of fifty rather than fifty individual requests. They reasoned, too, that this strategy might coerce Welfare into making certain kinds of grants more automatic, or, rather, less discretionary.

And so it was, after three years, that the center on Stanton Street decided to hire a "community organizer" to bring together people in the neighborhood around their most commonly shared interest—their problem with public welfare.[53]

By 1964 SIF's policy was to limit intake to specific welfare problems with public assistance clients having a high priority. MFY subsequently shifted from worker advocacy to the organization of client groups in a further attempt to force the welfare department to modify its operations.

Several reasons have been given for this shift in tactics. Some of SIF's leaders felt it was necessary if the welfare department were ever to become responsive to its clientele. Participation in social action was also thought to be highly therapeutic to the client.[54] In general, there were two schools of thought about the purpose organizations of welfare clients would serve. One was political; the other legal. The political school of thought viewed welfare client organizations as the beginning of a social movement with a large mass membership and the potential for effecting basic changes in the nation's social welfare system. The legal school of thought saw welfare client organizations as a means of achieving benefits for individuals and families and, simultaneously, broadening the procedural and legal rights of welfare recipients by controlling the welfare bureaucracy's behavior toward its clients. Other, external factors were also influential in the decision by MFY to organize client groups. The 1962 amendments to the Social Security Act established a legal precedent for organizations of welfare recipients in providing for advisory committees at local welfare centers as a means of establishing communications between clients and administrators. New York City's Department of Social Services did not comply with the 1962 amendments until late 1966, after the formation of a number of welfare client groups and the City-Wide Coordinating Committee.[55]

The Social Services Employees Union (SSEU), representing the city's caseworkers, also supported the formation of organizations of clients. In discussing a 1965 strike by caseworkers, the union noted:

We the union suffered the effects of the lack of communication with our clients; had our clients been more organized and had they more of a voice, they might have given our charge of bureaucratic strangulation a dramatic and favorable press. Instead we learned that most of our clients cannot really separate us from the barriers that surround them.[56]

A militant, client-oriented faction succeeded in gaining control of the union. Because of this, the SSEU was rather unique. Among other things, it created a full-time staff position for a worker to organize welfare clients and to assist in their training about welfare policy and law. The SSEU, unlike other municipal unions, has been strongly client-oriented rather than concerned primarily with the interests of its members.

The reason for MFY's extraordinary concern with welfare is that problems involving public assistance were at the base of most of the difficulties of persons appearing at MFY's intake centers.[57] By helping to solve these problems, MFY was able to provide tangible benefits to its clients. These problems centered on questions of eligibility; unmet needs; inadequate allowances, particularly for large families; late checks; and unsatisfactory social casework services.[58]

The Neighborhood Service Center Program served as a vehicle for identifying a significant group of city residents with needs not adequately met by the welfare system. Between 1962 and 1965, this program evolved from social service planning to advocacy on behalf of clients to the organization of clients.[59] This change in emphasis was a victory for those advocating confrontation with the welfare bureaucracy and delegation of a greater share of decisionmaking to emerging community groups and their leaders.[60] Out of this tactical shift emerged the welfare rights groups on Manhattan's Lower East Side. The MFY staff continued to help organize and direct client groups until November 1966, when pressure from city hall, the commissioner of the

Department of Social Services, and the Office of Manpower Training forced MFY to end its activities.[61] However, by the time the MFY had to lower its visibility, five welfare rights groups had been organized on the Lower East Side.[h] By early 1967 these groups joined together to form the Lower East Side Emergency Winter Clothing Council. In addition, several multi-issue organizations, some funded by MFY, others by churches, were following the lead of the MFY-sponsored welfare groups and, from time to time, were involving themselves in welfare campaigns.

Early Welfare Rights Activity in Brooklyn

At the same time, grass-roots welfare rights activity developed in Brooklyn, in part through organizations created directly or indirectly by the federal government's War on Poverty. The first welfare rights organization in Brooklyn can be traced back to 1964 when Frank Espada, a middle-class Puerto Rican activist, formed a group called East New York Action. East New York Action was composed of local members of the old Brooklyn CORE organization.[62] This group, as well as others affiliated with the War on Poverty, sought to end a wide range of problems affecting their communities: poor housing, lack of heating, slum landlords, and inadequate schools, welfare services, health care, and sanitation. East New York Action organized several rent strikes against landlords[i] and engaged several professional social workers for counseling a few nights each week. The counseling service soon proved inadequate to the need; the large number of clients made any solution to the problems of the poor based on a case-by-case approach impractical.

Espada's group discovered that between 80 and 85 percent of its problem cases were concerned with welfare. For this reason, in late 1964, it was instrumental in forming tbe Welfare Recipients League, the first of its kind in the city since the depression. Subsequently, a campaign was mounted against the local agent of the welfare department, the neighborhood welfare center. Sit-ins and demonstrations at the Brownsville center in 1964 won the support of activists and low-income groups in other parts of the city, as well as sympathetic elements within the SSEU and welfare department itself. One of the organizers of the Brooklyn welfare rights movement described what happened:

So we got together. And we only had three or four things going—with only a few people connected up with us. So we started a welfare recipients league. I think it was the first in the city. In any case, the thing started to catch fire. It started

---

[h]These were the Committee of Welfare Families (CWF), the Welfare Action Group Against Poverty (WAGAP), and the Citizens Welfare Action Group (CWAG), all within the SIF Division; the Sixth Street Welfare Group, within the Community Organization Division; and the Action for Progress Group.

[i]One associate of Espada and an organizer ot early rent strikes in the Brownsville section of Brooklyn was Major Owens, a community leader who later became the chief executive officer of the City's Community Development Administration.

with three people. The first chapter was predominantly black, but it was a good mix, black and Puerto Rican. Before we knew it the thing caught fire. In the late summer of 1964 and in the early fall of 1965 a friend from the Department of Social Services dropped off some of the regulations that had to do with minimum standards. At this point it became almost eerie because it was happening on the Lower East Side also. I had no contact with the Lower East Side. I knew MFY very well and I knew generally that they were to do something with welfare clients. We made no attempt to make contact.[63]

A caseworker and SSEU community action leader also explained:

I was very interested in what became the client movement from being a public assistance caseworker in Brooklyn. It was mid-1964 and by mid-1965 the thought that the welfare clients had organized was the most exciting thing I had ever heard of because, for a couple of years, I had seen people totally apathetic. Nobody could believe clients were organizing.[64]

By January 1966 six welfare recipient leagues were in operation in central Brooklyn. These leagues were engaged primarily in mimimum standards campaigns directed at the neighborhood welfare centers. The leagues began to attract publicity and outside support from such groups as the radical faction of the SSEU. This faction, headed by Judy Mage, had recently taken control of the union.

At first there was little contact between the Brooklyn welfare leagues and the groups operating on the Lower East Side of Manhattan. However, by January 1966 Espada had established close contact with Richard Cloward. As a result, the Espada-initiated groups in central Brooklyn were linked to the MFY-initiated groups on the Lower East Side. Through this contact, Espada and the Brooklyn leagues were introduced to city-wide and national developments in the then incipient, although rapidly developing, welfare rights movement.

Another organization that helped to lay the groundwork for the Brooklyn welfare rights movement was a private, nonsectarian self-help group, Christians and Jews United for Social Action (CUSA). CUSA began in late 1965 as a service organization with a middle-class program, dominated by white lawyers, law students, radical young Catholic priests, organizers, and a few black professionals and community residents. In December 1965, CUSA opened a storefront on Legion Street in the Brownsville section of Brooklyn, its operations financed by funds raised from among its membership. By early 1966, after shifting its location to Strauss Street, CUSA hired a staff of three people and involved itself in a wide variety of issues that plagued depressed areas of the city like Brownsville. At first, CUSA concentrated on problems connected with slum housing and winter heating. A rent strike was begun in early 1966 after a landlord's refusal to supply heat in an apartment despite repeated complaints by CUSA's staff to the landlord and the city's Buildings Department.[65]

Young priests, frustrated in their efforts to effect meaningful social change, cold and dissatisfied tenants, and lawyers, law students, and professionals, all joined together in CUSA to promote the strike. Meetings and demonstrations were held in Brownsville at local churches and storefronts, and landlords were picketed at their homes whenever possible. Because of severe winter conditions, the news media picked up the story that entire clusters of building units in Brownsville were without heat.[66]

However, CUSA soon lost its momentum in organizing low-income communities in Brooklyn. First, the advent of spring caused tenants to lose interest in the problem of heating.[67] Second, internal discord, particularly between the white organizers of the CUSA groups and black militants in the emerging "poverty leadership," forced a reorientation and reorganization of many CUSA groups. The surviving CUSA groups became neighborhood organizations, many dominated by nonwhites from within the community. The CUSA groups were, as it happened, all located in the high-density welfare areas of Brooklyn. The surviving CUSA groups also became the nucleus of the local welfare movement, the Brooklyn Welfare Action Council (BWAC), formed in 1967.[j]

Prior to 1966 CUSA survived on contributions primarily from the National Maritime Union, the Clothing Workers, the UAW, and other AFL-CIO unions. One solicitation in the *National Catholic Reporter* raised $4,000. After 1966, however, many CUSA groups had access to OEO or private nonunion funding.

Elements within the Catholic Diocese of Brooklyn were also influential in the development of CUSA and the emergence of welfare rights activity in Brooklyn. Organizers and financial and technical assistance were provided by the Catholic Charities to locally based welfare rights groups. Local groups in Brooklyn were given information about their rights and other forms of organizational assistance by young Catholic priests.[68] Several clerics were arrested at recipient demonstrations.[69] One of the Diocese's militant young priests described his early involvement in organizing low-income communities:

I went through the anti-poverty bit for two years, and then one day I was transferred to Bedford-Stuyvesant and got involved in the welfare rights movement. This was in October 1966 and it was a very small thing at that time. People would come to a storefront looking for a couple of bucks and I realized that I wasn't really doing anything for them and that they would be back in the same shape. And then I would call the DOSS and make sure that a special grant was taken care of. But there were too many poor people around, and too little resources that I had, and it seemed to me that what had to be done was that people had to help themselves. They really wanted freedom and justice in their own situation so they would have to do for themselves. So we started a storefront on Gates Avenue and collected stories of the daily DOSS outrages. We began to organize around minimum standards. We had a storefront and things like African culture, sewing, and the like. You can't do much with that so we started a welfare league and had nuns around visiting and telling people to come to the storefront or be interviewed in their homes. At first people were

jAmong the CUSA groups that survived and became key local units of the NWRO through the Brooklyn Welfare Action Council were CUSA-Marion, CUSA-Nostrand, and CUSA-East New York.

reticent . . . but slowly they began to talk about the advantages of organization and welfare client strength. We got a training program and two ex-caseworkers to speak about people's rights and in a very short time mothers who were high school dropouts and didn't know the country's geography were quoting page after page of welfare legislation because it was meaningful to their lives. My role in the beginning was to lead it and as the thing grew my role was to move a little further out into the middle and act as an advisor. . . . And so it grew from one store to another. Other priests were doing the same thing elsewhere. In September 1967 we came together and decided that the best thing that could happen was that we should begin to develop a number of stores in Bedford-Stuyvesant and that the storefront movement was very important. And so we began with this network of storefronts.[70]

The Brooklyn Diocese also gave substantial financial assistance to the Brooklyn Welfare Action Council. Indeed, the Diocese was for some time the sole funding source for many of its affiliates. For a while, it also paid the salaries of two full-time BWAC organizers and allowed the BWAC to use its facilities and communications equipment.[71]

The Beginnings of the Welfare Rights Movement in Upper Manhattan

In upper Manhattan an analogous experience was taking place. Several welfare rights groups grew out of the Stryckers Bay Neighborhood Council, an Upper West Side, OEO-funded community project heavily influenced by a Catholic priest, Father Harry Browne.[72]

The formation of the West Side Welfare Recipients League (WSWRL) and the United Welfare League (UWL) are typical. Jeanette Washington, a founder of the WSWRL, became involved in Stryckers Bay because of her refusal to move in order to make way for an urban renewal project. After her initial contact with Stryckers Bay, she attended several poor people's conferences and the 1966 meeting from which a city-wide organization emerged. Later, because no welfare rights group existed in their neighborhood, she and Beulah Sanders formed the WSWRL. One of the founders described the early mood of the organization.

Many people had the same feelings but never expressed them in a unified way. Suddenly they began to admit that they were on welfare and they were relieved and willing to go out and express the community feeling to the state and city. They said they were sick of conditions on welfare and were now ready to band together and fight welfare. Many meetings were held with quite a few professionals where we got together and talked about our basic needs. We noticed it more in our own community where families were being moved in and out and we found that five or six people were living in one room and when they moved into a two room apartment there were certain things they needed. We sat down and looked in the welfare manual and it said there were minimum standards.[73]

By early 1969, WSWRL had a membership of about 600. Later, it merged with other neighborhood groups to become Community Development Incorporated (CDI).

The United Welfare League on Manhattan's Upper West Side was also formed through the efforts of professional organizers and community residents affiliated with the Stryckers Bay Neighborhood Council. In the winter of 1966, a storefront was opened with a paid staff to organize for the UWL. One of the founders of UWL described her initial involvement:

It was a job getting people to mingle with other people, but by going to meetings we found we had things in common such as caseworkers who visited and did nothing. We were told of forms where people could get clothing and furniture and began to look at the forms and we couldn't believe the things that were in them. Coats and sweaters. We just couldn't believe that we could get this just for filling out a form. A lot of us did it and went to sit in at the center. There was a law in the books that said you were entitled to these things and we were going to try to get them. We arranged a time and sometimes the people didn't show up because of fear. Those that did so gave the others a little more courage and we were sort of stirred up behind this because, as one person would tell another about it, that person would tell somebody else and before you knew it the store front was full and it stayed full day in and day out.[74]

Through the Stryckers Bay Neighborhood Council, CDI and UWL received substantial funding from OEO.

Other welfare rights groups have been organized in most low-income sections of the city, including sections of the Bronx and Queens. The heart of the movement in New York City was, however, the neighborhood groups formed on the Lower East and Upper West Sides of Manhattan and, especially, central Brooklyn. It was here that many of the city's welfare rights members have been recruited and most of its welfare rights activities concentrated.

Summary

A complex set of forces account for the emergence of organized recipient groups in New York City. Startling conditions of degradation and unmet needs in the areas of health, education, food, and shelter were certainly a necessary condition for the sudden surge of protest activity among the welfare poor. However, they were not a sufficient condition. Civil rights activity, a liberal city administration politically allied with the city's ghetto communities, and the activities of aggressive activist intellectuals in the social welfare profession were all influential in the emergence of political radicalism among the welfare poor. Finally, and perhaps most important, the federal government's War on Poverty provided a new institutional framework complete with staff, funding, and new organizations for ghetto residents and their allies to mount a political campaign to bring about social change. As a result, storefront operations sprang up in different parts of the city to mobilize the urban poor and to establish communications with the city-wide and national organizations. From these storefront operations, a number of groups developed, all seeking to advance the interests of welfare recipients in their dealings with the city's welfare bureaucracy.

Interestingly, many of the local groups were to focus, independently of each other, on obtaining higher grant levels and, in particular, special grants. As we shall note in later sections, this focus on grant levels was to become the principal organizing tool of the city's welfare rights movement. Higher grant levels were, more than anything else, to provide, in Olson's terminology, the "private good" upon which the movement's growth was based.

The new poverty workers also had two important characteristics not shared with the earlier southern civil rights movement: legitimized public disorder as a viable protest strategy, at least among the poor, and social and political activists trained and experienced in implementing this strategy in an urban environment. The federal government's War on Poverty not only introduced some of the poor to the movement, but also identified target populations within poverty areas, isolated their primary needs, and sought to direct large numbers of people to welfare and other public agencies capable of ameliorating their conditions. One study of the activities of community action programs in New York City concluded:

Without exception, the largest single area in which CAP agencies provide service is welfare. Usually welfare complaints make up 50 percent of all individual services provided by these agencies. Often the handling of welfare complaints serves a dual purpose for the CAP agency: it gives the agency an issue to organize people around, and it enables the agency to demonstrate quickly that it can deliver. . . .[75]

This same study found that roughly one-third of New York City's Community Development Administration budget was devoted to welfare activities and that many neighborhood centers had their own welfare rights organizations founded by block workers and supplied with volunteers from the CAP program.

An evaluation of the Bushwick Neighborhood Coordinating Council in Brooklyn also found that

there is every indication that callers coming to BNCC's Center for welfare services found it warm, welcoming and helpful. The Center's main target population is the individual welfare client. Between September 1966 and January 1968, 1,213 cases were registered.[76]

One-third of these cases were concerned with minimum standards of assistance or other entitlements under the law.[k]

---

[k]The evaluation also tried to analyze whether the community action worker provided a direct service (by dispensing information), acted as a broker (by linking the client with resources), or served as an advocate (by pressuring the department). By far, the worker's role as an advocate was predominate, followed in order by his role as a broker and a provider of direct services.

From their origins in the city, we now move to an analysis of how these early welfare rights groups were to develop into a city-wide movement that by 1968 was to have a major impact on the city's and the state's welfare programs.

The City-Wide Coordinating
Committee of Welfare Groups

From the late 1930s until November 1965 no New York City commissioner of welfare had met with representatives of the city's welfare recipients.[1] The administration of public assistance involved little if any client participation. However, this noninvolvement ended after the formation of local welfare rights organizations and, especially, the City-Wide Coordinating Committee of Welfare Groups (City-Wide) in New York City. Since 1965, face-to-face contact between the welfare department and client groups has become a common occurrence in the city's political life.

On June 30, 1966, welfare recipients, social workers, clergymen, and members of public welfare unions from all parts of New York City demonstrated as part of a coordinated national protest against welfare policy.[2] This protest was the first concerted act by the city's welfare rights organizations and led, eventually, to the formation of an organization and its affiliation with the NWRO. From this protest has evolved a genuine city-wide client movement that, according to its supporters, has had a notable impact on public assistance policy both in the city and the nation.

It was, perhaps, inevitable that the various welfare rights groups in different parts of New York City would establish communications and, eventually, formal ties with each other. Yet ironically the event that was most directly responsible for the formation of City-Wide occurred outside New York City.

The Syracuse Experiment with
Maximum Feasible Participation

The City-Wide Coordinating Committee of Welfare Groups emerged from the attempt under the War on Poverty to organize and involve the poor in the management of their own affairs. Although the origins of the phrase "maximum feasible participation" are obscure, its impact upon the development and direction of the poverty program has been substantial. From the president's message on poverty on March 16, 1964, to the passage of the Economic Opportunity Act of 1964 several months later, there was little public debate about the clause calling for participation of the poor even though there were many participants in the drafting of the poverty legislation—departmental representatives from HEW, Labor, Agriculture, and Commerce; the President's Committee on Juvenile Delinquency; and numerous legal, community relations, poverty, and welfare experts.[3] Nevertheless, only a short time after passage of the act, OEO programs in city after city were enmeshed in bitter and often protracted disputes over the proper representation of the poor in the Community Action Programs' governing bodies. Participation by the poor had its origins in community development programs in underdeveloped countries, the civil rights movement in the United States, and welfare policies that "debilitate rather than rehabilitate."[4] Together, these forces led to several CAP demonstration projects emphasizing citizen participation.

The idea of involving the poor in the antipoverty program was a departure from past practice.[5] For the first time in recent American history, the poor were told explicitly by legislative mandate that they were to have a hand in managing their own affairs. To the bureaucracy, the limited involvement of ghetto residents in managing their own affairs meant that poverty programs would operate efficiently and with minimal opposition. To the poor, however, participation under legislative mandate meant control. Community action programs were often used to legitimize the drive by the poor for some form of self-determination.[6]

This process and the political conflict it engendered occurred in an early community action program in Syracuse, New York. In February 1965, OEO granted $314,000 to Syracuse University for a nine-month period, with additional financing for another fifteen months if the initial program appeared promising.[7] The project came to have two parts. The Community Action Training Center (CATC) was established to train twenty students for work in selected target areas. Saul Alinsky was hired by the university as a consultant to CATC, and an Alinsky protege was made head of the organizing team. CATC's organizing tactics were, to one observer, "rubbing raw the sores of discontent to mobilize militant neighborhood protest."[8] CATC attempted to implement what it preached, particularly its understanding of OEO's mandate to involve the poor. However, CATC soon incurred the wrath of the local press, civic groups, city departments, and eventually Mayor Walsh. The university was forced to create a second organization, the Syracuse Community Development Association (SCDA), to do the actual organizing under subcontract. More than 2,000 adults were subsequently mobilized through nine neighborhood groups.

The newly organized poor immediately picketed city hall, the city housing authority, and the welfare department.[9] A CATC worker was arrested at the housing authority. Eleven AFDC mothers staged a sit-in at the welfare department in protest over not receiving allotment checks for children's clothing. When OEO funds were used to bail them out, Mayor Walsh and other local officials deplored the "excesses of a Federal program using a local community as a social laboratory."[10]

SCDA also helped to register 2,500 new voters from among the poor. Almost all of these new voters registered as Democrats. The Republican mayor, who had at one time spoken with pride about the program, now expressed his opposition to it. A CATC leader noted:

We are trying to maintain very carefully the fact that we are not partisans. . . . Neither party's happy with the appearance of these organizations in the neighborhoods in which they had only themselves to worry about before.[11]

Nevertheless, OEO refused to refund CATC and SCDA, and suggested that they seek funding through the local city hall-controlled program, the Crusade for Opportunity (CFO), a service-oriented organization dominated by representatives of social agencies, the press, and political groups. Later, OEO relented and agreed to consider refunding CATC, the research and training arm of the university program, but not SCDA. SCDA, the neighborhood arm, was left to seek funds through the CFO. OEO's reasoning was that, because the initial organizing had been successful, it should now become a city responsibility. A bitter conflict ensued. The People's War Council Against Poverty (PWCAP) was organized nationally to protest OEO's decision. PWCAP charged OEO with "abandoning the idea that the poor should be helped to build organizations totally of, by and for the poor . . . without even giving it half a chance."[12] OEO's decision, declared the SCDA director, raised "a very serious national question—whether OEO is going to fund any independent programs anywhere."[13]

OEO's decision in Syracuse was prompted by mounting pressures from local political forces. In June 1965 the U.S. Conference of Mayors passed a resolution urging OEO to recognize existing or city-hall-endorsed agencies as local conduits for community action programs. An antipoverty committee headed by Mayor Daley of Chicago met a few days later with Vice-President Humphrey and OEO officials to express their growing concern. Subsequently, OEO exhibited greater awareness of the political repercussions of federally financed organizations created to aid and abet the poor in fighting city halls.[14]

The PWCAP was formed in January 1966 as a reaction to the retreat from maximum involvement of the poor by OEO under pressures from local politicians, civic groups, the press, and social welfare agencies. Over 600 delegates representing the poor from 250 organizations in twenty-one states decided "to band together to help each other organize neighborhood groups to fight against poverty independently from social workers, politicians, and the so-called recognized leaders of the power structure."[15] In particular, the January convention, the first national convention of the poor, sought support for the PWCAP-Syracuse, a coalition of neighborhood organizations formed to protest and seek a reversal of OEO's decision to deny refunding for the Syracuse CATC-SDCA.[16] At the time of the People's Convention for the Total Participation of the Poor, both New York City and Syracuse had already formed local councils. Grace Cade, chairwoman of the New York City War Council, summed up the purpose of the convention in her address to the delegates:

We have resolved to support Syracuse because we feel that all of the poverty programs all over the country are either in the process of being attacked or can expect this kind of attack from either their local City Hall or eventually some city government agency.... We understand today that the poverty money is really just buying votes. We are not going to be bought anymore. We're saying, all right, you want to get a poverty program for us. We want to operate it. We want the dominant voice, as a matter of fact, we want 100% total participation. No maximum feasible participation. 100%; we're the poor, we know what we need, it's our struggle, we want to operate and want our own programs. We want to make use of that money in the way we know how, better than any agencies, any official, any professional. Poor people can learn how to operate, they can be skilled and trained to operate their own programs. These are some of the many issues. If we work together in some kind of communication system across the country, nationwide, the thing that happened to Syracuse can be stopped.[17]

The Syracuse convention passed a number of resolutions that illustrate the spirit and temper of both the convention and the emerging leadership of the increasingly politicized poor:

Whereas the anti-poverty program as presently constituted does not attack the basic causes of poverty nor meet the needs of poor people,
Be it resolved that a national attack be made on OEO for a transferral of power from the politicians to the people by means of direct funding to neighborhood organizations.
We further resolve that a national demonstration be held by local groups to support the aforementioned.
Whereas independence of action and continuity of organization are largely dependent on a reliable and constant source of sympathetic income and
Whereas people who have a substantial and financial stake in their own future will work the best and most lasting change,
Be it resolved that all organizations working for social change develop their own independent sources of income.
Be it further resolved that we demand the Community Chests and United Funds across the nation provide operating funds for mass local community organizations controlled by the people to the same extent that they provide operating funds for existing welfare agencies controlled by the paternalists.
Whereas large numbers of our community people are members of local AFL-CIO unions and
Whereas the national AFL-CIO unions are providing massive financial resources for the Citizens Crusade Against Poverty,
Be it resolved that CCAP provide the necessary funds for recruiting and training local community organizers to insure participation of the poor in the War on Poverty policymaking.
We recognize that the realities of life seem to dictate that OEO will not fund any community organization project on a mass base that fits the needs of the people, and therefore,
Be it resolved that we call on the major denominations of our nation as one of the last hopes the poor have for obtaining funds to develop such organizations.
We urge the denominations to make these funds available for community organizations across the country.
Be it further resolved that each organization represented here confront their local churches with the specific needs of their community organization.[18]

The PWCAP was expected by the delegates to develop into a full-fledged, continuing organization dedicated to the protection of the interests of the newly involved poor. One observer noted the convention's "pervasive atmosphere of anger, ... an anger not born of despair, but of harsh vitality, fierce in its suggestion of suppressed violence."[19]

Besides illustrating the temper and growing political involvement of the poor, the Syracuse convention launched a new phenomenon, large meetings of the poor from different metropolitan areas. These meetings reflected a new concept of a community organizing for social action and the frustration felt by the poor and their allies when their goals and aspirations are denied. There were other conventions of the poor during this period.[20] Although most were organized along the lines of a typical middle-class convention, and carefully structured, they were often described as "instruments of fierce protest to express intense anger, suspicion, and bitterness toward the Establishment."[21] Their main purpose was to engage centers of power locally and nationally in order to attack the root causes of poverty.

The Organization of City-Wide

It was within the context of these developments that a coordinating committee of welfare families emerged in New York City. A founder of City-Wide recalled:

One of the things that came out of the conference was that we had not really acted on the welfare problem. Richard Cloward was also in Syracuse and we discussed that weekend his idea of a guaranteed annual income. He had a whole series written up. Several of us argued that people would not move forward over the guaranteed annual income, but that we had to move around immediate needs. We came back to the City and we moved on the welfare front. It just happened that this developed.[22]

On December 12, 1965, an organization of the poor, the People's War Council Against Poverty of New York (PWCAP-NY) was formed. PWCAP-NY was initially composed of between twenty and thirty local neighborhood organizations representing the boroughs of Queens, Brooklyn, the Bronx, and Manhattan. Its life span was short.

The Council was primarily concerned with supporting and encouraging paraprofessionals and the poor. It brought together the leaders of the various local welfare rights groups scattered throughout the city. Among these leaders were: Frank Espada, the organizer of welfare recipients in Brooklyn; Beulah Sanders and Jeanette Washington, the welfare recipients who were active in the Stryckers Bay Poverty Organization on the Upper West Side; Grace Cade from the Lower East Side; and Alex Epthim, Richard Cloward, and Ezra Birnbaum, all affiliated with the MFY on the Lower East Side. Through PWCAP-NY, these individuals came into contact with the personalities, ideas, and programs of each other. This was the beginning of a welfare rights movement throughout the city.

However, by early 1966, it was clear that PWCAP-NY was not developing a program around which the city's poor could be mobilized, despite its success in bringing together activists from all parts of the city and all aspects of city life. A leader of PWCAP-NY described its problems:

The War Council was falling apart. Our principles and bylaws were so strong that we really alienated people who wanted to help us. We were so up tight. We said we don't want your expertise. We want you to come and help us to do it ourselves. We made a lot of demands. We frightened a lot of people we didn't know, people who trusted us. We found ourselves without funds, falling apart and isolated. So in order for us not to lose what we had gotten together and the people who had gotten together, we said we would move on welfare. The poverty program was doing okay. Too many people were getting little pieces of the pie and were no longer willing to fight. A lot of leaders in our area were really just frustrated. A lot of groups had become frightened of what happened at MFY and HARYOU. So we got involved in welfare. I really wasn't involved in the welfare struggle at that time. I just didn't want the whole movement to evaporate into nothing. I was surprised to see the number of welfare groups around the city that were not just isolated and cut off from each other, but did not know basic things such as how to organize themselves. Although quite militant, they were not getting any help.[23]

In April 1966 a conference was held at the Judson Memorial Church jointly sponsored by the PWCAP-NY and the Welfare Recipients League of Brooklyn (WRL), headed by Frank Espada. The conference had the theme, "An Action Conference on Welfare and Poverty." A mimeographed handout described the purpose of the conference:

The purpose of this conference is to discuss common goals, and to plan common actions welfare recipients and their own groups can take to get their full rights—what they are entitled to under the law, *immediately.* It is also the purpose of this conference to organize to change a system that does not work—that keeps the poor, *poor.*

Already several groups in New York have begun to fight for their rights. They have even won concessions from Commissioner Ginsberg. It is up to all of us to spread this information so that all welfare recipients in the city join this movement—begin working and organizing in their own areas now.

The PWCAP and WRL want all who attend this conference to return to their neighborhoods and begin a movement the likes of which New York has never seen—building good solid organizations of the poor, run by the poor, giving voice to the poor. The poor will take their rights.[24]

Through PWCAP-NY, a small group of poverty warriors, dissident social workers, organizers, activists, intellectuals, and the leaders of the poor began to meet informally to map out action programs and strategies for the city. These meetings attempted to bring together the various groups emerging in the ghetto communities across the city around issues related to welfare and assistance problems. Out of this, it was hoped, would come a coordinated approach to the problems of the city's welfare recipients.

Two key resolutions adopted by the Judson Memorial Church conference were: (1) to concentrate a major campaign against the ills associated with the welfare system through a soon-to-be-established city-wide or state-wide co-ordinating committee;[25] and (2) to stage a major demonstration at either city hall or the city's welfare administration in early June.[26]

On May 12, a group met at the Metropolitan Urban Seminary Training Center (MUST) to form the City-Wide Coordinating Committee. Prominent among those in attendance were Frank Espada, Grace Cade, and Richard Cloward. Intense organizational activity ensued as a national and local welfare rights movement were built simultaneously. Weekly meetings followed the establishment of City-Wide. Richard Cloward, by all accounts, was highly influential at this point through his spreading of his ideas and fund-raising for both the incipient national and local welfare rights organizations. In May 1966 a conference on the guaranteed annual income was sponsored in Chicago by a leading midwestern school of social work. Robert Theobald and Richard Cloward both spoke at this conference. More important, present at this conference were persons active in poverty programs, including George Wiley who was soon to form PRAC in Washington. A caucus at this conference laid the groundwork for a national effort in welfare culminating eventually in the formation of the NWRO. A participant in these early endeavors described some of the activity:

Wiley came on the scene shortly after the Judson Memorial Church conference. First of all we said we were going to have a city-wide demonstration in early June. Then Cloward decided that there was a conference out in Chicago. They used that to bring about an anti-poverty conference, to try to bring some welfare groups together. It was a kind of a national thing. Se we went out to Chicago. I first met George Wiley there. He was organizing a poverty rights thing and he just appeared. Cloward said that Wiley was going to coordinate welfare rights on a national level to get things going.
At that point, Wiley said why don't we have a national thing June 30th. We had originally scheduled our demonstration for June 1, and then learned about a march the people in Cleveland were having. So we got keyed into that. We had demonstrations in 24 to 27 cities. We had a hell of a demonstration in here, one hell of a show. Cloward was instrumental in this early organizing.[27]

Just a few weeks after the official formation of the City-Wide Coordinating Committee on June 30, 1966, the committee initiated its first major action as a part of a national protest organized by George Wiley and PRAC in Washington. A demonstration was held at city hall with a heavy turnout of clients, students, caseworkers, and other persons associated with the incipient movement.[28] The committee demanded a redress of grievances, a 25 percent increase across the board in welfare budgets so that clients could be brought up to minimum standards, a special clothing grant for school-age children, with the threat of a school boycott if the grant were not allowed, burial expenses, the use of minimum standard forms, and negotiation with the welfare commissioner on a regular basis.[29] The committee received a promise of action after a ninety-minute conference between the Commissioner of Social Services Mitchell Ginsberg, Timothy Costello, and a delegation of twenty-five demonstration leaders led by Frank Espada. The officials assured the delegation that the school clothing grant would be increased by 10 percent that very day. Commissioner Ginsberg and Dr. Costello also agreed that the welfare allowances should be increased by about 25 percent to bring clients up to minimum standards. However, Commissioner Ginsberg pleaded, "Honestly, we haven't got the money."[30] Dr. Costello promised to accompany the welfare rights leaders to Albany in an attempt to persuade the legislature to raise the mandated budgetary allowances for welfare recipients. Furthermore, both men promised that the demand for use of minimum standard forms to streamline the processing of client demands would be met and scheduled a second meeting with the client groups for July 15, 1966.

Thus a welfare rights organization was launched in the city by the June 30th demonstration. Yet this organization was still far from having genuine representation throughout the city; nor was there yet an effective welfare rights movement throughout the city. Nevertheless, a beginning had been made.

7

The Winter Clothing Campaign

By and large, welfare rights tactics have been formulated at the local level. In New York City, the MFY-inspired groups on the Lower East Side were most instrumental in the early development of these tactics. They had a dual objective: to generate maximum pressure for change and reform by the welfare department and to utilize this change as a means of establishing and perpetuating organized client groups. In this section, we discuss at length the role of the MFY-sponsored Committee of Welfare Families (CWF). The CWF was the pioneer among the Lower East Side groups; for the most part, the other organizations followed its lead.

In September 1965 Ezra Birnbaum, a student of community development, joined the staff of MFY's Neighborhood Center-South as its community development worker. Shortly afterwards, the center decided to concentrate on problems connected with the public welfare system. Birnbaum was charged with organizing clients around welfare issues.

In October 1965 Birnbaum and his associates adopted two objectives: (1) to isolate a problem common to all clients which, if attacked successfully, could provide a basis for clients forming political groupings; and (2) to find an issue that offered an immediate solution and tangible results. The issue that the MFY staff took up was the need for winter clothing, a recurring problem for New York City's recipients despite the availability of special grants that, presumably, allowed clients in need to satisfy their requirements without delay. A meeting was called to discuss the problem of winter clothing. Welfare recipients using MFY's neighborhood centers were encouraged to attend, while the MFY staff prepared a winter clothing request form for clients to fill out, sign, and present to their welfare center. At the first meeting, held on October 8, 1965, 17 clients attended. At the second meeting, 28 clients appeared, and at the third, nearly 50. Between 45 and 120 clients attended subsequent meetings during the remainder of the winter clothing campaign.

At these meetings MFY workers urged clients to exercise their rights, band together as client groups, and end ineffective individual approaches to the welfare department.[1] The meetings focused on welfare problems and winter clothing; clients with nonwelfare problems were referred elsewhere. One guiding principle of the early organizing efforts by the MFY staff was that clients should seek benefits that the welfare department was legally mandated to deliver. A few weeks after the first meeting, a winter clothing campaign was launched and, with it, the CWF.

A number of clients filled out form letters to their investigators. These letters, prepared by the MFY staff, were detailed requests for winter clothing to meet the needs of their families. The CWF decided to wait twenty-one days for answers before taking further action. By early November 1965, after waiting vainly for responses to most of these letters, the CWF then sent another letter to New York City's welfare commissioner signed by twenty-one clients requesting winter clothing grants. This letter, according to a founder of MFY, had a "properly indignant and militant, yet measured tone."[2] It read, in part:

We members of the Committee of Welfare Families of the Lower East Side have written letters to our investigators requesting winter clothing.

Our members have already sent 70 individual letters to four local welfare centers. The first 21 letters were mailed between October 12th and 15th. Of these only nine have received any money at all and none of these nine have been given enough money to keep their families warm this winter. More important the other 12 families have received no money at all.

We feel that we are being neglected—especially since many of our -investigators haven't even been in touch with us to find out about the seriousness of the situation.

Winter is here; our children are cold. Many of us are unable to keep clinic appointments because we do not have proper clothing. Many of our children have caught colds which can lead to other serious illnesses. Some of our children haven't been to school since the weather turned cold.

In most years, many of us have had to wait until December, January, or even later to buy our winter clothing. This year we're not willing to wait that long and see our children have to wear thin summer clothing when it gets below freezing.[3]

The letter requested an answer within three days. The CWF's strategy was to generate some form of concerted action that would precipitate a publicly visible confrontation with the welfare department, while involving minimum risk to individual clients. Three days, although a reasonable time, was short enough to make a response difficult and to provide CWF's organizers with a justification for more direct action.[a]

After the three days elapsed without a reply, the CWF sent a strongly worded telegram to the Commissioner threatening to fill his office with angry clients, to establish a picket line, and to secure press coverage to find out why he was not meeting the clients' requests or answering their correspondence. The commissioner then sent a telegram to the CWF agreeing to a meeting with the client group. The commissioner's willingness to meet with CWF representatives was the movement's first victory. However, it did not deter the CWF from going ahead with its planned demonstration which was now intended more for organizational esprit de corps than its impact upon the welfare department.

On November 26, 1965, welfare administrators and welfare clients met to

[a]In fact, no response was anticipated because no welfare commissioner had met with a group of clients about client-initiated grievances since the depression.

discuss client grievances.[4] This meeting resulted in agreement on an immediate investigation, acknowledgment of request for winter clothing by clients and the establishment of a grievance procedure. Commissioner Louchheim, in a letter to the CWF, reaffirmed the right of all welfare recipients to receive the winter clothing to which they were entitled and suggested that any recipients with complaints should communicate directly with their caseworkers. The Commissioner also stated that he would ask each welfare center administrator to designate a liaison worker to handle complaints from the community action group. The liaison worker should not be approached, however, until the usual caseworker-client route had been tried. Commissioner Louchheim went on to say that the liaison worker must have at least ten working days to handle complaints and that laws requiring confidentiality prohibit discussion of one recipient's case with another, even though he may represent the group.[5]

A series of meetings between the CWF and local welfare centers followed. The welfare recipients were represented by client complaint committees consisting usually of four clients. These meetings were at times acrimonious. The complaint committees objected to their reception by the local welfare centers' liaison officers. More important, they objected to the composition of the client grievance committees. Commissioner Louchheim, in his letter of December 9, 1965, had suggested two client representatives; CWF wanted four. The welfare department objected to the attendance of MFY staff personnel, the CWF insisted that these personnel be present.

The complaint-liaison committees met for over a month. Clients were pleased with a system in which complaints went directly to the top administrators, bypassing lower-level bureaucrats. However, the difficulties involved in conducting these meetings soon forced the CWF to discontinue their use. The client complaint committee was required to have at hand all the administrative facts of each case.[b] Under this procedure, the client complaint committee was, in effect, asked to perform the task normally done by welfare department investigators, a function it did not request or want. The CWF also lacked both the skills and staff to obtain the amount of information required by the welfare center liaison personnel. Moreover, its leaders feared that this might change the CWF from a social action group to a service-oriented group. In mid-December 1965, the CWF sent a letter to Commissioner Louchheim and the administrators of the four local welfare centers informing them that it was terminating the meetings. However, it reserved the right to use the formal complaint procedure at a future date.

After this initial encounter with the welfare department, CWF's organizing efforts proved more successful. For a period of two or three months more clients were brought under the umbrella of the winter clothing campaign, and the trappings of a welfare rights organization began to emerge.

---

[b]These details included such items as the date of each request, whether grants were awarded or not, follow-up, and the number of caseworker visits.

Leadership talents were identified by staff personnel and weekly training and educational sessions were established for a selected cadre of potential leaders. At the initial meeting between the CWF and Commissioner Louchheim, the CWF was represented by a steering committee of five clients. The steering committee eventually became an executive committee with five elected officers. The leadership training sessions were deliberately kept small. Only ten to fifteen clients attended each session. In these sessions, clients were taught the mechanics, operations, and laws governing the welfare system, client organization and tactics, and the preparation of clients' budgets. The current programs and organizational problems of the CWF were also discussed in these sessions. A number of welfare experts spoke to these groups. These included several welfare department staff members, Social Service Employees' Union officials, professors, and community organizers.[c] From these sessions emerged a client leadership possessing an in-depth knowledge of the operation of the welfare system and the rights of recipients under the law.

From its inception, MFY's strategy for developing leadership was twofold. First, it sought to build a stable and committed leadership while at the same time permitting individual leaders to advance into higher positions in their community. Second, the mass membership, it was thought, would be less stable; it was expected to change over time with the particular benefit campaign being waged.

Thus a two-tier organizational structure developed. A founder of MFY noted:

We regarded our people in at least two different groups. One was a hard core group and this, in essence, was the decision-making guts of the organization. I had dinner with these people at their houses, and I got to know their families. They were people who could be called on any time. If someone had a fire at their house at two in the morning, I was called. In other words, they had complete access to me and, in turn, I had complete access to them. This wasn't just an organization that they came to once a week. They were people disciplined to the organization. This was their group and, whatever else they were doing, they would drop it and come running for the group.[6]

The leadership group manned the executive and grievance committees, met with welfare administrators, and later shared responsibility for negotiations with the MFY staff. At the start of the campaign, the CWF mailed request-for-aid forms to investigators. Subsequently, it delivered these forms personally. The tactic of disrupting welfare center activities, which was commonly employed by 1968, was not used at this stage. Nor did the committee try to flood local welfare centers with more clients than they could handle.[d] Instead, the committee

---

[c]Some of the participants in these training sessions were Richard Cloward and Frances Piven of Columbia University; Ed Sparer, the MFY legal services head and a noted expert on welfare law; and Clara Eisner, a thirty-year veteran of the New York welfare bureaucracy.

[d]This lack of militancy resulted, in part, from the newness of the organization and, more important, its emphasis on the traditional social work approach.

would approach a center with between eight and fifteen clients demanding winter clothing. Upon refusal of a request, the committee would then insist on seeing the center's administrator.

The winter clothing campaign became enmeshed in the complexities of the welfare system. It also faced bureaucratic hurdles erected by local welfare center officials trying to thwart the complaint committee procedures worked out with Commissioner Louchheim. Despite these obstacles, the campaign was successful in obtaining winter clothing grants for 80 of the 110 clients who applied for them. However, one of the CWF's major goals failed: to secure automatic dispensation of winter clothing grants in the same manner that New York dispensed school clothing grants.[e] Although the campaign was able to satisfy the winter clothing needs of only a handful of New York City's welfare families, it nonetheless served as a training ground for the fledgling welfare rights movement. The importance of the tactic of focusing on a tangible benefit to gain the allegiance of welfare clients was demonstrated. This tactic was to become a central principle in the movement's subsequent activities.

During the winter clothing campaign, the CWF depended heavily on the goodwill and financial and staff support of the MFY. MFY established the CWF in its storefront; it hired the organizer who was instrumental in the formation and subsequent development of the CWF. Most important, MFY's support was available continuously. The role of the MFY lawyer is illustrative. MFY's Legal Services Unit assigned a Puerto Rican lawyer, Ray Narral, to the CWF early in its development. The presence of Narral and his determination that welfare mothers should seek additional benefits confirmed the legality of clients, asserting their rights by participating in the winter clothing campaign. Narral also educated clients about the intricacies of welfare regulations and, in the beginning, aided Birnbaum in chairing CWF meetings. Many other forms of support were forthcoming from MFY. Mass leafleting required technical as well as distribution facilities. Client leaders had to be guided and advised about the skillful manipulation and timing of group activity with sufficient visibility to attract the attention of the communications media. MFY's staff, consisting of a variety of experts with important contacts, was particularly helpful in developing issues for protest activities as well as actual protest tactics and strategies.

The communications between Commissioner Louchheim and the CWF, followed by negotiation sessions with the central administration and local welfare center officials, constituted a form of de facto recognition on the part of the welfare department. The establishment of a complaint grievance procedure between clients was a further confirmation of this de facto recognition. To be sure, this interaction between the welfare department and a client protest group stemmed from different motives. The client leaders, encouraged by the MFY

---

[e]Under automatic dispensation, winter clothing grants would not be dependent upon caseworker investigation, but would be disbursed automatically by the welfare system at a specified time and in a stipulated amount.

staff, thought their organization similar to a trade union, with the organization attempting to publicize the grievances of its presumed constituency. This view was totally rejected by the welfare department which viewed the organization as a highly vocal, but localized group of clients of uncertain strength and with considerable encouragement and assistance by outsiders.

The winter clothing campaign also validated the CWF as an organizational structure. Client leaders were identified, instructed by a variety of experts on the operations of the welfare department and the intricacies of welfare law, and encouraged to assert their legal rights to benefits mandated under the welfare system. Formal organizational roles developed. Most important for the future, CWF's client leaders came into contact with members of other groups in other parts of the city. In January 1966 four CWF client leaders accompanied Ezra Birnbaum to the Syracuse meeting of the People's War Council against Poverty. In Syracuse CWF leaders met with similar leaders from Brooklyn and Manhattan. This led, ultimately to the formation of a branch of the PWCAP in New York City. From this would emerge the City-Wide Coordinating Committee of Welfare Groups. The CWF was also validated as a viable organizational entity by the establishment of its storefront. The importance of this office as a means of legitimizing the organization in the eyes of ghetto residents cannot be over-stressed. The office gave prestige to the leadership and, simultaneously, provided a contact point for mobilizing and coordinating the CWF's efforts.[f]

The winter clothing campaign was the first systematically organized effort by the City's welfare recipients. As such, it was an important means of experiment-ing with a variety of protest tactics. Clients had to be mobilized through mass meetings, exhortation, and positive rewards. Potential leaders had to be iden-tified, politicized, and educated about the details of welfare regulations. Specific tactics had to be developed that would simultaneously appeal to clients and result in concessions by welfare administration officials. The winter clothing campaign was, in most of these respects, a successful trial run. A small number of clients was organized around a specific, benefit-producing campaign with limited success. Mailings were suspended in favor of hand delivery of grievance requests to caseworkers. At mass meetings, CWF and MFY workers urged clients to seek their rights, and mass leafleting became the most widely used communi-cations vehicle of the movement. The social work approach of having a small number of clients present their grievances to a local welfare center, followed by negotiations with the center's officials, also proved to be an ineffectual means of placing pressure on welfare centers to bring about meaningful institutional change. Clients would have to make the same effort to get adequate winter clothing the following year.

---

[f]The establishment of the storefront was a major event in the development of the CWF. It took well over a month to open this storefront and a series of problems attended its opening. At issue were MFY's role in the running of storefront, who was to work in it, who was to possess a key, and how it would deal with visitors, particularly welfare center caseworkers. An elaborate set of ground rules was eventually established governing how the storefront would be operated.

During the campaign, the subsequent tactics of New York City's welfare rights movement began to evolve. The logical next step was for the movement to advance from winter clothing to other types of special grants. Having emerged, on the whole successfully, from the winter clothing campaign, the movement now turned to the broader issue of minimum standards.

8 The Minimum Standards Campaign

Many participants in the winter clothing campaign also obtained special grants for furniture. Following their lead, the CWF initiated a furniture campaign in late 1965, printing a furniture request form on the opposite side of the winter clothing form. The furniture campaign continued after winter clothing grants ended in mid-April. In succeeding years, an annual clothing-furniture campaign was staged throughout the city by the City-Wide Coordinating Committee of Welfare Groups.

The CWF's experience with the two campaigns identified the most salient issue between the client and the welfare administration—the client's budget. Many welfare families had never seen their own budgets; nor did they know what they were receiving or whether their budgets reflected the legally-mandated "minimum standard" lifestyle. The fulfillment of clients' needs covered by the regular or basic grant such as food, rent, and certain utilities was of less immediate interest to the CWF than the fulfillment of special needs presumably met by various special allowances. These special grants were supposed to enable caseworkers to correct specific financial difficulties confronting a welfare family and, in this way, bring the family's living conditions up to minimum standard requirements. Table 8-1 lists the special grants that New York City's Department of Social Services was authorized to dispense during the mid-1960s.

The special grant had two important characteristics as far as the welfare rights movement was concerned. First, while the regular grant was fixed according to schedules established by law, and varied only with the size and composition of the welfare family, the special grant, being based on the peculiar needs of the family, was variable and theoretically limitless. Second, while the regular grant was set by the state legislature, the special grant was determined by the caseworker. Because of this, the special grant was to prove highly responsive to pressures by local welfare rights organizations. The special grant was intended to provide caseworkers with sufficient flexibility to help meet the individual needs of their clients. It became, instead, the most important organizing tool of the welfare rights movement, providing, in Olson's terminology, the essential private benefit from welfare rights membership that, while it continued, would assure the membership's commitment to the movement.

Table 8-1

Justification for Special Grants in Force as of July 20, 1965

Proration of regular allowance

Payment of regular budgetary allowance to clients not receiving their
allowance through normal channels

Supplementation of current period

Supplementation of previous period

Special clothing allowance

Household furniture, furnishings, and equipment

Replacement of lost or stolen check or cash

Replacement of cancelled check

Rent arrears

Utility arrears

Surgical or orthopedic appliances (including minor repairs),
batteries for hearing aids, and delivery costs

Approved essential, verified transportation needs within New York City

Expenses incident to securing employment

Installment payment or payment on loan

Transportation (to points outside New York City)

Housekeeping services

Other expenses connected with securing and maintaining housing

Day care fees

Dispossess fees and related costs

Storage charges

Moving expenses

Expenses connected with rehabilitation

Guide fees

    Shelter and/or repair allowance for Homeowners

Telephone service

Expenses incident to camp attendance

School expenses

Security deposit

Brokers' and finders' fees

Accrued rent

Accrued utilities

Disaster; sustenance

Disaster; clothing

Disaster; household furnishings and replacements

Disaster; shelter (temporary hotel accommodations)

Disaster; transportation to the home of a friend or relative or to a
shelter

Other

Source: New York City Department of Welfare Procedure No. 65-28, July 20, 1965.

The CWF's Role in the Minimum
Standards Campaign

The CWF discovered during the winter clothing and furniture campaigns that many welfare families were not being maintained at the minimum levels required by welfare law. This realization led to the minimum standards campaign in 1966 and focus by the welfare rights movement on a wide range of special grants. The CWF's primary campaign goal was to persuade the Department of Health, Education, and Welfare to force New York City to adhere to HEW's minimum standard levels.

The minimum standards campaign was similar in organization to earlier campaigns. It was launched by a series of mass meetings and heavily publicized through verbal communication in the neighborhood, posters, mass leafleting, and, most important, the network of storefronts established by the MFY and its affiliated organizations. Welfare rights protest activities also attracted substantial free publicity by the local press, radio, and television, as well as various community and ethnic modes of communication. The CWF kept its work visible by having its leadership on radio and television and in the press on at least twenty occasions during the first six weeks of the minimum standards campaign.

Attendance at the first six meetings of the campaign ranged between 90 and 225. Organizers used these sessions to explain the campaign and to exhort clients to participate in it. Emphasis was placed on obtaining household and personal items mandated by welfare legislation. Rabagliati and Birnbaum describe the process:

This meant, for example, one chair per person, a certain number of beds according to the sexes and ages of the children, and specific items for cooking and housework, many of which were known to be missing in the homes of most welfare recipients. When the list of items was read out, it was evident that most of the people present did not possess many of these items and were overwhelmed at the long enumeration.

The leaders asked people to talk about what they had or did not have, and suddenly people were on their feet telling everyone—the other recipients, the social workers, the television cameras, the newspapermen—what they had and how their requests had been ignored or refused by their caseworkers. A mother of four told of having only one bed for the whole family; an elderly lady living alone in a dark basement described how she had been refused extra money for electricity; another woman said she kept her light burning all night to keep away the rats and took the money for the electricity out of the food budget; another complained that her children could not attend school because they lacked sufficient clothing, particularly in the winter. None of these tales was new to the listening clients of the Department of Welfare.[1]

Clients sent letters requesting particular items to their local welfare centers. These letters demanded that the recipients' living conditions be raised to legally mandated welfare standards. In addition, petitions seeking a redress of grievances were directed to the commissioner of welfare. For over a month, mass meetings were held to persuade clients to join and participate in the campaign. The CWF made ample use of MFY's resources. Approximately 5,000 leaflets were printed for each weekly meeting; roughly a thousand were mailed to recipients announcing each meeting. Through MFY, the CWF had unlimited paper, postage, and other technical resources.

On April 5, 1966, a CWF delegation, accompanied by about eighty recipients, demonstrated at the city's welfare department at 250 Church Street and presented a list of demands for minimum standards to the new Welfare Commissioner Mitchell Ginsberg. The commissioner agreed to the enforcement of departmental regulations and an investigation of complaints, with a two-week limit between the time of a legitimate request and the receipt of a check by the client. This concession by Commissioner Ginsberg was a significant short-term victory for the CWF. It legitimized the minimum standards campaign to other groups scattered across the city.

The CWF, with some reluctance, agreed to sponsor a city conference of welfare client groups.[2] On May 21, 1966, about 300 individuals representing forty organizations, including the Urban League, the NAACP, hospital groups, settlement houses, and other welfare client groups, met to discuss common issues. The names of the panels and workshops at this conference are indicative of its purpose: "Why and How Clients Are to Organize"; "Welfare Law and Client Benefits"; "New Budgets"; "Client Rights to a Normal Social Life"; "How to Set Up a Minimum Standards Campaign"; and "Discrimination in Municipal Hospitals."[3] Besides disseminating technical and organizational materials, the conference also served as a forum for communication and an exchange of ideas between activists and client leaders throughout the city. The conference ended with an invitation to all groups present to participate in the newly created City-Wide Coordinating Committee's first demonstration at city hall on June 30, 1966.

During the summer of 1966, the CWF secured a $19,000 grant from the New York City Office of Economic Opportunity for a training program, a children's program, and family and adult outings.[4] The CWF thus obtained its first measure of independence from the MFY apparatus, and its first experience with running programs of this type. The OEO project was used to maintain and enhance the organizational structure and leadership of the CWF.[5]

Other Client Groups on the Lower East Side

There were other developments on the Lower East Side. Foremost among these developments was the formation of two other MFY-sponsored welfare client organizations, the Welfare Action Group Against Poverty (WAGAP) and the

Citizens Welfare Action Group (CWAG). Eventually, all three groups would pool their efforts in the Emergency Welfare Council for Winter Clothing.

Marty Eisman, a unit supervisor in the Neighborhood Service Center—South and a founder of the CWF, was the driving force behind the WAGAP.[6] WAGAP started by organizing elderly clients who had health, medicare, or other problems common among the aged. WAGAP served a more limited clientele than the CWF and was handicapped by the fact that many of its members were illiterate or semiliterate and generally less sophisticated than CWF members.[7] Thus, although Eisman had initially sought to develop an autonomous organizational structure, in the end WAGAP was to become more heavily dependent on MFY than the CWF.

The tactics and subsequent development history of WAGAP were determined largely by its distinctive membership. Its first task was to define the problems facing older people, many of them physically handicapped. By and large, the elderly wanted to make their lives less difficult and to communicate their grievances to a sympathetic audience.[8] Issues developed around whether clients had to obtain caseworker approval prior to making dental and eye clinic appointments, or whether clients could use local drug stores for medicines instead of having to travel outside their neighborhoods. Despite meetings with welfare department representatives and demonstrations at the welfare department's main offices, WAGAP did not have a significant impact on the system. Because of its small active membership, it simply could not muster the mass force required to make the welfare bureaucracy take its efforts seriously.[9] WAGAP's membership peaked early and then declined rapidly because it could produce few tangible benefits to maintain the interest of existing members and to attract new members.

WAGAP eventually turned to the minimum standards campaign, drawing heavily in the efforts of staff volunteers, social-work students, and two permanent VISTA volunteers. However, even the minimum standards campaign, used successfully by the CWF in building up and maintaining its organization, failed to stem the decline in WAGAP's membership.

Finally recognizing that the composition of its membership raised insurmountable difficulties in mounting mass campaigns, WAGAP decided to focus on "home groups."[10] It would hold meetings in small groups on a neighborhood basis rather than stage mass public meetings. By having selected WAGAP members invite friends and neighbors to their homes, WAGAP would convey information to the welfare community on such matters as welfare and tenants' rights. This, it was thought, would locate welfare clients with problems, develop WAGAP leadership, educate and mobilize clients for social action, and generate new ideas for a program for WAGAP.[11] WAGAP subsequently pursued its "home policy" in a well-defined membership target area by moving from its storefront to a settlement house. However, despite the hopes of its staff and organizer, it never developed into an independent and autonomous organization.

The third major welfare-oriented MFY-inspired group was the Citizens Welfare Action Group (CWAG), formed in late March 1966.[12] At first, the CWAG drew its members primarily from MFY's Neighborhood Service Center-North. Later, members walked into CWAG's office or were drawn to it by word of mouth. Barbara Lounds, an MFY community organizer, started CWAG in response to clients' repeated complaints about the lack of needed services by the Department of Social Services. Approximately sixty clients attended the first meeting. Many of these clients had had some contact with earlier CWF activity.

The organizer, Barbara Lounds, had the full range of MFY support behind her. Most important was the advice of the CWF organizer, Ezra Birnbaum. The CWAG started in March 1966 with the minimum standards campaign as its major organizational effort. It followed a procedure similar to that used by the CWF. An interview was held with each client at which the group's goals were discussed, client rights were outlined, and client grievances articulated. After the client agreed to join CWAG, a minimum standard form was completed and signed. This form was then mailed to the local welfare center. Between March and November 1966, CWAG generated 598 letters to twelve welfare centers requesting special grants (see Table 8-2).

Ten days after mailing a letter, follow-up would begin. If clients reported no

Table 8-2
Minimum Standard Letters Sent by CWAG as of November 1, 1966, by Welfare Center

Center	Number of Letters
Yorkville	246
Gramercy	221
Nonresident	67
Lower Manhattan	45
Veterans	11
Tremont	1
Kingsbridge	2
Special Service	1
Dyckman	1
Amsterdam	1
Brooklyn	1
Williamsburg	1
	598

Source: Memo to Dan Morris, Assistant Executive Director for Programs, from Barbara Lounds, Community Organizer, Citizens Welfare Action Group, "Welfare Minimum Standards Campaign," November 7, 1966.

response or an inadequate response, subsequent letters would be sent by the MFY legal department to the administrators requesting further action. The legal department wrote 310 of these letters during CWAG's first seven months. If after five days the client again reported no response or an inadequate response, a second letter was sent by the legal department. During this period, 116 second and 14 third and fourth letters were prepared by the legal department. The follow-up letters served to alert the welfare administration to the clients' unmet needs and the possibility of legal action because of departmental inaction. Finally, if a response were still not forthcoming, a fair hearing procedure was begun.

Rarely was a full or adequate grant issued as a result of a client's request. According to CWAG estimates, actual grants averaged 40 percent of requests. Supplemental grants issued after the receipt of the lawyers' letters brought the total to 65 to 70 percent of requests. When fair hearings were instituted, clients received 90 percent of what they had originally asked.

At the end of 1966, CWAG's organizer reported that the program had resulted in 600 letters requesting household equipment and over 200 letters requesting clothing from welfare centers; 310 cases were known to have received $65,319 in grants for household items and $6,140 in clothing grants for a total of $71,459.[13] After seven months, CWAG claimed a membership of 600.[14]

Besides its minimum standards campaign, the CWAG ran a leadership development and training program designed to locate leaders and, through community workshops, to acquaint these leaders with the administrative details of the welfare system and techniques for organizing welfare rights programs. A newsletter supervised by a VISTA volunteer, a bazaar, and educational meetings and trips were all part of the group's agenda. CWAG maintained close liaison with the CWF and other emerging client groups in the city, particularly after its participation in the June 30 demonstration at city hall.[a]

Evolution of Tactics

From the beginning, there was disagreement within the MFY over the appropriate tactics to be used in forcing the welfare department to implement desired reforms as quickly as possible. Two competing styles of advocacy—the traditional, professional social-work approach and a more militant disruptive style of protest—were considered by the founders of the city's welfare rights movement.

The former emphasized quiet orderly protest, using such methods as mailing in aid requests and documentation of client grievances and the welfare depart-

[a]Other groups participated in welfare-related programs on the Lower East Side. For example, MFY's Community Organization Division started the Sixth Street Welfare Group and the Negro Federation. Several other ethnic groups also participated in welfare campaigns. In terms of members, however, none of these groups approached the CWF, WAGAP, and CWAG.

ment's response to these grievances. This documentation would then be used in negotiations between client leaders, MFY staff, and the Department of Social Services. Above all, this approach rejected illegal activity of all types, particularly disruption of local welfare centers. The emphasis throughout was on seeking an orderly redress of grievances through negotiations on a client's legal entitlements.

The more militant approach was first suggested as early as December 1965 when Martin Eisman proposed that the CWF "flood" one welfare center with mailed requests for winter clothing and, in this way, generate administrative chaos. His goal was to create a crisis situation as a way of forcing serious thought by welfare department officials about computerizing winter clothing grants.[15] In late 1966, in summing up the year's activity, Eisman concluded:

Unfortunately, we were not able to inundate any one center with either winter clothing requests or the minimum standards letters that began going out in March 1966 and are still being mailed out. Lots of people got lots of things, but we were not making much impact on any one welfare center, let alone the system itself. One of the great positives to come out of both these campaigns was the proliferation of welfare client groups around the Lower East Side and the City. But aside from these important results, the two campaigns meant that the groups were really doing the work for the welfare department.[16]

Eisman then went on to suggest that there were advantages to be gained if, instead of mailing in requests, clients brought them to the welfare center. This would flood a few welfare centers with clients asking to be served. Eisman also suggested that the issue around which the next campaign might be organized should be the demand for winter clothing, an issue involving an immediate felt need by welfare clients.[17]

This tactical approach received further support in May 1966 when Richard Cloward and Frances Fox Piven, professors at the Columbia University School of Social Work, published what was to become a highly influential article.[18] Cloward and Piven argued that the present welfare system functioned only because it did not give recipients their legally mandated benefits. This was accomplished by not informing recipients of the full range of benefits available under federal, state, and local laws, and intimidating those recipients who did know their rights and dared to apply for them. The Cloward-Piven solution called for a massive, twofold campaign: to enroll eligible nonrecipients and simultaneously to seek the full range of benefits and entitlements for those already receiving assistance. It outlined a strategy calling for a massive educational campaign describing welfare benefits; the dissemination, through the mass communications media, of information about the inefficiencies and injustices of the welfare system; and, finally, publicly visible disruption of welfare centers. This disruption had the dual aims of creating a militant climate that would combat the feeling of helplessness that many recipients had toward the system and of imposing administrative and fiscal hardships on local and state governments.[19] The long-term result of this strategy, it was hoped, would be the replacement by the federal government of existing state and local welfare administrations and institution of some form of guaranteed income maintenance system.[20] Cloward and Piven did not think that the success of their strategy depended on the existence of cohesive, dues-paying membership groups, but simply on large numbers of recipients seeking legal benefits and participating in mass demonstrations.[21]

Early in 1966 a draft of the Cloward-Piven paper was circulated among welfare organizers and activists on the Lower East Side. This draft had a major influence on individuals involved in organizing welfare clients. A founder of the New York City welfare rights movement described its impact:

At the very beginning when we first saw the draft, I was excited. It provided an intellectual rationale and thought for what we were doing. The main thing that it added, aside from intellectual support, was the idea of flooding the system. It pressed the idea of forcing the system to break down as a basic strategy. This is something that we had thought of, but we didn't plan on putting it into effect because it sounded more militant than what our people were willing to accept. Once that appeared and started to influence what was happening around the city then we put it into effect the following fall of 1966.[22]

By October 1966 the various client groups on the Lower East Side were well staffed and supported, in large part, by OEO. The strongest groups, by far, were those associated with MFY and, particularly the CWF, WAGAP, and CWAG. In the fall of 1966 these groups decided that a new strategy was needed on the Lower East Side. It was agreed to attempt total mobilization of energies and resources for a single benefit campaign, winter clothing. Although the winter clothing campaign was not new, an added twist was agreement to seek a confrontation with the welfare system in order to force the Department of Social Services[23] to alter its existing policies and practices.[24] The new strategy would flood the local welfare centers with more grievance requests than they could cope with administratively. Clients would no longer wait for an official investigation of individual cases, but would demonstrate and cause disruption at the local centers until everyone was taken care of. "Our purpose," a leader of the campaign stated, "was to force the machinery to a halt, to force the centers to negotiate with us."[25] In short, the basic difference between the winter clothing campaigns of 1965 and 1966 was that the latter would be "very militant and very political, aimed towards television and radio, aimed towards the welfare department, and aimed towards a deliberate use of tactics that would disrupt those centers."[26]

All of this was to be accomplished by the concerted efforts of the major Lower East Side groups and their allies.[b] A coordinating committee consisting of

[b]The major groups were the Committee of Welfare Families, Welfare Action Group Against Poverty, the Citizens Welfare Action Group, the Sixth Street Welfare Group, Action for Progress, and several smaller organizations.

leadership and staff held weekly planning sessions from which emerged the Lower East Side Emergency Welfare Council for Winter Clothing. The basic minimum standard form was used, along with an instruction sheet and an information leaflet. Clients sent letters to their local centers asking to be brought up to minimum standards by the first week of November, the time of a planned demonstration. Beginning in November, and for several weeks afterwards, hundreds of clients appeared at the four Lower East Side centers with seven demands:[27]

1. That they be brought up to minimum standards immediately.
2. That the special home visit be eliminated, constitutional rights of privacy guaranteed, and illegal searches of drawers and closets ended.
3. That red tape be cut by eliminating the need for the caseworker to consult a home economist and by letting the unit supervisor approve minimum standard needs no matter what the cost.
4. That winter clothing grants be issued automatically, as is done with school clothing grants.
5. That on a caseworker's regular visit four times a year, a checklist be used to guarantee that clients are kept up to minimum standards.
6. That when a new item is added to the Department of Welfare's minimum standards, all clients be given this item immediately and automatically.
7. That special grants for clothing be given over and above the clothing allowance in the regular check.

The demonstrating clients disrupted normal operations at all four centers and succeeded in closing one.[28]

The centers failed to process most individual requests for clothing allowances within the ten-day period promised by the welfare administration. For this reason, the Emergency Welfare Council for Winter Clothing sent Commissioner Ginsberg a telegram demanding that all "welfare clients be brought up to minimum standards for clothing as stated in bulletin No. 66-38, dated September 29, 1966, and as guaranteed by welfare law."[29] This telegram was followed by a demonstration at the Central Complaint Bureau on November 22 and a meeting between Commissioner Ginsberg and a committee of several representing the council.[30]

Disturbed by the activities of the welfare rights organizations, Commissioner Ginsberg sent letters to the local welfare centers that were under siege.

I know that you and your staff, in making their statutory visits, have been trying to bring our clients up to standards in clothing and furniture. With enough time, we could have eliminated this as a grievance. But time is a commodity of which we do not seem to have a surplus. Instead, we are forced to use our limited resources to meet crisis after crisis, which are generated from outside the department, sometimes out of a desire to help our clients; sometimes out of a desire to exploit our clients.[31]

Commissioner Ginsberg also issued a new statement of his department's commitment to the principle that clients should be brought up to minimum standards, as defined in the welfare manual, and the manner in which this was to be accomplished.[32]

The winter clothing campaign created a policy conflict between the Department of Social Services and the Social Service Employees' Union (SSEU) representing the caseworkers.[33] Client demonstrations on the Lower East Side and in upper Manhattan posed a dilemma for the caseworker. Both the union and the department agreed that clients should be brought to minimum standards, but disagreed on how clients should be handled upon arrival at the local center. Departmental procedure called for the client to leave a message for the caseworker and then go home. The worker would then investigate the legitimacy of the request. The SSEU insisted that the worker see the client personally, determine from existing records whether the request should be met, and inform the client immediately about the disposition of the request. Cash grants would be made through normal procedures. In response to the massive winter clothing campaign, the union, in a seven-point advisory document to its membership, urged caseworkers to reduce home visits and adjust their caseloads to give themselves maximum time to work on minimum standards grants. The city's welfare commissioner publicly disagreed with this position.[34]

The Emergency Welfare Council for Winter Clothing was well organized. Besides providing busing for hundreds of clients daily, it also set up gigantic coffee urns, prepared hundreds of sandwiches, installed a telephone call-in system, and appointed a spokesman for press relations. A budget of several thousand dollars was also used to transport, feed, and organize the demonstrators.

Essential to the long-range success of the new strategy was publicity going beyond the MFY apparatus on the Lower East Side. The campaign was covered extensively by the local press. Publicity was vital to the fulfillment of the two objectives of the council. The first was to disseminate information about the welfare movement and the benefits it provided to clients; the second, to interest the incipient City-Wide Coordinating Committee of Welfare Groups in sponsoring a similar city-wide campaign. Extensive coverage by such newspapers as *El Diario* and the *Daily News* helped the council achieve these objectives.

The conscious effort to flood the welfare centers with requests for special grants ended shortly after Thanksgiving. There were several reasons for its termination. The Lower East Side welfare centers eventually met the demands placed upon them by bringing many applicants up to minimum standards.[35] The localized nature of the winter clothing campaign also meant that clients in other neighborhoods got less. Finally, and perhaps most important, the MFY came under strong attack for its assistance to welfare client groups.[36] Responding to external criticism, MFY placed a senior staff member in the Emergency Welfare Council's winter clothing campaign to "ensure a level of consistency in decisions made by those engaged in the giving of direct service."[37] In discussing illegal behavior by its staff, MFY's executive director declared:

MFY has long had a policy which holds that staff members cannot aid, abet, nor participate in any illegal act. This means that when they are working with a group and the group wishes, for example, to conduct a sit-in, the staff member will try to help the group see the consequences of the action and possible alternatives. If the group wishes to proceed to have the sit-in, the staff member cannot accompany the group.[38]

Although MFY stressed its determination to resist official blandishments, its subsequent involvement in the welfare rights movement was clearly affected. MFY's administration foresaw a new direction for the MFY, toward the goal of increasing adult employment and experimenting with various forms of income maintenance. This new direction, the administration thought, would be of greater benefit to the individual than an organized welfare rights movement.[39]

MFY had now reached a crossroad. The essential issue was to what extent a public agency supported by public funds could organize against the welfare department. MFY chose to withdraw from its involvement in the welfare rights movement. However, the movement it had spawned did not disappear. From the welfare bureaucracy's point of view, the damage had been done and its problems were only beginning.

Summary

The federal government's antipoverty programs were primarily responsible for launching New York City's welfare rights movement. From early 1965 to late 1966, MFY played a pivotal role in this process. It began with staff workers acting as middlemen, helping their clients to obtain benefits from local welfare centers. That approach did not prove productive and gradually the MFY staff took on an advocate's role, providing legal services and administrative assistance in an effort to aid clients and change the welfare department's policies and procedures. Finally, MFY began to organize clients in the belief that the client group itself should bring pressure to bear on the welfare department. From its organizational efforts evolved a set of tactics that were used with some success in the Lower East Side. The most important of these tactics was emphasis on securing higher benefit levels for welfare recipients.

MFY provided financial and technical resources to the newly formed welfare rights groups. It also provided an institutional framework within which the early organizations of welfare clients were allowed to experiment with different tactics and, in this way, grow. Much of the early welfare rights activity was directed toward informing welfare clients of what was available under the law. MFY supplied welfare consultants who were knowledgeable about welfare policies and procedures. MFY prepared a manual of welfare procedures which was kept up to date and used by the neighborhood organizations. MFY supplied organizers experienced in working with the urban welfare poor. Lawyers from

MFY's Legal Services Unit played a critical role in assuring clients of the legality of their actions and in bargaining with department officials. Finally, MFY provided financial and other support through which forms, instruction sheets, training materials, and leaflets were printed and distributed.

The minimum standards campaign exposed the vulnerability of the welfare system to planned welfare rights activity. With the end of MFY's interest in organizing welfare clients, the stronger of the Lower East Side groups turned their attention to a broader, city-wide effort and participation in the newly formed City-Wide Coordinating Committee of Welfare Groups. By the end of 1966, minimum standards campaigns were also begun in the Bronx, Brooklyn, and upper Manhattan. Aside from the MFY groups, such antipoverty and civil rights organizations in the city as HARYOU, the East Harlem Triangle Project, University Settlement's Action for Progress, the South Bronx Community Program Center, and CORE were active in the campaign.

The publicity generated by the minimum standards campaign spread to other groups working in the city's low-income areas. Activists and welfare organizers began to learn of each other's existence, to communicate with one another, and to plan common strategies. Soon, the minimum standards campaign became a concerted effort to build an effective city-wide movement in the welfare area. Knowledge of welfare rights groups and their success in obtaining minimum entitlements spread rapidly in the lower-income areas of the city through the mass media and the network of storefronts and umbrella organizations which, by early 1967, were to be found in almost all parts of the city. Many diverse and structurally unrelated organizations, with different programs, different sources of funds, and different constituencies, initiated some form of minimum standards campaign. Some saw in the minimum standards campaign a way to serve individual recipients in their communities, while others used the campaign as an organizing tool to build durable client organizations. It was at this juncture that the City-Wide Coordinating Committee of Welfare Groups became the major impetus for welfare rights activity in New York City.

In this way, MFY's short-lived attempt at organizing welfare clients produced a successful model for other poverty groups in the city. This model had both an intellectual rationale and proven track record. The staging of well-timed, periodic campaigns for legally entitled benefits, backed up by appropriate legal action, was to dominate the city's welfare scene during the next year and a half.

Creation of a City-Wide
Movement

From its inception in May 1966 until late 1967, the City-Wide Coordinating Committee of Welfare Groups, although nominally the leader of the city's welfare rights movement, functioned in organizational chaos with little control or influence over the growing and disparate number of local client groups.[1] One leader of City-Wide complained to NWRO headquarters about these difficulties:

In the past year we have not worked in such a way as to solve our organizational and structural problems; we just make do. We have established few definite organizational relationships that welfare groups can latch on to; no definite principles of operation; no financial reports; no rules for voting at opening meetings; no by-laws or constitutions, nor anything that is on the way to such by-laws.[2]

Among the changes needed were a city-wide conference of welfare groups to plan an action program, elections, bylaws, payment of dues, and an efficient organizational structure.[3]

To survive, City-Wide had to develop its leadership, a reason for its existence, and (above all) a working relationship with the local groups that were springing up throughout the city's poverty areas. City-Wide also had to develop reliable sources of funds and technical expertise needed to maintain a protest organization.

Yet City-Wide's organizational structure was ambiguous, amorphous, and wracked by internal dissent. Until late 1967, when a workable operational structure was finally established, the City-Wide Coordinating Committee experienced repeated crises over leadership and funds. Numerous disputes and personality conflicts created disunity. The turnover in its leadership and staff was appallingly high.[a] City-Wide did not have a staff director for prolonged periods. Even when it did manage to hire a director, chaos continued because there were no guidelines for staff authority or responsibility. A leader in City-Wide described these problems:

For a long time we had no structure. It got too big too fast and we had no money. It simply mushroomed. Welfare recipients came and got minimum standards. Some went away; some remained. Actually, many community leaders

---

[a]For example, Frank Espada, Shirley Spears, and Virginia Smythe, all chairmen of the Executive Committee, left City-Wide during this period for better jobs. Other key staff members who left City-Wide between 1966 and 1967 were Grace Cade, Cheryl Covian, Alex Epthim, and Frances Julty.

who had not found any place to move in the social action arena got involved in this whole thing. It was crazy, wild, no structure, no nothing. We moved mostly on emergency crisis activity, and there were always emergencies. We were sitting in, picketing, demonstrating, and getting arrested. That was the kind of thing that went on.[4]

City-Wide's executive board, instead of being elected, included by appointment the more aggressive clients who insisted on participating fully in the decision-making process or clients who staff organizers thought possessed strong leadership potential. Incredibly, City-Wide's first elections did not occur until early 1968. Moreover, to many welfare recipients the potential usefulness of the City-Wide Coordinating Committee remained unclear. A number of the established local welfare rights groups were actually hostile to City-Wide and thought it a competitor for membership and funds.

Yet despite this early organizational chaos, the City-Wide Coordinating Committee managed to develop into an effective and genuine organization by the end of 1967. Among the reasons for this was the establishment of an Advisory Committee separate from the Executive Board. This committee included lawyers, social-work students, professors, and others interested in welfare protest activity. Perhaps its most influential member was Richard Cloward. A major function of this committee was the political education of City-Wide's leadership.

Although survival of City-Wide was a feat in itself, another development was even more remarkable—the spontaneous growth of local welfare rights organizations throughout the city. Many of these organizations were inspired by the initial successes and publicity received by the MFY groups on the Lower East Side. Another explanation for City-Wide's survival was the continuing need for and interest in City-Wide's support by some of the organizers of these groups. Only City-Wide addressed itself solely to welfare issues; it was a logical place to which the local organizers might turn. As a result, the demand for City-Wide's services overwhelmed its ability to supply these services. City-Wide's headquarters, manned by a few volunteer workers, were inundated with requests for information, organizers, minimum standard forms, and other technical information. Yet instead of meeting these requests and providing a strong leadership model, City-Wide's organization produced chaos and internal schisms which in turn encouraged the local groups to drift into and out of City-Wide's orbit. By the spring of 1967, support for City-Wide at the local level was waning.

City-Wide's early tactics were also in error. Its efforts centered on the welfare commissioner and the welfare department's central headquarters. Yet the welfare department was highly decentralized, with considerable administrative discretion and power being vested in the administrators of the local welfare centers. Many of the local groups soon discovered this. By the end of 1967, it had become increasingly clear that if City-Wide were to survive and successfully coordinate the activities of the many groups now scattered across New York City, major changes would be necessary.

**The Emergence of a Successful
City-Wide Movement**

Three events occurred in late 1967 that would bring to an end the organizational chaos of the City-Wide Coordinating Committee, enable the committee to gain some measure of authority over local groups and in the process broaden the base of the welfare rights movement in New York City. First, City-Wide hired a young, energetic, and aggressive staff director. Second, by adopting the dues requirements of the NWRO, City-Wide and its affiliates became part of the larger national movement. This helped to resolve its financial problems and to establish an organizational identity separate from other War on Poverty groups. Finally, City-Wide's organizational structure was decentralized and roles were more clearly delineated with the result that an imperfect but operational structure was finally established. This structure, for the first time, allowed City-Wide to perform its primary function—coordination.

The Staff Director

In November 1967, City-Wide hired a twenty-five-year-old black activist, Hulbert James, as its staff director. The staff director's background typified the talents that were often united under the welfare rights banner. James was a graduate of Hampton Institute in Virginia and had been an early participant and organizer in black student civil rights protests throughout the South. Subsequently, he gained additional organizing experience under Dr. Martin Luther King in the Southern Christian Leadership Conference. Besides having had direct experience with the civil rights movement, James also participated in the War on Poverty and community organization programs by serving as an antipoverty coordinator and director of the West End Community Council in Louisville, Kentucky. In addition, James had legal training at the University of Louisville and Howard University Law Schools. In short, James brought to the job a combination of organizing experience and legal training that would greatly influence the later development of the City-Wide Coordinating Committee.

Adoption of a Dues-Paying Membership System

The second event that helped to establish City-Wide on a sound basis was the adoption of the NWRO's dues-paying membership system in June 1967 (see Chapter 4). According to BWAC's organizer, the national membership plan proved invaluable in forging a degree of unity among diverse Brooklyn groups.[5] NWRO's membership plan allowed participation with the larger movement without depriving the local groups of the autonomy needed to operate successfully local welfare rights campaigns. Membership cards, kits, badges, buttons, and dues requirements all created the necessary paraphernalia of a viable organization. Most important, they provided a parallel system of book-keeping for each group and a mechanism through which groups and individuals could exchange information about activities and tactics.

Organizational Decentralization

City-Wide's several attempts to manage special benefit campaigns in 1966 and 1967 demonstrated clearly its need for greater organizational efficiency. City-Wide was able to mount large demonstrations at a single target. However, its early efforts to mount simultaneous demonstrations throughout the city were not overly successful. To perform its function as a coordinator, City-Wide held weekly meetings with representatives of the local groups. However, because of difficulties in communication and transportation, these representatives failed to show up at these meetings on a continuing basis. Nor could City-Wide's chairman and staff maintain their day-to-day or even week-to-week personal contact with each local group and still perform their City-Wide functions.

Hence, in late 1967, a proposal for decentralizing the City-Wide structure was widely discussed and debated. This proposal resulted in part from the fact that the main targets of the local groups were increasingly the local centers and not the head offices of the city's welfare administration. A consensus developed that City-Wide, as it was then structured, was too loosely organized to coordinate effectively the activities of the sixty to eighty local welfare rights groups operating in the city.[6]

The proposed solution to City-Wide's organizational problems became known as the borough model. This model envisioned City-Wide at the apex of an organization encompassing the entire city, with borough councils linking City-Wide with the local groups. The development of borough councils, it was thought, would lessen problems of communication between City-Wide and the community groups. These councils would also have primary responsibility for the mobilization of clients for meetings and demonstrations and the organization of new groups. Through City-Wide, the borough council would have links with the NWRO. Communications between City-Wide and the local groups would flow through the council. The borough council was, in short, to become the critical link in the New York City welfare rights movement's chain of command.

The Brooklyn Model

The City-Wide borough model was first established in Brooklyn. The decision to organize Brooklyn's many different welfare rights groups into a cohesive movement was heavily influenced by the extraordinary growth in membership in that borough.[b] By 1967 Brooklyn had supplanted the Lower East Side as the center of welfare rights activity in New York City. The sudden emergence of a large number of new groups produced organizational needs in Brooklyn that City-Wide could not meet.

After protracted negotiations with City-Wide, the Catholic Charities agreed to support a full-time organizer in Brooklyn. Rhoda Linton, an experienced organizer, was assigned to this position by City-Wide. The Brooklyn experiment began on April 1, 1967.[7]

The Brooklyn Welfare Action Council (BWAC) was faced with the immediate problem of locating groups and identifying client leaders from among the many organizations now functioning in Brooklyn. Twenty-seven groups were isolated during the first few weeks of BWAC's existence. These groups were operating in communities scattered throughout the borough. The pluralism of the Brooklyn welfare rights movement is illustrated by the fact that fifteen of the twenty-seven groups were aided or sponsored by the clergy or church organizations, eight were sponsored by antipoverty agencies, one by a settlement house, and two by VISTA volunteers and local housing office employees. One group had organized independently in a Brooklyn housing project.[c]

Styles of operation also varied from organization to organization. Strong groups held weekly meetings and developed minimum standard forms which they then presented to welfare centers, sometimes by mail, sometimes by personal delivery. Other groups placed staff members in storefronts to fill out forms for clients who would then mail these forms or present them personally to their caseworkers. Some groups negotiated with local welfare center administrators; others with caseworkers, unit supervisors, or the center's liaison officials. While some groups dealt with a wide range of client problems, others concentrated on one central goal, getting additional money grants from the system. Some groups had friendly contacts and allies among welfare department personnel who provided valuable technical information; others encountered hostility from these personnel. Some groups were involved in nonwelfare issues; others were solely welfare-oriented. Most groups operated on a shoestring, securing financial assistance from churches, or wherever else it might be obtained, to pay for such minimum essentials as the rent, supplies, and telephone services. Some groups operated out of offices and storefronts; others out of private apartments and church basements.

Group rules and membership also varied widely. Some required regular payment of dues and issued membership cards; others did not. Some did not require dues but, instead, insisted on participation in meetings and activities. Still others held no regular meetings but considered all welfare clients in the

---

[b]For the membership in local welfare rights groups in 1967 and 1968 by welfare districts, see Table B-1, Appendix B. In June 1967, Brooklyn accounted for about 53 percent of the city's welfare rights membership; in June 1968, 57 percent.

[c]A year and a half later only eleven of the twenty-seven groups were still in existence.

community to be members. Leadership ranged from trained community workers to clients who were particularly aggressive in demonstrations at the local centers. Some groups required that the group leaders be clients, while others set no specific standards for their officers.

From April to August 1967 the groundwork of the Brooklyn organization was laid. The identification of local groups was completed, new groups were organized, and the benefits from joining the City-Wide and national movement publicized. To accomplish this, the staff coordinator participated in local group action, with City-Wide providing support by means of a regular newsletter and communications with local groups.[8] By August 1967 there were thirty-seven organizations affiliated with BWAC. Thirteen were able to send delegates to the NWRO convention in Washington. The introduction of the local leaders to the national movement resulted in their return to Brooklyn with a greater understanding of the need for closer organizational ties within the borough and between the borough and other parts of the city and nation.[9]

BWAC's first major protest activity was the school clothing campaign in the fall of 1967. In Brooklyn, this was to be a "unity" campaign. Weekly meetings were held to assess what had happened during the current week and to plan for the following week. Between fifteen and forty people attended these sessions. From them emerged a program for recruiting new members as well as securing greater benefits from welfare center officials.

The effort to recruit new members began with two local groups erecting tables outside their centers. Welfare rights workers sitting at these tables handed out leaflets and informed persons entering and leaving the centers about special grants for school clothing and furniture and what the welfare rights groups were doing to obtain them. Interested persons were referred to the welfare rights group nearest their residence. A few groups were so successful that clients signed up at the centers, even paying the national membership dues. The activists at the tables also helped clients to fill out clothing forms, asking them to return a few days later to enter the centers as a group to get their special grants. On the target day, large crowds appeared which were then organized by group leaders. There was initial agreement that group action would prevail until all those who entered the center were satisfied. Group leaders gave direct assistance to clients encountering especially recalcitrant caseworkers. Finally, lists of clients were prepared for future recruitment of members and participants in later campaigns.

These actions produced instant results. Many clients received checks on the same day that they applied for them.[10] Although this type of action had been tried before in Brooklyn, BWAC's leaders felt that the school clothing campaign was more successful because of an unprecedented degree of cooperation between widely different groups. The campaign conducted by BWAC was credited with substantial membership as well as benefit gains.[11]

As the school clothing campaign waned, the idea of converting BWAC into a permanent organization of local groups on a borough-wide basis began to receive serious attention. A "congress" of all local groups was planned for November 9, 1967, at which time BWAC's planning committee would present an organizational plan. Local groups would each be allowed one vote and ten representatives.[12] For six weeks the coordinator continued the weekly sessions, drafting a constitution, making arrangements, and publicizing the upcoming congress through leaflets, newsletters, and word of mouth.[13] Seventeen different groups participated in these planning sessions.

Of thirty-five Brooklyn welfare rights groups invited to the congress, twenty-one attended. Five others asked to be included, but were unable to be represented. Altogether, 130 clients, guests, and advisors attended the congress. On November 9, 1967, after a spirited debate over several drafts of the constitution, the twenty-one local groups voted unanimously to establish and affiliate with a borough-wide organization of welfare rights groups. BWAC's major purpose was described in the constitution:

The primary aim of the Council will be to work on problems of welfare recipients directly related to the Department of Social Services. . . . The Council will coordinate joint group actions and organize leadership training programs for the benefit of all groups. Other problems not directly related to the Department of Social Services, such as setting up co-op housing and action on school issues, may be dealt with as long as they do not interfere with the primary purpose.[14]

BWAC's officers would include a chairman, vice-chairman, secretary, and sergeant-at-arms, each elected for a term of one year. Only welfare recipients could hold council offices.[15] BWAC was also decentralized. Its local affiliates were organized on a regional basis parallel to the structure of the city's Department of Social Services (see Figure 9-1).

Adoption of the Brooklyn Model
Elsewhere in the City

After the formation of BWAC, City-Wide tried, without notable success, to organize similar councils throughout the city. Because welfare rights activity was virtually nonexistent in Richmond, this borough was ignored.

There were several strong and effective local welfare rights groups in Queens. However, their overall membership was small compared to Brooklyn. Queens was, and remains, a predominantly middle-class borough. Nonetheless, a Queens Welfare Action Council was formed and became quite active despite the small size of its membership.

Although many groups in the Bronx had participated in benefit campaigns, a viable council never really emerged despite several attempts by City-Wide. Efforts to organize the Bronx Welfare Action Council were thwarted by leadership problems, lack of paid staff, and the absence of personal contact

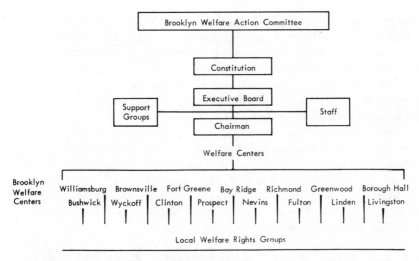

Figure 9-1. Brooklyn Welfare Action Committee Organizational Chart

between the local groups and the City-Wide and national welfare rights organizations.

A Manhattan council was also organized. However, despite intense welfare rights activity on the Lower East Side, the Upper West Side, and, to a lesser extent, in East Harlem, it too was never able to function effectively. The Manhattan welfare rights movement remained to the end a local and relatively uncoordinated protest activity.

The Queens, Bronx, and Manhattan councils were patterned after the Brooklyn model. Their primary roles were to coordinate joint group actions, to organize leadership training programs, and to affiliate with the NWRO.[d] To understand why BWAC was highly successful while the other councils were not, one must look to the kinds of support and allies that City-Wide and the local groups were able to muster.

Support for City-Wide

Following decentralization, City-Wide completed its own reorganization by drawing up and adopting a constitution at a convention held on March 9, 1968. By the end of 1967, City-Wide had a coherent organizational form. (See Figure 9-2.) It also had experienced leaders, new staff direction, substantial grass-roots support, and a local organization. Once it developed its own sources

[d]Constitutions of the Queens Welfare Action Council and the Manhattan Welfare Action Council, City-Wide files.

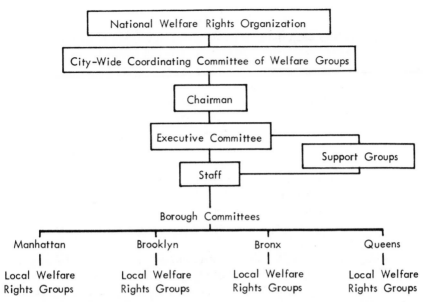

Figure 9-2. Organization of the City-Wide Coordinating Committee of Welfare Groups of New York City

of financial support, the stage would be set for what was to be the heyday of the welfare rights movement in New York City.

In the spring of 1967, City-Wide was still a relatively young political structure with a poorly defined financial base. It remained afloat through its own efforts and some assistance from the NWRO. Its support varied with the nature and effectiveness of its benefit campaigns, particularly its visibility in the communications media. City-Wide also developed alliances with academic and legal organizations,[e] local and national church institutions, trade unions, women's groups, social-work students, law students, and other community organizations. From among this heterogeneous group of supporters came financial support, staff, and technical expertise.

The NWRO has provided financial support to City-Wide since its inception, paying some salaries and providing certain essential services.[16] Several local unions have also provided financial aid to City-Wide. A series of meetings were held in July and August between City-Wide and a group of local union officials.[17] Out of these negotiations came a commitment of limited, although continuous financial assistance to the City-Wide organization.

Victor Gotbaum, Executive Director of the American Federation of State,

[e]Ironically, many of its legal services were provided by organizations spawned by the federal government's programs offering legal assistance for the poor.

County, and Municipal Employees, argued strongly that each local contribute $100 per month to keep the City-Wide office going. Several other unions made regular or periodic contributions to help cover City-Wide's special financial needs.[18] The contributions by unions played a critical role in maintaining City-Wide operations. Local union support was, however, primarily financial. For the most part, the unions did not provide manpower, technical expertise, or support for the welfare rights movement's position on certain issues.

Another important source of financial assistance was various church groups. City-Wide received a reduced rental for its offices in an Episcopal church in Harlem. Meeting space was donated by the New York Theological Seminary. The Interreligious Foundation for Community Organization (IFCO) granted $14,000 to City-Wide. The Episcopal Church, the Church of the Resurrection, Catholic Charities, the Interfaith City-Wide Coordinating Committee, the Foundation for Voluntary Service, and several other church-related groups also made contributions to City-Wide.

Besides support from such institutional sources as churches, foundations, and unions, City-Wide received many contributions from individuals. In tapping individual sources of money, Richard Cloward was once again a tireless friend of the welfare rights movement. In addition, client leaders, social workers, social-work students, and other supporters of the welfare rights movement such as the Upper West Side Friends sponsored fund-raising drives on City-Wide's behalf. City-Wide also benefited from the services of volunteer workers, particularly social-work and law students. Its staff was willing to work for minimal compensation. An advisory council of professionals and experts on the welfare system also helped to formulate strategy and provide legal assistance to City-Wide.[f] Other groups gave other types of assistance. Besides financial contributions, the Social Services Employees' Union provided City-Wide with office supplies and helped to prepare welfare manuals for clients. ARCH, a Harlem-based group of architects, developed and printed manuals on welfare regulations, while the Metropolitan Applied Research Center paid the salary of a staff member.

Despite all its sources of funds, City-Wide operated on a limited budget, with its expenses often out-running its revenues. For the most part, it did not receive federal funds. Yet City-Wide was able to survive.

---

[f]Among the groups with which City-Wide had contact were the Legal Aid Society, Mobilization for Youth, the Scholarship, Education and Defense Fund for Racial Equality, the National Organization for the Rights of the Indigent, the Columbia University Center on Social Welfare Policy and Law, the Community Action Legal Services Program in New York City, the New York State Americans for Democratic Action, the Law Students Civil Rights Research Council, and the Roger Baldwin Foundation of the American Civil Liberties Union.

**Support for the Borough Councils
and Local Welfare Rights Groups**

Several local welfare rights groups were successful in developing a distinct resource base of their own. BWAC also had a secure source of funding through its relationship with Catholic Charities in Brooklyn. This relationship was developed and nurtured by the earlier sponsorship, by Catholic priests and local parishes, of welfare rights groups in the central Brooklyn area. In that borough there happened to be a convergence of activist priests seeking to secure greater church involvement in social action, and activist recipients determined to improve their condition on welfare.

Because of Catholic Charities, BWAC's budget was generally sufficient to meet its operational expenses. In contrast to the OEO-funded groups, no strings were attached to the funds received by BWAC from its sponsor. It was free to pursue its own course relatively immune to outside pressures, including those emanating from City-Wide and the NWRO. It was also free to concentrate solely on welfare issues.

Some local groups in Brooklyn received funds from OEO on a regular basis. Others obtained OEO-funding for specific projects. Still others, no OEO funding at all. One Brooklyn welfare rights group, CUSA-MARION, is typical. It started with support from a local church for its storefront and telephones. Then BWAC was organized and the local Brooklyn affiliates were funded through the borough council. Finally, in 1968, CUSA-MARION was awarded an OEO grant for $7,000 for a summer education and culture project.

By contrast, the Bronx, Queens, and Manhattan councils were heavily subsidized by City-Wide. In Manhattan, several local groups developed independent sources of financial assistance, but on a more limited scale than in Brooklyn. Almost certainly, a major reason for the extraordinary success of the welfare rights movement in Brooklyn was the fact that BWAC and many of the local groups had their own secure sources of funds, while the other borough councils remained, by and large, the creations of the City-Wide Coordinating Committee. Because the Brooklyn groups were independent, they were better able to respond to the interests and desires of the communities they served.

10 The Movement at its Peak

In June 1967, New York City's welfare rights organizations launched a minimum standards-fair hearings campaign.[1] Unlike its predecessors, this campaign was staged throughout the city under the guidance of the City-Wide Coordinating Committee. The campaign again involved the simultaneous submission of household furniture and clothing grant applications. However, in a departure from past practices, clients were also encouraged to apply for fair hearings upon denial or excessive delays in receiving grants.[a]

The campaign was to last three months. It had as its immediate goal submission of large numbers of fair hearing requests to Mayor Lindsay during a demonstration at city hall on June 30, 1967. However, the campaign's overriding purpose was to "secure large sums of money for individual members of welfare rights groups."[2] Income is the most pressing need for most clients in New York. Emphasis on minimum standards would, it was thought, assure maximum commitment by the welfare population. The submission of large numbers of minimum standards and fair hearing requests would also overtax the welfare centers and simultaneously put pressures on the city and state welfare administrations for change. Finally, the fair hearings were expected to generate many cases that City-Wide's legal staff could appeal. Litigation on significant issues of welfare law, it was thought, would stimulate among recipients an awareness of the value of group activity on their behalf.

During the campaign, City-Wide encouraged local groups to proselyte non-members and to deepen the commitment of existing members. It urged unaffiliated groups to join City-Wide and the NWRO. It also urged local groups to use the campaign to demonstrate their own importance to welfare center administrators. The campaign was a calculated effort to establish City-Wide as the sole bargaining agent for New York City's clients.

The 1967 Minimum Standards-Fair Hearings Campaign

City-Wide's staff began to plan and coordinate the campaign in the spring of 1967. Its first job was to locate and inform the local groups. To do this, City-Wide drew up a master list of welfare rights organizations and then urged

---

[a]Both federal and state law provided for a hearing if a client believed she was being denied legally mandated grants by the local welfare department.

each organization to send representatives to weekly meetings. Several thousand leaflets were distributed and numerous speeches made at these meetings discussing the potential of the minimum standards-fair hearings campaign and the welfare rights movement in general. City-Wide also passed out membership kits designed by the NWRO specifically for use in the New York City campaign. Besides literature on protest activity, these packets included NWRO's simplified membership form which enabled a client to affiliate simultaneously with a neighborhood group, City-Wide, and the NWRO.

The Columbia University Center on Social Welfare Policy and Law, an OEO-funded project, provided a staff lawyer, Dave Gilman, who, with other lawyers and law students, planned and coordinated the fair hearing part of the campaign. Up to this time, City-Wide had used the fair hearing only in a few cases not involving minimum standards. Among other things, Gilman and his staff developed a simplified form to enable the processing of large numbers of applicants at one time. Because of the efforts of City-Wide and the local groups, thousands of forms were prepared and submitted to the welfare centers in June and July 1967 requesting clothing and household furniture grants. These submissions were accompanied by picketing as a show of strength and, often, demands to see local administrators. Direct action of a disruptive type was neither planned nor encouraged, and little occurred. Client fair hearing requests were submitted several weeks later, to conform with departmental procedures and to provide time for the anticipated negative response by welfare officials. Almost invariably, these requests were submitted for recipients who were either members or thought to be members of local welfare rights groups. There was little organized effort on behalf of nonmembers.

In July, the city terminated its automatic $20 clothing grant to each school-age child. The $20 grant had been initiated in August 1966 after welfare rights demonstrations at city hall.[3] In explaining its move, the city cited a recent cost-of-living increase in the regular welfare allowance. Efforts by City-Wide officials, lawyers, and advisors to obtain restoration of the automatic school clothing grant proved unsuccessful. A caucus of the New York leadership at the August NWRO Convention decided to continue the minimum standards-fair hearings campaign into the fall. By terminating the automatic school clothing grant, the leadership reasoned, the welfare department had handed City-Wide an issue about which welfare mothers were highly emotional and around which they could be readily mobilized.

At the same time, City-Wide began an evaluation of the ongoing campaign. This evaluation was to result in the adoption of a new set of tactics. The June campaign focused on clothing and household furnishings; the September campaign on back-to-school clothing for children only. In the June campaign, clients filled out minimum standards forms which were then submitted to the welfare centers. Fair hearings requests were submitted later. However, many local groups lacked the time and resources to complete and coordinate all of the request forms. For this reason, in the fall campaign, the fair hearings application would accompany the minimum standards application, thus ending the grace period given the welfare department to respond to a request for a special grant. The fair hearings form was redesigned to be consistent with state regulations. It now declared that the client was requesting minimum standards while at the same time filing a request for a fair hearing because she had not been informed of her entitlements and consequently was not receiving minimum standards. The request argued, in effect, that the welfare department was already guilty of unfair actions. The main benefit of this new procedure, as far as the welfare rights groups were concerned, was that it simplified the administrative task confronting the local groups.

There were also important differences in the objectives and organization of the summer and fall campaigns. The fall campaign had as a specific goal reinstatement of the automatic school clothing grant. Moreover, this campaign placed greater stress on city-wide mass action at the local centers. It was hoped that this action would not only build local membership and strengthen relationships between local groups, City-Wide and the NWRO, but also lead to greater recognition by welfare officals of the importance of City-Wide. Finally, the fair hearing request was given a different meaning during the fall campaign. A major goal was to obtain state and city agreement that, if a client lacked the standard clothing and furniture items to which she was entitled, this was *prima facie* evidence of unfair action by the welfare department and the client's entitlement to a fair hearing.

Another important difference between the summer and fall campaigns was the role played by the borough organizations. In the fall, coordinators were assigned in each borough and all functions involving the boroughs were handled through these coordinators. This simple organizational change proved to be of great significance. It freed City-Wide officials and staff to concentrate on other critical tasks such as the development of press contacts and public relations, negotiations with city and state officials, and improvements in City-Wide's own organizational structure. Decentralization of the campaign also placed greater responsibility for local actions on the local groups. This encouraged innovation. An example was provided by the Brooklyn group, the Neighborhood Action Center (NAC), which set up tables in front of two welfare centers to recruit clients entering and leaving.

These changes led to a more intense form of political activity in the fall than in the summer campaign. During the fall, the local groups did more than appear in large numbers to picket and submit minimum standard forms. They actually initiated activities and experimented on their own with new forms of protest. Many of these groups also resorted to such highly visible, direct action techniques as sit-ins and face-to-face confrontations with welfare administrators.

The Results of the Fair Hearings Campaign

By September, City-Wide submitted 760 fair hearings requests directly to the state welfare administration. Although most local groups acted on behalf of their clients through City-Wide, some did not. Altogether, more than a thousand fair hearings requests were submitted by September. Table 10-1 indicates the geographic origins of these requests. Most came from Brooklyn and Manhattan and, within these boroughs, Ft. Greene, Crown Heights, Bedford-Stuyvesant, and

Table 10-1
Fair Hearings Forms Filed by City-Wide as of September 30, 1967

Borough	Number of Reporting Groups	Number of Fair Hearings Requested
Manhattan		
East Harlem	21	6
Central Harlem	8	15
Upper West Side	5	—
Lower West Side	5	40
Lower East Side	11	303
Brooklyn		
Brownsville/East New York	15	10
Crown Heights/Bedford Stuyvesant	6	144
Bushwick	3	60
Williamsburg	6	—
South Brooklyn/Red Hook	5	32
Ft. Greene	5	32
Coney Island	4	4
Bronx		
East Bronx	6	45
South Bronx	4	49
North Bronx	5	19
West Bronx	1	1
Total	110	760

Source: See Gene Rothman, "Welfare Rights Groups of the 1930's and 1960's: An Essay in Comparative History," M.A. thesis, Columbia University, 1969. Gene Rothman was a volunteer worker at City-Wide in charge of keeping records of early fair hearings requests.

the Lower East Side.[b] According to one state welfare official, subsequent changes in the fair hearings procedure were inspired by this "shift in agitation of welfare recipients and a number of complaints."[4] City-Wide was highly critical of these changes. It wanted, instead, more far-reaching reforms like those proposed by such groups as the Columbia University Center on Social Welfare Policy and Law and the Metropolitan Applied Research Center.[5]

Despite this dissatisfaction, the new rules were a distinct improvement. They extended the right to a fair hearing to Home Relief cases. They required that information on the right of appeal be given to all recipients. Finally, they clarified the appeal procedure.[6] In effect, in changing its rules, the state met many of the objectives of the fair hearing campaign.

State and city welfare officials tried to meet with lawyers associated with the welfare rights movement to work out procedures for scheduling and holding fair hearings. The lawyers refused. Instead, they referred these officials to City-Wide. As a result, a historic meeting occurred. In September 1967, the City-Wide Executive Board met with state and local welfare administrators to discuss procedures to be followed in granting fair hearing requests. For the first time, the state, in effect, recognized City-Wide as spokesman for the organized client movement.[c]

From this meeting came a procedural framework through which the fair hearing mechanism would operate. It was agreed that the state and city would honor all requests and would begin on September 18 to schedule hearings. It was further agreed that the state would provide translators for Spanish-speaking clients and pay for baby-sitters and carfare so that welfare mothers could attend. Night hearings would be scheduled for working mothers. The hearings would be scheduled from mid-September until early January 1968 at the rate of fifty per day.

Table 10-2 indicates what happened to the number of fair hearings in the face of organized client pressures. In 1964 and 1965, the fair hearings process was rarely used. Even then, few cases actually reached the review board, most being disposed of by abandonment, withdrawal, or adjustment.[d] Moreover, at that time, the department did not maintain a fair hearings office of its own, but assigned personnel from other offices to conduct these hearings. Fair hearings

---

[b]The several available accounts vary widely as to the number and exact timing of fair hearings requests. However, all indicate that the total number was substantial and far more than the state's fair hearing apparatus could handle.

[c]Among those representing the state were Joseph Louchheim, now the state commissioner of social services, and Felix Infausto, general counsel and secretary to the state board of Social Welfare.

[d]In 1964 and 1965, the state welfare department would seek a resolution of a dispute by adjustment. Only after attempts at adjustment failed was an aggrieved client finally scheduled for a hearing. One result of subordinating the fair hearings to the adjustment process was a delay of about six to twelve months before a hearing would be scheduled.

Table 10-2
Fair Hearings in New York State, 1964-67

Year	Numbers of Hearings Requested[a]
1964	188
1965	199
1966	650
1967	4,233
January	170
February	105
March	100
April	141
May	129
June	109
July	139
August	443
September	906
October	435
November	1,193
December	363

[a]In 1964, 14 fair hearings were actually held; in 1965, 16; and in 1966, 20.
Source: New York State Department of Social Services.

requests rose in 1966, primarily because of the Medicaid program. At that time, four hearings officers were formally designated by the state.

However, 1967 was clearly the year of change. In 1967 there was a virtual explosion in fair hearings requests. This explosion resulted primarily from the activities of the organized client movement.[7] Almost all new requests were from New York City. Many were sent in packages. Most complained about the inadequacy of money grants for AFDC cases.

This increase in requests led to the appointment of four additional hearings officers and, in December 1967, the opening of the New York City Office of Fair Hearings. Clients were represented at the hearings by lawyers, volunteer law students, and some trained lay advocates. At no time, however, was there enough legal support to meet the needs of the recipients. Over 3,000 hearings were scheduled between September and January. However, 90 percent of these hearings never occurred. Oftentimes, local centers contacted clients before the dates scheduled for their hearings and granted their requests for special grants. In one-half of the cases in which hearings were actually held, clients received substantially all of their requests, while most of the remaining clients received at least partial grants.

The Results of the Minimum Standards Campaign

Large numbers of clients applied for special grants during the latter half of 1967. According to City-Wide, most of these clients were successful in obtaining additional allotments from the welfare administration.

By the middle of October several million dollars were recovered through special grants. Of this amount, $500,000 was actually tabulated by our groups through report-back meetings. The remainder was the constant "ripple effect" we had throughout the City.[8]

A City-Wide spokesman has also asserted:

I would estimate that $5,000,000 now has been paid to welfare clients since the hearings before welfare officials began on September 18th. Some got as much as $1,000, and no one got less than $150.[9]

Gilman and Birnbaum, in their report on the campaign, also claimed that the Department of Social Services granted nearly $5 million in special grants because of pressures by the organized client movement.[10]

In addition, the minimum standards campaign led to changes in departmental procedures. The welfare department had to abandon its requirement that caseworkers conduct home visits in order to verify a client's special need for clothing or household furniture. The home visit was replaced by a simple check of the case record to determine the time of the last money grant for the item requested. Departmental policy had also required that the client show proof of purchase after receiving a grant. Where money awards were substantial, the grant was issued in two parts, with the client receiving the second installment after giving a receipt to the caseworker for expenditures under the first installment. In addition, the state required that clients authorized grants for consumer durables such as washing machines must get written estimates after which the lowest estimate would be accepted. Partly because of the backlog of paper work created by the welfare rights movement, each of these requirements had to be eased by the welfare administration.

The Movement at Peak Strength

The 1967 campaigns also resulted in far greater strength and cohesiveness for New York City's welfare rights movement. Local groups gained valuable experience in organizing. This would prove useful in later campaigns. Leaders were identified and received training and, in a few instances, groups were able to establish themselves as client representatives at welfare centers.

Relationships with the welfare administration varied widely. At several centers, meetings between client representatives and officials became routine, while at others no continuous relationship could be developed. At several Brooklyn centers welfare staff members were assigned the full-time function of maintaining liaison with the client leadership. In some, again in Brooklyn, client group representatives were allowed inside the centers' waiting rooms to assist existing members and recruit new members.[11] A few groups were even given office space and the right to use the centers' telephones.

The campaigns also resulted in a sharp increase in the number of recipients belonging to welfare rights organizations (see Table 10-3). Membership more than doubled between 1967 and 1968. Although this growth occurred in all boroughs except Staten Island, Brooklyn accounted for over half of the city's membership as well as half of the increase in membership during this period. Just as Brooklyn dominated the city, so, too, New York City dominated the nation. In 1967, 51 percent, and in 1968, 59 percent of the NWRO's total membership lived in New York City.

Moreover, state and city welfare agencies, in effect, recognized City-Wide as a bargaining agent for the city's welfare recipients by negotiating with it on important policy matters affecting the entire public assistance caseload. These negotiations exposed the client leadership still further to the operations of the welfare bureaucracy and the decision-making process.

Recognition by the welfare administration was accompanied by increasing press coverage of the movement's activities. The media began to treat City-Wide as the nerve center and spokesman for the entire welfare population and even credited it with activities sponsored solely by local and unaffiliated groups. Some of City-Wide's protests were deliberately timed to create maximum press coverage.[12] The movement's greatest publicity success occurred in October 1967 when the *Daily News* ran a three-part series describing the activities of the welfare rights movement and, in particular, City-Wide.[13]

Table 10-3

Approximate Membership in Welfare Rights Organizations (Number of Families)

Area	1967	1968	1969
United States	5,000	10,000	22,500
New York City	2,550	5,870	4,030
Brooklyn	1,350	3,370	2,440
Queens	100	380	330
Manhattan	1,070	1,400	500
Bronx	30	720	760

Source: Membership data have been obtained from the National Welfare Rights Organization. These data have been supplemented by information on a few nonaffiliated groups obtained from these groups themselves. NWRO membership data are collected around June of each year. For membership by district, see Table B-1 in Appendix B.

In the past, only welfare caseworkers knew the mysteries of the [public assistance] handbook. But the client groups put their experts to reading the book and ... discovered that only about 2% of all welfare recipients were completely at standard levels.

This fact has resulted in the tea strainer-potato masher approach. Such items as tea strainers, potato mashers and fruit reamers are listed in the book, and client groups have set out to make sure every reliefer has one of each.[14]

This series and the many other articles that appeared at the time helped to spread the word about the movement's activities throughout the city's low-income community.[15]

Publicity by the press, radio, and television was supplemented by literature disseminated by City-Wide and the various local welfare rights organizations.[16] Thus, despite the fact that City-Wide and its affiliates had not had as a primary goal the recruitment of new members in the 1967 campaign, the publicity generated by their activities, as well as their notable successes, resulted in many nonmembers joining the movement.

As 1967 came to an end, there was a publicly visible welfare rights movement in New York City with organizations in four of the five boroughs. This movement concentrated almost solely on securing financial benefits for its clients and, in conjunction with the NWRO, on building a formal organizational structure. This movement also developed and tested a highly successful, although narrow, set of tactics. It focused on the special grants for clothing and household furnishings. It threatened welfare center officials with the specter of massive disruption of their activities if its demands for higher grant levels were not met. Finally, it confronted an essentially liberal welfare administration which itself professed to support many of the goals of the movement.

The second half of 1967 was the beginning of the New York City welfare rights movement's golden age. This age continued until the second half of 1968, at which time its triumphs would give way to setbacks and decline.

11 The End of an Era

For several months after the minimum standards-fair hearings campaign, New York City's welfare rights movement paused and took stock of itself. The fair hearings campaign, despite its successes, had demonstrated several weaknesses in the movements' ability to plan and undertake a massive campaign. There was a serious shortage of legal talent. Clients were often unable to give competent presentations at hearings. There was still a less than ideal relationship between City-Wide and the local groups. Many clients were unaccustomed to the hearings process and were upset by their inability to present their own cases. Often the welfare rights attorneys did not try to involve the clients in this process. It was also apparent that a well-executed fair hearings campaign required the exclusion of virtually all other activities.[1] Finally, contrary to expectations, the fair hearings campaign did not produce good issues for test cases. There was little uniformity in the handling of cases and lay advocates were often inadequately prepared.[2]

Despite these difficulties, the welfare rights leadership was at first reluctant to abandon the dual objective campaign. In late 1967, George Wiley suggested that both minimum standards and fair hearings be emphasized throughout the coming year.[3] The imperfections in the fair hearings process could be corrected, Wiley felt, by greater use of professional volunteers and law students and the establishment of a leadership training program to prepare welfare group leaders to be effective lay advocates at fair hearings. Wiley envisioned both types of campaigns being used "for winter clothing, spring, summer, camp and school clothing, for furniture, and for any other benefit and entitlement which lends itself to a massive approach on a City-wide basis."[4]

In November 1967 Hulbert James, City-Wide's new staff director, mapped out a strategy for the coming year. There would be a continuing, year-round benefit campaign. A partial solution to the problem of staffing would be provided by an intensive leadership training program for clients in order to lessen dependence by the movement on irregular volunteer support.

In early 1968 BWAC established just such a program.[a] This program was financed by Catholic Charities.[5] Three terms were held, one in February and March, one in May, and one in August. Each had several separate classes of instruction. Class A, taught by client leaders, was directed toward new members and older members who had not had an opportunity to learn the basic rights of

---

[a]BWAC's constitution listed its two major functions as serving as a coordinating body for joint local group actions and providing leadership training for all local groups.

welfare recipients and procedures of the welfare department. Such matters as minimum standards, the right to fair hearings, eligibility requirements, and burial allowances were explained in this course. How to deal with the welfare department on an individual as well as a group basis was also stressed. The remaining classes were taught by experienced staff organizers. Class B was directed to potential or existing group leaders who needed a better understanding of how best to organize their groups, develop contacts, recruit new members, establish an effective committee structure, run meetings, and prepare agendas. It also explained the use of the NWRO membership kit and how to keep records and use minimum standards as an organizing tool. Class C taught how to plan and carry out direct action activities and to deal with emergencies as they arose. It also explained the legal rights of demonstrators and how legal assistance could be obtained. Finally, Class D was a general course that explained the origins of welfare rights organizations and placed the movement in the perspective of national politics.

Altogether, 150 clients signed up for these courses; 95 attended regularly.[6] The second and third terms were held during actual campaigns, thus providing trainees with valuable field work. The primary purpose of the training sessions was to arm client leaders with a technical knowledge of welfare laws, benefits, rights, and procedures that would enable them to represent their local groups in discussions with recalcitrant caseworkers and welfare center administrators.[7] The trainees were often treated by the local groups as group officers. In this way, the programs also enhanced the prestige and status of the trainees. In short, as a result of these programs, BWAC's administration functioned more smoothly and client leaders acquired a better understanding of the job they had to do. They also became more deeply committed to the welfare rights movement.

The 1968 Campaign

Storm clouds appeared in early 1968. Through its contacts with friendly politicians and members of the state and city welfare administrations, City-Wide began to hear rumors of impending changes in the system of special grants. Although these changes had not yet been made public, their broad outlines were clear; they would eliminate the special grant and the client's right to appeal for additional assistance on the basis of individual need. They would also eliminate caseworker discretion in determining benefit levels. Instead, special needs would be met by a "flat grant" or fixed payment for every family based on its size and composition.

City-Wide's leaders immediately understood the implications of this change in policy for the organized client movement in New York City. The movement's success in organizing and recruiting recipients rested on its success in securing tangible benefits for its members. These benefits were obtained by demanding legally mandated entitlements from the welfare bureaucracy and by threatening or actually using disruption at welfare offices if these demands were not met.[b] The changes would, in effect, bring to an end the incentive to join the welfare rights movement.

In response to these rumors, City-Wide decided to mount a new campaign with a twofold goal: (1) to prevent the proposed termination of special grants and payments based on individual need, and (2) while the system lasted, to extract from it as many benefits for its membership as was humanly possible. The principal weapon, far more than in the past, would be repeated demonstrations at the various city and state welfare offices.

Organizationally, City-Wide was now far better prepared to mount an effective campaign throughout the city than it had been in 1967. Its new management was more aggressive and experienced in the politics of protest. Its membership had developed an unprecedented *esprit de corps*. Most important, however, was the threat of the termination of the special grant itself which, if fulfilled, would deny the organized client movement its primary organizing tool. City-Wide and the movement were, in a very real sense, fighting for their lives.

The campaign was launched in late April 1968. The procedures used in past campaigns would be used again. There would be City-wide coordination through borough councils, mass leafleting, preparation and distribution of thousands of minimum standard forms, recruitment through NWRO membership kits, demands for fair hearings, and the provision of legal assistance. Client leaders, especially those in Brooklyn, were also instructed in more aggressive, direct action techniques. Friendly social workers, union leaders, law students, and other allies of the movement were asked to join in the campaign. In April the welfare rights organizations focused on spring clothing; in May on Mother's Day clothing; in June on school graduation clothing and expenses; in June and July on camp clothing and camp expenses; and in July and August on telephones. However, far more than in the past, clients were encouraged to demand any items to which they felt entitled and not to restrict themselves to the particular items that happened to be the focus of group activity at the time.

The different character of the 1968 campaign soon became apparent. Clients armed with minimum standards checklists descended upon local welfare centers, particularly in Brooklyn and the Bronx. However, instead of presenting their requests for minimum standards peacefully to caseworkers or other center officials, they more often than not staged sit-ins, some lasting several days. As a result, the work of caseworkers and other center personnel was disrupted and, in some instances, had to be suspended.

Jack Goldberg, then New York City's commissioner of social services, described what was happening and what had to be done to correct it:

---

[b]The mere threat of disruption proved to be a powerful lever in the hands of the movement because it raised the specter of a wider and more serious confrontation between ghetto and minority communities and the rest of society.

The sometimes unruly demonstrations which have included sit-ins of several days duration and the closing of centers are the kind of problem we're going to have until we really face the issue of changing our system.[8]

In May, five weeks after the campaign began, City-Wide claimed to have won $3 million for its clients.[9] Demonstrations at the Melrose and Kingsbridge Centers in the Bronx, which involved a three-day, two-night sit-in, were alleged to have secured $135,000.[10] At the Tremont Center in the Bronx, 70 clients held a sit-in in July, while another 200 clients demonstrated outside. Welfare workers reported that processed client demands averaged $300 or $400 per family, with grants in exceptional cases reaching $1,200.[11] In both the Bronx and Brooklyn, caseworkers, in turn, demanded that the city's Department of Social Services cut red tape in order to process the flood of client demands. They backed up these demands with the threat of a strike.[12]

The welfare department's headquarters was also a target of protest. On July 1, 1968, 38 clients and their allies were arrested for blocking the doorway to the Department of Social Service's head offices. During the demonstration, they succeeded in keeping from their jobs approximately 200 workers. The three-day sit-in was ended only after the intervention of mounted police.[13] One week later, a group of 200 clients blocked noon traffic near DOSS's headquarters after their request to see the welfare commissioner was refused. On July 15, another group of 200 demonstrators closed completely three Brooklyn welfare centers for three hours in a demand for faster processing of special grant claims. As a result, four-fifths of the center's casework staff remained off the job.[14] In July City-Wide warned Mayor Lindsay that "the clients and the City's Department of Social Services were on a collision course."[15]

By this time, Mitchell Ginsberg, now head of the city's Human Resources Administration,[c] was conceding that "recent demands by welfare clients were costing $10 to $12 million a month in special grants."[16] The press was also giving extensive coverage to the successes of the campaign. A good example was the *New York Times*, which wrote:

The drive started in April, with special grants for the month reaching a total of $8,072,485, and mounting in May to $11,567,163. This compared with special grants of $3,082,842 in April 1967, and $3,174,406 in June 1967, and a monthly average of $3,863,790 through all last year.[17]

In June and July, the welfare rights movement focused on camp clothing and expenses. A recent change in the state law authorized relief payments for attendance at summer camps; the previous law had allowed only school clothing grants for children attending camps sponsored by philanthropic groups.[18] City-Wide was determined that its members receive all they were entitled to.

[c]HRA has nominal supervision of the city's Department of Social Services.

In mid-July City-Wide, in close association with a local affiliate, the United Welfare League, launched a campaign for telephones.[19] The telephone campaign illustrates how the movement was able, by now, to manipulate welfare regulations, to use the welfare bureaucracy, and to motivate welfare rights members for a prolonged confrontation with the welfare system. Departmental regulations required evidence of a serious medical ailment or a need by the recipient to maintain contact with welfare or other agencies, friends, or individuals as part of a social service plan before a client could receive a special grant for a telephone. City-Wide built its case around this regulation. The client's argument for telephones was simple. Telephones were essential in high-crime areas, in areas with housing that is a distinct fire hazard, in health emergencies, particularly for children, and in cases where it is necessary to maintain contact with teachers, landlords, employers, and caseworkers. The Social Services Employees' Union, which was sympathetic to City-Wide, instructed its members to process and approve quickly all the requests for telephone grants.[20] Representatives from the Board of Education, the New York City Youth Board, and community groups also joined in the campaign. A timely report issued by a CUNY sociologist disclosed that only one in four New York City welfare families possessed telephones.[21]

By August the city's welfare system was near collapse. The *New York Times* reported:

Since April, bands of organized clients have descended on welfare centers demanding special grants for items provided for under the law but in practice rarely given out. The demonstrators have jammed the centers, sometimes camping out in them overnight, broken down administrative procedure, played havoc with the mountains of paperwork, and have been increasingly successful.[22]

The *Times* concluded that the drive had "thrown the city's welfare program into a state of crisis and chaos."

The Beginning of the End

In June the worst fears of the welfare rights leadership were confirmed. The state announced its proposed abandonment of most special grants and establishment of the flat grant system. September 1 was the target date for adoption of the new system.[23]

The state plan was immediately hailed by leading politicians and State and local welfare officials. Mayor Lindsay, for example, called the plan "a very positive thing."[24] The client movement, however, strongly condemned any changes that did not bring clients up to standards and expressed its concern with the projected amounts of the flat grants.[25] Almost immediately, the movement intensified its demonstrations against the plan, while continuing to carry out its minimum standards campaign. A meeting between federal, state, and local welfare officials to discuss ways of implementing the new plan was harassed by a City-Wide group.[26] On July 23 about thirty persons representing the Citizens Committee for Children, United Neighborhood Houses, the Methodist Board of Missions, the American Jewish Congress, and several women's peace groups responded to a plea by Mrs. Martin Luther King, Jr., to support the organized relief recipients. Beulah Sanders, City-Wide's chairwoman, threatened that if City-Wide's demand for a guaranteed annual income of $6,500 per year were not met, demonstrations would continue to interrupt operations at all city agencies.[27]

On August 27, 1968, New York City's Department of Social Services announced the receipt of both federal and state approval to establish a simplified payments system. Each recipient would receive $100 annually in four equal installments. This would pay for clothing and household furniture. In addition, there would be a 6 percent hike in the basic grant.[28] Among the few exceptions permitted were:

1. Expenses related to the birth of a child
2. Replacement of possessions destroyed by fire or other disaster
3. Expenses related to graduation from school or special camp equipment
4. Expenses related to moving from a furnished to an unfurnished apartment

However, these exceptions were limited in the amount of the money grants allowed. The aim of the flat grants, according to state officials, was to help recipients to plan their budgets better and "to aid everyone, instead of those most insistent in demanding special grants."[29]

The reaction of the organized client movement was swift and fierce.[30] Several days earlier, the impending announcement was leaked to City-Wide. Approximately 15 recipients demonstrated at city hall within hours. Weekend sit-ins were also held at the Linden and Brownsville Centers in Brooklyn, with city police having to be summoned to the latter center.[31] On August 27, after the announcement, a massive demonstration was staged at city hall with 200 policemen, some mounted, dispersing over 600 client protesters. Four protesters and 5 policemen were injured and 13 protesters were arrested.[32] On August 28, renewed demonstrations led to clashes between protesters and the police. Eighteen demonstrators were arrested.[33] On August 29 police again had to be called to two welfare centers. As the first week of reaction to termination of the special grant ended, several centers had been closed and one center in the Bronx vandalized.[34] By the end of August, two-thirds of the city's thirty-eight centers reported some form of incident and, as a result, the Department of Social Services was forced to establish an emergency communications room.[35]

Other black community groups, including the Black Panthers and CORE, began to participate in demonstrations in early September.[36] In mid-September, a group of 75 recipients descended on Linden, Ft. Greene, and Prospect Centers in Brooklyn, overturning furniture and barring 600 staff members from entering.[d] The *New York Times* described what happened:

The protesters, mainly women, ripped telephones from walls, scattered papers and threw desks onto piles in the middle of the intake rooms of the three centers, which are in the same building in downtown Brooklyn. There were no arrests in the day long protest. Policemen who watched some of the disruption said they were helpless without a formal complaint from a welfare official.[37]

The reaction of the establishment was also swift. State Senator William E. Adams, chairman of the Joint Legislative Committee to Revise the Social Service Law, announced hearings to probe the welfare system top to bottom. Critical editorials appeared in New York city's papers.[38] The Department of Social Services and Mayor Lindsay issued new policy directives to both welfare personnel and the police to assure a tougher response to future demonstrations.[39]

The total number of demonstrations staged each month by welfare rights organizations has been recorded by City-Wide since April 1968 (see Table 11-1).

Table 11-1
Total Demonstrations at New York City Welfare Centers and Other Welfare Offices, April 1968 through March 1969

April 1968	18
May	188
June	172
July	217
August	213
September	113
October	28
November	15
December	60
January 1969	16
February	7
March	2

Source: City-Wide Coordinating Committee of Welfare Groups. For data on demonstrations at each welfare center, see Table B-2, Appendix B.

---

[d]In Brooklyn, several welfare centers are colocated in the same building or in proximity to each other in the downtown area. While administratively convenient, this also made it very easy for welfare rights groups to stage massive demonstrations at several centers simultaneously.

These data indicate the magnitude of the 1968 protest movement. There was a notable increase in the number of demonstrations from 18 in April to 188 in May. Demonstrations peaked in July and August and then, after termination of the special grant on September 1, dropped off sharply. In other words, the number of demonstrations accurately reflects the fortunes of New York City's welfare rights movement. On September 1, 1968, the golden era of the movement (in New York City at least) came to an end.

Denouement

In succeeding months, most remaining special grants and the flat grant itself were also terminated. As a result, local caseworkers no longer had an appreciable influence over the monthly grant level. As a result, also, the local welfare rights organizations lost their organizational focus and much of their influence. They were no longer able to provide as tangible a benefit to their membership as they did prior to September 1, 1968.

Not surprisingly, membership in New York City's welfare rights organizations has fallen. In 1968 there were nearly 6,000 dues-paying members; in 1969, only 4,000 (see Table 10-3). At the same time, national membership has continued to rise. New York City, which provided 59 percent of the national membership in 1968, provided only 18 percent one year later.

Since 1968, the movement has continued to focus on immediate, tangible gains for its membership. It has explored alternative ways of increasing the grant level. It has staged protests in Albany in support of an increase in the basic grant and other welfare reforms. It has challenged unsuccessfully the flat grant system and levels of assistance in the courts. Welfare rights leaders have proposed rent strikes and expenditure of rental allotments on other goods and services, in effect raising the real grant level paid to participants. However, no satisfactory replacement for the special grant has been found, either in bringing the grant levels received by members back to their 1968 levels or in restoring the essential private good character of special grants. The unfortunate fact, as far as the welfare rights movement is concerned, is that efforts to obtain an increase in grant levels from the state legislature or Congress, were they successful, would benefit all recipients and not just welfare rights members only. These efforts would result in public benefits which, by their very nature, are not as likely to provide as great an incentive to membership in welfare rights groups as did special grants. One can understand why, since 1968, the movement has declined in New York City.

At this point, let us return, once again, to our discussion of the various theories of protest by the poor in Chapter 2 and especially the basic question posed in that section—can successful protest be launched by an essentially weak and powerless segment of society? In the case of New York City's welfare rights movement, the answer would appear to be "yes and no."

Following Lipsky, the New York City movement at its peak was able to manage several constituencies simultaneously: its own members, the communications media, and the welfare administration.

Following Von Eschen, Kirk, Pinnard, and other adherents of the democratic participation model, the movement was able to focus on an obvious dilemma, the welfare system as it is and is supposed to be. It found allies in the press, trade unions, universities, and the welfare bureaucracy itself. It created disorder to persuade the welfare administration to resolve this dilemma in its favor. And finally it found in the special grant and the local welfare centers targets able to yield easy victories.

Following Olson, the movement chose as its organizing vehicle an essentially private good. To obtain special grants one did not have to be a member of a welfare rights group. However, it most certainly helped. The welfare rights organizations were able to provide information, legal assistance, and some of the muscle necessary to bring home all the benefits permitted under the law. This fact, while it lasted, helped to secure the commitment of the membership.

Yet, in the end, Wilson and the pessimists won out. While the special grant was critical to the short-term success of the movement, it was also a highly vulnerable organizing tool. What the state gave, the state took away. The establishment reasserted its control over the welfare system and its authority over recipients by the simple expedient of terminating the special grant.

What has the welfare rights movement accomplished? Here, observers are divided. Some argue that it did raise benefit levels significantly and brought a larger percentage of eligible nonrecipients onto the rolls. At the very least, it gave a measure of self-assertion and pride to an otherwise abject segment of society. Others argue that, in the long run, recipients were no better off than before the movement began. They may even be worse off because of the termination of the special grant and the loss of the flexibility that this grant once provided to caseworker-client relations. In the remaining chapters of our study we try to measure some of the impact of welfare rights activities on the city's grant level and caseload.

12 The Impact of the Welfare Rights Movement on the City's Welfare System

Up to this point we have examined the origins, growth, and activities of the welfare rights movement in New York City. We now attempt to measure, as best we can, the impact of this movement on the city's caseload and grant level.

Many writers have asserted that welfare rights organizations have had a major impact on the city's welfare system. For example, Banfield declares:

In my opinion, the principal underlying causes of the increase in the welfare caseload [in New York City] have been these political ones—first, the general ideological change produced by the civil rights movement and the war on poverty and, second, the efforts of militant organizations created under OEO and other auspices to encourage the poor to demand all that they are legally entitled to. These causes have, by liberalizing regulations, increased the number of persons eligible for welfare; they have increased the proportion of eligibles applying; they have increased the proportion of applicants found acceptable.[1]

A similar opinion was expressed by two officials of New York City's Human Resources Administration, the agency that runs the city's welfare program,[2] and an ad hoc group of New York area scholars formed to rebut a report critical of the city's welfare administration.[3] Cloward and Piven have also argued that, "taken as a whole, there is little reason to doubt that the many-faceted welfare rights movement has had a crucial impact on the rolls."[4]

Similar claims have been made for other welfare jurisdictions and for the nation as a whole. For example, an HEW-sponsored report, after surveying the caseload increase in eleven cities, declared:

There was evidence that the higher the number of AFDC recipients who belonged to WRO's, the larger the number of poor persons using AFDC, but the evidence was not statistically significant. However, the number of AFDC women who reported that they belonged to WRO's was very small in all cities. For example, only 4.1 percent of all AFDC women in New York City belonged to the local WRO. These small percentages could, however, lead to false conclusions. A slight increase in the number of WRO members might have had a great influence on the attitudes of all AFDC recipients. To illustrate, there was a strong inverse relation between the percentage of WRO members and the number of recipients who felt helpless. The more WRO members in a city, the fewer the number of recipients who felt powerless.[5]

A study of Baltimore has also concluded that eligible families have been encouraged to apply for assistance because of welfare rights activity.[6]

Others have argued that the influence of welfare rights organizations on the city's caseload has been minimal or nonexistent. Perhaps the most explicit statement of this view is found in a controversial report by Lawrence Podell.

[The organized poor] thesis attempts to explain the recent caseload increase by claiming that it was the direct result of campaigns by neighborhood anti-poverty organizations and/or welfare client groups to publicize eligibility requirements. It is very difficult to obtain evidence either to support or refute this claim. However, relevant inferences may be drawn from the following:

(a) Contrary to media-produced images, the number, size, influence and campaign-effectiveness of such organizations and groups seem to have been relatively small. In addition, they were involved in a multiplicity of programs, most of which had far higher priority than welfare-connected efforts per se; the few groups that were militantly engaged in such activities tended to have concentrated their energies on organizing those already on welfare and attempting to better their condition, rather than on recruiting non-clients for the rolls. Besides, it may be argued that few ghetto residents did not know about welfare already and about where to go to apply for assistance—too few to account for the caseload increase of the dimensions experienced by New York City.

(b) Neighborhoods within New York City with more structured and/or militant organizations do not show a significantly greater caseload increase than neighborhoods without them. In addition, other cities in the State have well-organized, militant, anti-poverty programs. Yet, they have not experienced the caseload increase that New York has.

(c) Certain organizations have had a direct effect upon the caseload due to their "fair hearings" activity. (A client whose case is about to be closed by the City may request such a hearing from the State; until the matter is decided, the City cannot close the case. In effect, this may add to the total caseload by lessening exits from it.)

In 1966, there were 386 requests for "fair hearings" and 12 were held. (Most requests were resolved before the hearing.) In 1967, there were 3,332 requests for "fair hearings" and 183 were held. This certainly indicates an increase in such activity.

However, in 1966 there were 108,764 case closings. In 1967, there were 116,477. In other words, while the increase of "fair hearings" activity was considerable, the numbers involved were quite small compared to the number of case closings. Besides, this activity delayed closings far more than it prevented them. In any case, "fair hearings" activity did not contribute significantly to the case load increase of the magnitude that has been described.[7]

What, in fact, has been the impact of New York City's welfare rights movement? Has it affected the city's caseload and grant level and, if so, how? To answer these questions, it is essential that we understand why welfare rights organizations have functioned as they have and what they have tried to accomplish.

First, welfare rights organizations are recipient-oriented; they are primarily concerned with the interests of the welfare population. For this reason, they have tended to stress higher benefit levels, better treatment by caseworkers, and other matters of immediate concern to welfare families. The first organized effort in New York City was the winter clothing campaign. This evolved into the minimum standards campaign and a concerted effort to increase the size and to speed up the delivery of welfare allowances. Yet the grant level was not the only concern of welfare rights organizations in the city. More dignified treatment by caseworkers, less inconvenience in dealing with welfare officials, and greater protection against termination or threat of termination of a case have also been important group objectives. In each instance, however, the groups' objectives have been recipient-oriented; they have sought to improve the position of existing welfare families and not the poverty population as a whole.

We stress this because welfare rights organizations are often said to have campaigned to persuade eligible nonrecipients to apply for assistance or to have pressured welfare officials to accept a larger number of applicants. In fact, these have not been major activities of the movement. Being recipient-oriented, the local groups, at least, have not been primarily concerned with adding non-recipients to the welfare rolls.

This does not mean, however, that welfare rights organizations have had no influence on openings. Rather, this influence, if it has existed, has been more a "by-product" of efforts to obtain higher benefit levels and other concessions for the membership. Welfare rights groups have publicized the availability of welfare by word of mouth and demonstrations at various city offices. They have also helped to reduce the stigma attached to welfare dependency and to increase the self-confidence and even militancy on part of the poverty population, perhaps emboldening some segments of this population to apply for public assistance. Finally, to the extent that welfare rights activities have influenced the grant level, they have increased incentives for nonrecipients to apply and for recipients to stay on welfare and, in this way also, may have affected applications and closings. In other words, it would be a mistake to assert, as the Podell Report has, that welfare rights organizations have had little or no influence on the caseload because they are client-oriented.[8]

A second major point is that welfare rights groups have also been member-oriented, particularly at the local level. The local groups consist primarily of mothers banded together to advance their own immediate interests. Membership gave these mothers an advantage over other welfare recipients in receiving special or supplemental grants, once available under New York State's welfare law, as well as other benefits from the welfare administration. It provided them with knowledge of what they were entitled to and how they could obtain it, as well as some organizational backing in getting it. It provided, in other words, a benefit that bore the essential characteristics of a private as opposed to a public good. This, in turn, contributed to the rapid growth of the welfare rights movement in New York City.

Again, this does not mean that welfare rights organizations were exclusive groups or that they denied information and support to nonmembers. Rather, members were in a better position to obtain and use the information and the support provided by these organizations. Through word of mouth and neighborly contact, nonmembers probably benefited from welfare rights activities. However, they almost certainly benefited much less than did members.

Finally, there have been important changes in welfare rights tactics over time. There were from the beginning demonstrations at welfare centers and other city office buildings. There were also city-wide conferences and protest meetings. However, prior to 1968, when the welfare rights organizations were building their strength in the city, much of their activity was conducted at the local level. Groups held meetings at which the members were informed about what they were entitled to under law and were urged to demand their rights from their caseworkers. Checklists of items that could be obtained through special grants were circulated to the membership. In this way, the welfare rights movement provided a service to members that the welfare administration should have provided; it interpreted and explained the law to the members to ensure that recipients obtained that to which they were entitled.

There was a major change in welfare rights tactics in April 1968 when the movement began an intensive city-wide campaign of demonstrations at various welfare centers and city offices (see Table B-3, Appendix B). There were several reasons for this change in tactics. First, there was growing militancy in the ranks of the welfare rights movement. There was also growing strength. The movement had the manpower or, more properly, the womanpower, to undertake daily demonstrations in all parts of the city. Perhaps most important, the state legislature had become aware of the growing strength of the welfare rights movement and, in particular, its ability to take advantage of special grants and was considering putting an end to the system. The demonstrations were a conscious effort by the welfare rights leadership to build popular support for the movement and for retention of these grants.

This change in tactics also affected how the welfare rights organizations influenced both grant levels and caseloads. The demonstrations served to publicize both the availability of special grants and of welfare in general to the poverty population. Both members and nonmembers received this information. For this reason, the benefits of welfare rights activities also became a public good.

13 Decision Variables Affecting New York City's Caseload

It is no easy matter to determine whether welfare rights activities have affected New York City's caseload. To begin, we first break down the caseload increase into three components or what we call "decision variables." At any point in time, the change in the caseload ($\dot{C}$) can be expressed in terms of three decision variables: the acceptance rate (r), the applications rate (a), and the closings rate (k). This relationship is given by the difference equation:

$$\dot{C} = raN - kC$$

where N is the number of eligible nonrecipient families, C the caseload, and $N + C$ the total number of families eligible for welfare in New York City. This equation states simply that the increase in the caseload is equal to openings less closings. The level of openings and closings, however, also depends on the overall size of the caseload. The more families that are on welfare, the fewer that will apply; the more that are on welfare, the more that are likely to leave.

The opening of a welfare case involves a joint decision. The judgment that a family will be on the welfare rolls must be made by both the family and the welfare administration. The potential recipient must first decide to apply for public assistance; the welfare administration must then decide whether or not to accept the family's application. Both parties may also be instrumental in the family's withdrawal from dependency status. However, the decision to close a case is not likely to be made jointly. Withdrawal may occur either because the welfare family decides, for one reason or another, that it no longer needs assistance or the welfare administration decides that the family is no longer eligible.

Because two decisionmakers are involved in both openings and closings, the various factors thought responsible for the caseload increase are likely to affect each of the decision variables in different ways. For example, welfare rights activists may have persuaded nonrecipients to apply. Or, they may have encouraged caseworkers and other welfare center officials to increase their level of acceptances. One cannot determine how the welfare rights movement has affected the caseload unless the three decision variables are examined separately.

In Table 13-1 we present annual averages of the three decision variables in New York City between 1966 and 1970, the period of maximim growth in the caseload and, parenthetically, maximum growth in the welfare rights move-

Table 13-1

Decision Variables Affecting New York City's AFDC Caseload, 1966 through 1970

Year	Annual Acceptance Rate (r) (Percentage)	Applications Acted upon (A) (Number)	Annual Closings Rate (k) (Percentage)
1966	69.6	66,401	32.6
1967	76.1	78,744	28.4
1968	79.1	91,139	25.6
1969	72.8	81,366	25.4
1970	72.1	97,079	21.3

Source: Computed from data presented in New York City, Department of Social Services, *Monthly Statistical Report*, various months.

ment.[a] All three variables have changed since 1966 and in ways that would increase the city's AFDC caseload. The acceptance rate rose sharply between 1966 and 1968, but then dropped somewhat in 1969 and 1970. The level of applications increased throughout most of the period, while the closings rate fell steadily.

We start by estimating the direct impact on the city's AFDC caseload of changes in each of the three decision variables. For example, by holding the acceptance rate constant at its 1966 level and allowing applications and the closings rate to vary, one can determine what the caseload would have been if there had been no liberalization of acceptances during the five-year period. One can also estimate the effect of higher applications and lower closings rates by performing a similar calculation.

This computation is not as easy as it might appear. Although the change in the AFDC caseload depends, in part, on the level of closings, this level will itself depend on the size of the caseload. As the caseload falls, because one or more of the decision variables is held constant, the level of closings will drop independently of any changes in the closings rate. This induced increase in the caseload, which follows from the initial decrease, must be considered in our computation.

In Table 13-2 we present estimates of the AFDC caseload at the year end, holding each of the decision variables at its 1966 level.[b] In Table 13-3 we

[a]Because there is no published information on either the applications rate or the number of eligible nonrecipient families, we measure changes in the level of applications (A) where $A = aN$.

[b]A unique solution for the effect of changes in each of the three decision variables can be obtained by iteration. One set of estimates of year-end caseloads is used to determine a new set of estimates of annual closings. This new set of estimates of closings is used, in turn, to adjust the previous set of estimates of year-end caseloads. And so on. In making this computation, we assume a lag of one year, i.e., that: $C_t = rA - kC_{t-1}$.

Table 13-2

Estimates of the Impact of Changes in Decision Variables on New York City's
AFDC Caseload, 1966 through 1970 (Number of Cases)

Year	Actual AFDC Caseloads as of December 31	Hypothetical Caseload Assuming No Change since 1966 in:			
		Acceptance Rates	Applications Acted upon	Closings Rates	All Three Decision Variables
1965	84,699	84,699	84,699	84,699	84,699
1966	103,525	104,109	104,109	103,509	104,109
1967	135,549	130,833	126,558	131,176	117,869
1968	175,374	163,230	149,139	163,000	128,116
1969	194,670	182,928	164,126	173,632	137,093
1970	224,212	212,562	178,071	188,073	139,645
Caseload Increase	139,513	127,863	93,372	103,374	54,946

Source: Computed from Equation (13.1) and data contained in Table 13-1.

indicate the relative importance of each of the three decision variables for the
entire five-year period. Changes in all three variables contributed to growth in
the city's AFDC caseload. The most important was applications. Had there been
no increase in the level of applications between 1966 and 1970, about one-third
of the growth in AFDC caseload would not have occurred. The rise in
applications was followed in importance by the reduction in the closings rate,
which accounted for one-fourth of the caseload increase. Far less significant was
the increase in acceptance rates. Liberalized acceptances explained only 8
percent of the rise in New York City's welfare rolls during the five-year period.

This last finding may come as a surprise. In the popular view, increasing
laxness in administration and liberalization of welfare policies have been major

Table 13-3

Percentage of the AFDC Caseload Attributable to Changes in Decision Variables
Between 1966 and 1970

Component of the Caseload Increase Due To:	Percentage of the Caseload Increase
Higher acceptance rates	8.4
Higher number of applications acted upon	33.1
Lower closings rate	25.9
All three variables working simultaneously	60.6

Source: Estimated from data contained in Table 13.2

reasons for the recent growth in New York City's welfare caseload.[1] The evidence suggests, however, that the increase in the rate of acceptances was a minor factor in the city's caseload increase during the second half of the 1960s. The basic reasons for this increase were, instead, higher numbers of applicants and lower closing rates, both only partly or indirectly related to the liberalization of welfare administration policies.

We have also estimated what the caseload would have been if all three decision variables had remained constant at their 1966 levels. Sixty percent of the caseload increase between 1966 and 1970 can be attributed to the collective change in these variables. Put differently, 40 percent of the increase would have occurred anyway. The reason for this is that openings exceeded closings in the base year, 1966; in effect, changes in the decision variables subsequent to 1966 merely added to what was already a positive rate of growth in the city's AFDC caseload at the beginning of the five-year period.[c]

This exercise is only a beginning. The important question to which we now turn is why each of these three decision variables has changed over time, resulting in an unprecedented growth in New York City's welfare rolls in recent years.

[c]Several perceptive readers have observed that the percentages obtained holding each of the decision variables constant do not add up to the percentage obtained holding all of the variables constant simultaneously. There is no reason why they should. Because of interaction between the acceptance rate and the applications, one would expect the latter percentage to be lower than the former.

14 Some Reasons for the Growth in Welfare Dependency in New York City

The major purpose of this and the remaining chapters of this study is to determine as best we can whether welfare rights activities as well as several other factors thought to have affected the city's caseload have had an impact on each of the three decision variables and, if so, what this impact has been. To do this, we use multiple regression analysis, a method of inferring from historical data whether the decision variables (the dependent variables) and welfare rights activity (an independent variable) are so strongly correlated that it would be extremely unlikely that this relationship could occur by chance. If so, the measured relationship between the dependent and independent variables would be "statistically significant"; the available data would suggest that welfare rights activity has, in fact, influenced applications, acceptances, or closings.

In Appendix A we describe at length our use of multiple regression to measure the impact of welfare rights activities and other factors on the three decision variables. In this section we discuss the various factors that are likely to have influenced each of the decision variables, or independent variables. In the remaining sections we discuss the results of our analysis.

Many explanations have been given for the rising welfare caseload both in New York City and the nation as a whole. Migration from rural areas and the South has brought formerly self-sufficient poor families from states with stringent welfare standards to states with generous standards. There has been a general relaxation in eligibility rules, either because of governmental policy, administrative laxness, or litigation brought by community groups and other organizations concerned with the legal rights of the poor. Many of the new jobs created during the decade were inappropriate for the nation's urban poor, partly because they were located in relatively affluent suburban communities and partly because they required skills not possessed by the typical welfare family head. Welfare rights and other community organizations, the War on Poverty, Medicaid, and civil rights activities during the decade publicized the availability of welfare assistance and helped to destroy much of the stigma attached to dependency status.

The list of possible explanations for the caseload increase could be extended much further. However, our purpose in this study is limited; it is to determine, first, whether one of these explanations—welfare rights activity—has been an important determinant of the caseload increase in New York City. At the same time, we also consider two other explanatory variables—rising grant levels and changes in the admission standards or stringency of the welfare administration. There are many additional reasons for the caseload increase. However, given the formulation of our model, the nature of our data, and the scope of our study, we cannot give these other explanations the analysis they deserve.

Because a number of factors affect the caseload, one cannot say, as some have,[1] that other metropolitan areas have experienced the same caseload increase as New York City but not the same level of welfare rights activity, and thus this activity has had little influence. Nor can one say that because several communities have had the same level of welfare rights activity but not the same caseload increase, welfare rights activity has been inconsequential. This activity varies from area to area as do welfare laws, attitudes of welfare administrations, grant levels, and other determinants of the size of the caseload. Simple regional comparisons of the growth in the caseload prove nothing because different variables may operate with different force in different areas.

Moreover, a particular factor may affect a decision variable in several ways. For example, welfare rights activity has probably had both a direct and an indirect effect on applications. The direct effect has resulted, among other things, from the spread of information about the availability of welfare by word of mouth and the publicity given to welfare rights activities; the indirect effect, from the welfare rights organizations' influence on the grant level and the likelihood that higher grants have, in turn, encouraged some families to apply for public assistance. The analyst is, in short, faced with a problem of separating from each other the several effects of welfare rights organizations on a particular decision variable if he is to understand properly how these organizations have functioned and what they have accomplished.

Finally, not only are the various factors responsible for the increase in welfare dependency in the city not mutually exclusive, but several factors may have to operate simultaneously if an indigent family is to become a recipient family. It is particularly important to distinguish between the underlying causes of poverty and the particular circumstances that have led to a family's entry onto the welfare rolls. A family may be deserted by the father because of his inability to find a well-paying job in or near the city. However, the family may decide to apply for welfare only after it has come in contact with welfare rights activists and is accepted because of a change in welfare rules that allows the mother to supplement her own employment income with public assistance. The distinction between the underlying causes of poverty and the particular reasons why individuals may apply and be accepted as welfare recipients is especially important in considering policy measures to counter the rapid increase of welfare dependency in recent years. The solution to the dependency problem, in the particular case cited, is not the curtailment of welfare rights activities or adoption of more stringent standards of acceptances, but correction of the basic social and economic reasons for the father's inability to find employment.

In short, there is no simple cause and effect relationship between the caseload increase and the factors responsible for this increase. We are faced with a complex, multivariate problem. Nor do we have any illusions that we have satisfactorily overcome all the difficulties posed by this problem. Our analysis is only a beginning. We have done the best we can with the data, time, and resources available to us.

In the remainder of this chapter we discuss the independent or explanatory variables and how they might affect each of the three decision variables. We also discuss some important explanatory variables that are, necessarily, omitted from our analysis.

Welfare Rights Activity

We have already discussed at some length the activity of welfare rights organizations in New York City. We need only repeat here how these organizations may have influenced the caseload at different points in time.

Welfare rights groups are local community organizations. Most have been active in only one welfare district; some in two or three districts. None serves a clientele throughout the city or even throughout a borough. This makes it possible to identify membership in each welfare district by aggregating the membership of organizations active in that district (see Table B-1 in Appendix B). Membership best reflects the dominant type of activity during the first phase of the movement's operations, that is, during the months prior to May 1968. At that time, the various welfare rights organizations sought primarily to provide information and organizational support to members in their quest for special grants, more favorable treatment by caseworkers, and other benefits from the city's welfare administration. One would expect the grant level and growth in the caseload to be higher in a district the larger the proportion of welfare recipients belonging to welfare rights organizations.

A second measure of welfare rights activity is the number of demonstrations held per month at each welfare center (see Table B-3, Appendix B). The available data tell us only of the existence of a demonstration at a welfare center. They do not indicate the intensity of the demonstration, who was involved, or which objective the welfare rights groups had in mind. Despite these limitations, demonstrations should provide a reasonably good measure of welfare rights activity during the more militant phase of the movement's existence, the four months between May and August 1968 when the welfare rights organizations sought, by staging widespread demonstrations, to forestall the abandonment of the special grant.

Given the primary focus of New York City's welfare rights movement on obtaining higher grant levels for its members, one would expect a strong positive relationship between welfare rights activities and the grant level in a district. It is less certain, however, that there has been a significant relationship between welfare rights activities and each of the three decision variables.

The acceptance rate should be least influenced by the welfare rights movement. This rate affects nonrecipients. Once again, local organizations, at least, have been recipient-oriented. They have not lobbied or demonstrated in an effort to bring about greater liberalization of acceptances by the city's welfare administration. Similarly, applications also involve nonrecipients; the local organizations have not, for the most part, been directly concerned with bringing nonmembers into the welfare system. However, efforts by the welfare rights movement to secure higher benefit levels for members and the publicity generated by their activities, particularly after May 1968, may well have had that effect. It would not be surprising to find some relationship between the intensity of welfare rights activity in a district and the number of people seeking public assistance. Finally, one might expect the welfare rights organizations to have had some impact on the closings rate. A secondary welfare rights activity has been the instigation of fair hearings to reinstate members whose welfare status has been terminated by the welfare administration.

Grant Levels

During the 1960s, and particularly between 1966 and 1968, there was a substantial increase in the average grant level paid to the city's AFDC families (see Table 14-1). Prior to 1968, this increase reflected a rise in both the basic and special grant levels. In 1968, however, the increase in the special grant was dominant.[2]

The reasons for this secular increase in grant levels include changes in payment standards brought about by the Congress and the New York State legislature and activities of welfare rights organizations which, as we will argue, affected the special grant and, therefore, the average payment to welfare families. One possible result of this increase in grant levels was an encouragement to applications and discouragement to closings, both contributing to the increase in the city's welfare caseload during the decade.

The basic grant schedule is determined by the state legislature, with financial support and guidelines provided by the federal government. Once a family is admitted to a particular category of assistance and its needs relative to its resources established by the caseworker, the basic grant level is determined. It varies only with the size and age structure of the family. In New York City, holding the category of assistance, family size, and age structure constant, the basic grant level should be more or less identical for most families.[a]

[a]There are some exceptions to this rule. For example, where welfare payments supplement the earned income of a family, the family's welfare grant will be lower than the state's payment standard. There is considerable latitude for caseworker discretion in setting the grant level to reflect the nonassistance income of the recipient. In our study we assume, implicitly, that this exception is relatively minor in importance. Because few AFDC mothers in New York City are reported to hold jobs, this would seem to be a fairly realistic assumption. See Appendix B for further discussion.

Table 14-1

Monthly AFDC Grant per Case in New York City, 1967 and 1968 (Dollars)

Period	Total Grant	Basic Grant	Special Grant[a]	Special Grant as a Percentage of Total Grant
1967				
First Quarter	229	178	51	22
Second Quarter	230	172	58	25
Third Quarter	232	170	62	27
Fourth Quarter	249	172	77	31
1968				
January	255	184	71	28
February	246	185	61	25
March	249	184	65	26
April	267	184	83	31
May	284	183	101	35
June	304	188	116	38
July	196	179	117	40
August	375[b]	270[b]	104	28

[a]Data on special grants include all allotments above the basic grant.

[b]In August 1968 the first quarterly flat grant was paid to the city's welfare recipients. At the same time, welfare recipients received their last monthly special grant. As a result, the total grant level for August appears to be unusually high; similarly, the percentage of the total grant accounted for by the special grant is unusually low.

Sources: Data on total grants have been taken from: City of New York, Department of Social Services, *Monthly Statistical Report*, various months. Data on special grants are unpublished and have been obtained from the Department of Social Services.

Prior to August 1968, the special grant was given to the recipient over and above the basic grant at the discretion of the caseworker, unit director, or some other local welfare official. In theory, the special grant depended on the peculiar needs of the family such as costs of moving, replacement of a lost or stolen check, or a requirement for a particular type of clothing. The rationale for the special grant was that the caseworker needed flexibility in establishing a satisfactory relationship with the client. One way of creating this flexibility was to provide him with the power to add to the client's basic allotment if a special need arose.

The special grant became the most important organizing tool of the city's welfare rights organizations. It provided a tangible benefit that could be clearly associated with welfare rights membership. Consequently, many of the organizations' activities prior to mid-1968 were intended to obtain from the city and the various welfare centers higher special grants. Not surprisingly, the level of special grants rose sharply in late 1967 and 1968. As a result, these grants became highly controversial and in August 1968 many types of special grants were terminated by the state legislature. In their place, New York State established a flat grant that could not be influenced by caseworker discretion. In succeeding months, most remaining types of special grants were also ended.

An increase in the grant level can be expected to influence the caseload in two ways. First, if it is an increase in the basic grant, it automatically makes more low-income families eligible for public assistance. The basic grant level for a family of a given size, with no outside support, is also the income eligibility level for that family.[3] Therefore, one would expect this increase to result in greater applications and acceptances and fewer closings simply because more families have become eligible for welfare assistance. Second, a higher grant level may induce a greater number of eligible nonrecipients to apply and a lower number of existing welfare recipients to withdraw from dependency status. The welfare payment level acts as a supply price in the sense that this word is normally used by economists. The greater this price, all other things remaining constant, the greater the number of individuals who will offer their "services" as welfare recipients.

The relationship between the grant level and welfare recipient supply[b] has been widely discussed by economists in recent years.[4] Two general observations can be made. First, welfare recipient supply has for the most part been treated as an adjunct to labor supply. Economists typically begin by assuming leisure to be a positive good and the individual's decision to enter the labor force as involving a choice between this and all other goods that can be purchased with employment income. The availability of welfare imposes a lower limit on the wage rate necessary to induce an individual to work. A "stigma discount" is generally included because, given the general attitude of society, a dollar of welfare income is less desirable than a dollar of employment income.

For our purposes, it may be better to think of welfare recipient supply as involving a choice between the dignity resulting from self-sufficiency, treated as a positive good, and other goods, including leisure, that can be purchased with welfare income. Welfare rights activity can, in this way, be viewed as affecting an individual's preferences so that he no longer considers dependency demeaning, that is, he no longer perceives a tradeoff between dignity and the other goods that can be purchased with welfare income. Alternatively, an increase in the grant level can be thought of as an increase in the opportunity cost of dignity. In a sense, every individual has a price at which he will no longer be willing to buy the dignity stemming from self-sufficiency.

There is no reason to prefer one or the other formulation of a welfare recipient supply model. Whichever is used depends ultimately on the purpose of the analyst. For some purposes, however, the alternative formulation may help

[b]"Welfare recipient supply" is often referred to in the literature as the "demand for public assistance." For our purposes, the two terms have the same meaning.

the reader to understand more clearly what we are attempting to do in this study.

Second, studies of welfare recipient supply using data generated by existing welfare programs have foundered on a common obstacle—their inability to distinguish between the two effects of changes in the grant level discussed above.[5] This results from their use of different welfare jurisdictions as units of observation in cross-sectional analysis. Even if individuals were totally unresponsive to an increase in the grant level (i.e., welfare recipient supply is totally inelastic), one would still expect, with the methods of analysis that have been used, to find a positive relationship between welfare incidence and grant level. The reason for this is that in each jurisdiction the basic grant level is, in effect, the income eligibility level. The higher the grant level, the greater the number of individuals who are eligible for public assistance and, therefore, are likely to receive it.[6]

One objective of our study is to demonstrate how, by performing the analysis within one welfare jurisdiction, this problem can be avoided in cross-sectional analysis. For this purpose, the existence of the special grant is essential. Eligibility levels in New York City are determined by the state legislature through the basic grant level. However, prior to the termination of special grants, the actual grant level—the basic grant plus the special grant—was determined by both the state legislature and by caseworkers operating out of the various welfare centers. By examining the effect of variation in grant levels between the welfare centers of a particular welfare jurisdiction at a particular point in time one can, in effect, hold constant basic grant levels and, therefore, income eligibility levels. One can, in this way, measure the actual supply response by potential or actual welfare recipients to changes in welfare benefit levels.

Administrative Stringency

We also consider whether differences in the attitudes of various welfare center officials may explain variation in the caseload and the grant level over time. We use as a measure of stringency closings for failure to comply with departmental policy as a percentage of total closings.[c] Caseworkers, unit directors, and other welfare center officials have the power to terminate a welfare family if that family is found to have violated welfare rules. The willingness of the welfare administration to enforce the rules varies from one center to another with the general attitude of the center's staff toward its clients. For this reason, cases closed for failure to comply with departmental policy should provide a reasonably good surrogate for departmental attitudes.

[c]We are indebted to Elizabeth Durbin of New York University, who has written several studies of welfare in New York City, for suggesting this measure to us. Unfortunately, we have had to use data based on monthly Home Relief closings for failure to comply with departmental policy. Comparable data for AFDC have not been published by New York City's Department of Social Services.

The Acceptance Rate

Changes in the acceptance rate may also have had an impact on applications for welfare assistance. As the acceptance rate increases, more nonrecipients may apply because the probability of admission to welfare status has risen.[d] A low acceptance rate may also reflect long lines, demeaning questions, and other means used by certain welfare centers to discourage applicants. It may, in other words, provide a measure of the nonmonetary costs of seeking welfare assistance at particular centers. It was a relatively straightforward matter in Chapter 13 to determine whether changes in the acceptance rate have had a direct effect on the city's caseload. It is more difficult to determine whether these changes have had an indirect effect. By analyzing applications separately, one is able, however, to measure this indirect effect.

Our analysis may also help to clarify what has been a rather controversial issue in New York State—whether recent increases in acceptance rates have been a result of factors outside the city's control, such as welfare rights activities, or a result of changes in city policies and attitudes. If one accepts the latter, there is a second issue—whether it has been a result of the deliberate implementation of the liberal philosophy of recent New York City welfare administrations or a result of an unintended relaxation of standards and general administrative neglect.[7] We cannot hope to provide definitive answers to each of these questions. We can try, however, to throw more light on these issues than has been visible thus far.

Explanatory Factors Excluded from
the Analysis

To study the growth in the city's caseload, we use cross-sectional regression analysis with the city's welfare districts serving as units of observation. For the particular explanatory variables included in the model—welfare rights activity, grant levels, administrative stringency, and acceptance rates—cross-sectional analysis is feasible. It is also desirable because there are a number of relatively intangible factors likely to cause variation in the caseload over time but not between welfare districts. For example, there have been, almost every month, administrative changes influencing the caseload. These include changes in eligibility requirements, investigative procedures, and coverage by a particular category of assistance. Many of these changes cannot be readily accounted for in

---

[d]It has been suggested by one reader that the opposite may also hold: The greater the number of rejections, the greater the number of reapplications, simply because hopeful applicants will try again. Our own inclination is to discount this possibility, an inclination based on the hunch that, despite the growing militancy of the poverty population, most members of this population continue to feel inhibited and even intimidated in their dealings with welfare center officials.

time-series analysis. Fortunately, they are neither relevant nor essential to cross-sectional analysis. In general, the specification of a cross-sectional welfare incidence model is much simpler and, for this reason, preferred.

There are, however, some additional factors that may explain variation in the three decision variables between welfare districts. These factors should be included in our analysis, but for various reasons cannot. For our purposes, the exclusion of these factors does not matter to any great extent; it does, however, deprive some of the explanatory power of the model. Given the absence of meaningful data, we have no choice in the matter. If there is scope for fruitful extension of our work, it is here.

In-Migration

There is a widespread belief that the migration of low-income families from other areas of the country to New York City has been a factor in the recent substantial growth in the city's welfare caseload. This belief underlies recent efforts by New York State to adopt a residency requirement. It is also stressed by some proponents of the family assistance plan once supported by the Nixon administration. Although this plan would not provide significant additional federal assistance to the city's welfare recipients, it was thought that, by bringing about greater equality in payment levels in different regions of the country, the plan would discourage the movement of people to areas such as New York City that now have relatively generous welfare standards. It would also provide greater incentives for out-migration from the city, in this way encouraging dispersal of the city's welfare burden.

A study by The New York City-Rand Institute finds that, even though a relatively large percentage of the city's welfare recipients were born outside the New York metropolitan area, there is little evidence to support the view that in-migration has been a factor directly responsible for the recent increase in the city's caseload.[8] Most in-migrants receiving public assistance have been long-term residents of the city. Moreover, most recent in-migrants are self-sufficient. This study also finds that only a small percentage of in-migrants receive welfare and that in-migrants show no greater propensity than the native-born poor to go on public assistance. Also, by the time in-migrants come to depend on public assistance, they are likely to be dispersed throughout the city. In short, the exclusion of in-migration as an explanatory variable does not seem to be too serious a problem.

Job Availability

Applications and closings may also reflect the geographic distribution of job opportunities in the city. If, for the sake of argument, there are fewer jobs vacancies in Brooklyn than elsewhere in New York, one might expect that, all other things being equal, applications would be greater and closings lower in Brooklyn than elsewhere. Again, there are no usable data on job vacancies or other relevant measures of employment opportunities for the various sub-divisions of New York City. Therefore we have no way of incorporating geographic variation in job availability into our study.

One may derive some encouragement from the fact that the city has a relatively well-developed public transportation system and, because of this, most sections of the city are, effectively, part of a single labor market. Thus regional variation in applications and closings may not bear as strong a relationship to regional variation in job availability as one might expect. Even so, commuting to work within the city could be difficult, time-consuming, and costly for the poor, and may discourage job-holding and, particularly, job-hunting by welfare recipients.[9] All things considered, the omission of regional variation in employment opportunities would seem to be an unfortunate but not critical limitation of the study.

The Distribution of Minority Groups and Family Instability in the City

The New York City welfare population is drawn disproportionately from minority groups. Nearly 50 percent of the city's AFDC recipients are black; about 40 percent, Puerto Rican.[10] Should one expect greater applications and lower closings in sections of the city in which these minority groups are most heavily concentrated?

To some extent, the racial composition of the welfare population merely reflects the fact that minority groups receive lower incomes and experience higher unemployment than other segments of society. By dividing applications by an estimate of the eligible nonrecipient population based on income to obtain an applications rate, the study accounts for some of the racial biases in applications.

However, are there factors other than income that might explain the heavy concentration of minority groups on welfare? There has been at least one celebrated "yes" to this question—the controversial Moynihan Report.[11] Basing its analysis on the earlier work by Frazier,[12] this report concluded that the heritage of slavery and poverty has created a pattern of family instability among blacks. This, in turn, has resulted in a greater tendency for black families to become dependent on public assistance.

AFDC has an eligibility criterion other than income, the absence of an able-bodied male head of the household. One would, therefore, expect AFDC applications and closings to vary from one part of the city to another with concentrations of female-headed households. To the extent that the Moynihan hypothesis is correct, applications might also vary with concentrations of black residents.

The incidence of desertion appears to have been abnormally large in New York City. Between 1961 and 1967, nearly two-thirds of the increase in the nation's AFDC families with a man listed as "deserted" occurred in the city (estimated from data presented in Table 14-2). By contrast, the city accounted for only about 17 percent of the increase in the nation's AFDC caseload in which the status of the man was listed as other than deserted. For some reason, new dependency because of desertion has been way out of proportion in the city relative to other parts of the nation.

In our measure of the eligible nonrecipient population we include an approximate estimate of the number of families headed by women. We have little confidence, however, that this measure satisfactorily takes into account the geographic distribution of deserted families in the city. This is, we think, the greatest weakness of our analysis.

Desertion and Job Change

Why has there been so sharp an increase in New York City's caseload during the 1960s when, at the same time, there have been unprecedented, high levels of

Table 14-2
The Status of the Father of AFDC Families

Status of Father	1961 Number	%	AFDC Caseload 1967 Number	%	1968 Number	%	Percentage of Increase by Status of Father 1961-67	1967-68
New York City								
Deserted	12,138	23.7	52,855	39.7	79,147	46.2	49.8	41.6
Not Married	19,914	38.9	40,141	30.2	46,406	27.1	24.7	16.3
Other	19,153	37.4	40,005	30.1	45,838	26.7	25.5	42.1
Total	51,205	100.0	133,001	100.0	171,391	100.0	100.0	100.0
United States								
Deserted	171,000	19.6	236,000	19.2	NA[a]	NA	18.2	NA
Not Married	196,000	22.5	348,000	28.3	NA	NA	42.6	NA
Other	505,000	57.9	645,000	52.5	NA	NA	39.2	NA
Total	872,000	100.0	1,229,000	100.0			100.0	

[a]NA indicates that the data are not readily available.

Source: Committee on Ways and Means, U.S. House of Representatives, *Report on Findings of a Special Review of Aid to Families with Dependent Children in New York City*, September 24, 1969, pp. 64-65.

prosperity and employment? Consideration of this question has led to speculation that, given the nature of recent job change in the New York region,
prosperity may actually encourage desertion and contribute to growth in the
AFDC caseload.

The New York area, like most of the nation's metropolitan areas, has
experienced suburbanization of low- and middle-income, blue-collar jobs.[13] The
major difference between New York and other regions, however, is in the
distances involved. Whereas the flight to the suburbs may entail a ten-mile shift
in the Detroit or Chicago metropolitan areas, in New York it could involve as
much as a fifty-mile move. Commuting from the central city is much more
difficult and, for some suburban areas, all but impossible in the New York
region.

There are many reasons for the suburbanization of jobs. One of the most
frequently mentioned is prosperity itself. As firms' activities and profits increase,
they expand. However, in expanding, many firms located in central cities must
contend with the constraints of antiquated transportation systems and the
nonavailability of contiguous land. The result, frequently, is a decision to
relocate in less highly concentrated suburban areas.

Commutation from New York City to many of these areas is difficult. The
region's commuter transportation system is designed to carry passengers from
the suburbs to the central city and not in the other direction. Suburban zoning
and urban renewal in many suburban communities are thought to have restricted
the supply of low-income and, particularly, minority housing.

Despite these difficulties, a disproportionate share of new suburban job-
holders in the New York area have been members of minority groups.[14] How,
then, have minority workers filled suburban jobs? One possibility is that
desertion has become, in the New York area at least, an alternative way to
commuting and permanent relocation of the man and his family. Because of the
increase in job opportunities at substantial distances from his residence, the
low-income male living in New York City may find separation from his family,
either on a temporary or permanent basis, the only feasible way of taking
advantage of suburban job growth.

This pattern of migration, if it exists, is not unique to the New York area. For
many years, men migrating into New York City in search of jobs have left their
families in Europe, Puerto Rico, and the South. The only difference now is that
New York City may be experiencing the tail end of this pattern of movement.
The city would, in other words, be inheriting the worst of both worlds. Not only
would it be losing employable residents, it would also be faced with the burden
of providing municipal services, including public assistance, to their dependents.

15 The Grant Level

In Chapter 16, we estimate the impact of welfare rights activities on the acceptance rate, applications rate, and closings rate. Before doing this, however, we must first measure the impact of welfare rights activities on the grant level. Our primary purpose is to determine whether the welfare rights movement has influenced the New York City caseload directly or indirectly (because of its impact on the grant level and the impact that the grant level has, in turn, had on the caseload).

Unlike the basic grant, which is given by schedules established by law, the special grant was paid out at the discretion of the caseworkers, unit director, or other welfare center officials. The special grant, being determined at the local level, was especially susceptible to activities of local welfare rights organizations and, for this reason, gave these organizations some measure of control over welfare payments. During the first eight months of 1968 there was a significant increase in the grant level (see Table 14-1). Virtually all of this increase resulted from growth in the special rather than the basic grant. Much of it was concentrated in mid-1968, the period of particularly intensive welfare rights activity. It would not be surprising, therefore, to find that the two phenomena were related.

To analyze the grant level and caseload increase, we have had to make a number of assumptions. These are necessary if we are to use the limited data that are available. For the most part, our results make intuitive sense. This, in the final analysis, is the best test of any empirical work. When our results do not make sense, we alert the reader to this fact and try to explain, if possible, why this is so.

To the nonstatistician, we urge patience and endurance to the end; this chapter and the chapters that follow will not be as easy reading as preceding sections. To make them as readable as possible, however, we have put in three appendixes our discussion of the model explaining the impact of the welfare rights movement on the grant level and welfare incidence. In the main text, we restrict ourselves to discussing the results of our analysis.

Welfare Rights Activity

The estimated parameters of a linear grant level equation are presented in Table 15-1.[a] Our results suggest that welfare rights organizations did, indeed,

---

[a]In tabulating our results, we include equations containing only those variables, discussed in Appendix A, which prove statistically significant or marginally significant explanators of the grant level. Throughout, we have applied Occam's razor to avoid the needless proliferation

have an influence on the grant level and that the nature of this influence changed over time with changes in welfare rights tactics.

We use two basic measures of welfare rights activity: the percentage of AFDC mothers belonging to welfare rights groups in each district and the number of welfare rights demonstrations in each district each month. From January through April 1968, the grant level was a positive function of membership, as expected.[b] However, in May, when the basic change in welfare rights tactics occurred, the grant level ceased to be a function of membership and appears, instead, to be a function of demonstrations. This relationship held for only one month, however. From June until August there was no apparent relationship between the grant level and either membership or demonstrations. It would appear that welfare rights organizations did, indeed, affect the grant level and that the nature of their influence varied closely with changes in their tactics.

The apparent lack of relationship between the grant level and both measures of welfare rights activity after June 1968 may at first sight seem rather curious. The special grant continued in existence until August 31. Both membership and demonstrations also continued at high levels. Yet this lack of relationship in later months seems reasonable; it is consistent with the basic change in the character of the welfare rights organizations that accompanied the change in their tactics in May 1968. Because of its increased militancy and widespread use of demonstrations, the welfare rights movement became, much more, a force affecting all welfare recipients.

By April 1968 it was generally known that the state legislature would end the special grant. The demonstrations were intended, among other things, to forestall this development. The leadership hoped to create a wider basis of support for the special grant by opening it up, to a far greater extent, to nonmember welfare recipients.[c] Information about special grants, which had previously been disseminated at storefronts and organization meetings, was now spread by the publicity generated by welfare rights demonstrations. For this reason, organization activities reached a larger cross-section of the welfare population. For this reason, also, what had been primarily a private good became, much more, a public good. Information about the special grant began to be conveyed to welfare recipients whether or not they were members of welfare rights organizations and regardless of the district in which they happened to live.

The welfare rights movement almost certainly had some effect on the overall grant level after May 1968. However, because its influence became city-wide, our cross-sectional model, as it is now structured, fails to measure this effect.

of computer printout which one so often finds in studies of this type. The exclusion of insignificant variables also simplifies out subsequent analysis of applications and closings.

[b]The relationship for February was, however, very weak and significant at somewhat less than 90 percent confidence.

[c]Perhaps for this reason, one finds a consistently low correlation between the membership rate and demonstrations and an equally low serial correlation in demonstrations between April and August. (Neither exceeded 0.50 for any one month.) The movement entered neighborhoods where it was not well established and concentrated on welfare centers that had been relatively unresponsive to recipients' needs and welfare rights organizations' demands.

Table 15-1
Estimated Parameters of Linear Models Explaining AFDC Grants per Case, January through August 1968[a]

Month	Constant Term (β_0)	WRO Membership as a Percentage of the AFDC Caseload (β_2)	Demonstrations (β_3)	Closings for Noncompliance with a Departmental Policy as a Percentage of Total Closings (β_4)	Average Family Size (β_5)	Corrected R^2	Sample Size
January	57.191	0.995 (2.39)	NA[e]	-1.067 (-1.93)[b]	51.383 (7.30)	0.71	32
February	76.386	0.809 (1.62)[c]	NA	-1.516 (1.85)[b]	45.298 (5.48)	0.59	33
March	44.985	0.928 (2.44)	NA	-2.568 (-4.09)	55.800 (9.06)	0.79	33
April	-91.235	3.480 (3.68)	6.111 (1.72)[b]	-3.570 (-2.83)	92.685 (5.78)	0.72	33
May	97.792	d	3.720 (5.40)	d	48.680 (2.67)	0.59	33
June	d	d	d	d	d	d	d
July	d	d	d	d	d	d	d
August	d	d	d	d	d	d	d

[a]Coefficients (t-values) are shown in parentheses. Unless otherwise specified, only those estimates are included that are significant at the 95 percent confidence level. Initial regressions were recomputed, dropping insignificant variables to yield the estimates presented in this table.
[b]Marginally significant at the 90 percent confidence level.
[c]Marginally insignificant at the 90 percent confidence level.
[d]No discernible relationship.
[e]NA indicates that the data for the month are not available.

One is also impressed by the speed with which welfare recipients and the welfare administration seem to have responded to welfare rights activities. In no instance does the introduction of a lag in demonstrations improve the explanation of variance in the grant level. In fact, lagged measures of demonstrations generally provide a considerably less satisfactory fit of the regression to the data than unlagged measures.[d]

The coefficients presented in Table 15-1 can be thought of as measures of the return to welfare rights activity. In January, for every percentage point increase in a district's AFDC caseload enrolled in welfare rights organizations, there was an increase in the average AFDC grant level of slightly less than $1. This return remained more or less constant until April, when a percentage point increase in the membership resulted in a $3.48 increase in the average welfare check. In May, a demonstration added $3.72 to the monthly grant level.

By substituting the means of the dependent and independent variables into these equations, one can separate the average grant per case per district into two components: that part determined by welfare rights activity and that part determined by all other factors. The results are presented in Table 15-2, as estimated from the parameters in Table 15-1 and means for the dependent and independent variables presented in Table 15-3. Between January and March, welfare rights membership accounted for slightly less than a 2 percent increase and, in April, a 5.5 percent increase in the average AFDC grant level. In May, demonstrations accounted for an increase of nearly 7 percent. Although

Table 15-2

Component of the Total AFDC Grant per Case Attributable to Welfare Rights Activity (Dollars)

		Average Grant Attributable to:		
Month	Average Grant per Case	WRO Membership	Demonstrations	Other Factors
January	253.25	4.27	–	248.98
February	244.33	3.42	–	240.91
March	248.18	3.92	–	244.26
April	266.12	14.68	3.33	248.11
May	304.15	–	20.40	283.75

Source: Estimated from parameters presented in Table 15-1 and means for the dependent and independent variables presented in Table 15-3.

[d]A dummy variable was included in the grant level equation for districts in which membership estimates were known to be understated. For each month, the coefficient of the dummy variable is positive, as expected, but very small and statistically insignificant. The underestimation of membership because some groups were not affiliated with the National Welfare Rights Organization, and data on their membership are unavailable would not appear to be a serious problem.

Table 15-3

Mean Values of Dependent and Independent Variables (Standard Deviation in Parentheses)

Month	Grants per AFDC Case (Dollars)	WRO Membership (%)	Demonstrations (Number)	Closings for Noncompliance (%)	Family Size (Number)
January	253.25 (15.486)	4.29 (3.9)	NA[a]	5.96 (2.9)	3.856 (0.227)
February	244.33 (16.049)	4.22 (3.8)	NA	6.50 (2.4)	3.850 (0.236)
March	248.18 (16.774)	4.22 (3.8)	NA	5.95 (2.3)	3.845 (0.234)
April	266.12 (35.193)	4.22 (3.8)	0.545 (0.904)	4.49 (2.8)	3.834 (0.224)
May	304.15 (35.221)	4.22 (3.8)	5.485 (6.073)	4.08 (2.4)	3.820 (0.229)
June	298.32 (30.094)	4.12 (3.8)	5.706 (4.687)	2.89 (3.2)	3.844 (0.220)
July	295.24 (32.875)	4.12 (3.8)	6.147 (6.397)	2.19 (1.7)	3.798 (0.223)
August	372.617 (38.462)	4.12 (3.8)	7.176 (8.159)	2.44 (1.8)	3.766 (0.222)

[a]NA indicates that the data for the month are not available.

Source: Estimated from data presented in Tables B-1 and B-3, Appendix B, and the *Monthly Statistical Report* published by New York City's Department of Social Services.

statistically significant, the returns to both welfare rights membership and demonstrations were small when compared to the total grant level.

There is reason to believe, however, that special grants were distributed unevenly and that welfare rights organization members received a disproportionate share of these grants.[1] Members of welfare rights organizations accounted for slightly more than 4 percent of the AFDC caseload in 1968 (see Table B-1, Appendix B). If, in the extreme, all or almost all of the return to the welfare rights membership accrued to members alone, which seems plausible, the increase in the grant for members would be roughly 25 times the average increase indicated by the regression coefficients. In April 1968, for example, membership in welfare rights organizations would yield a 138 percent increase rather than a 5.5 percent increase in a member's average monthly grant. It is impossible to determine with any certainty the exact return to welfare rights members. Our study suggests, however, that it was substantial for the period being examined. This fact probably contributed to the rapid growth in welfare rights membership at that time.

Administrative Stringency

During the first four months of 1968, the grant level bore a significant negative relationship to one of the two measures of administrative stringency, closings for failure to comply with departmental policy.[e] In no month, however, did we find a relationship between the grant level and the other measure, the rejection rate.[f] If one can assume that closings for failure to comply with departmental policy is a satisfactory surrogate for the administrative stringency of welfare centers, the picture prior to May is one of selective administration of welfare grants. An AFDC mother had a better chance of receiving a higher grant if she were a resident of a district that happened to have a relatively lenient welfare administration.

Closings for failure to comply with departmental policy fell sharply after May.[g] At the same time, the grant level ceased to bear a functional relationship to this rate. One might interpret this in several ways. Caseworkers may have been intimidated by widespread welfare rights demonstrations, both in allocating special grants and instituting closings for failure to comply with departmental policy. Or, caseworkers, aware of the impending end of most special grants, may have been more willing to authorize these grants as well as to overlook violations of departmental policy. Whatever the explanation, the evidence suggests a breakdown in the selectivity with which the special grant was administered after May 1968. It is possible that militant welfare rights activity was a major reason for this breakdown.

Family Size

As expected, during the first half of 1968 the grant per case was positively related to family size. Moreover, family size accounted for, by far, the largest percentage of explained variance.[h] What was not expected, however, is the apparent lack of any relationship between the grant per case and family size between June and August. This result is surprising, first, because under schedules established by the state legislature the basic grant increases with family size and, second, the basic grant accounted for about 60 percent of the total grant at that time (see Table 14-1). For some reason, the positive relationship between family size and the basic grant appears to have been offset by an opposite relationship

[e]In January and February, however, this relationship was only marginally significant at the 90 percent confidence level.

[f]To our surprise, there is no statistically significant relationship between the two surrogates for administrative stringency. The correlation between the two measures actually bears the wrong sign for most of the first eight months of 1968.

[g]See Table 15-3. The average rate per district was about 4 percent prior to May and 2 percent after May.

[h]About 90 percent each month in which family size was a significant explanatory variable.

between family size and the special grant in these months.[i] Parenthetically, after September 1968, with the establishment of the flat grant, the expected positive relationship between the grant per case and family size was restored.[j]

We have also regressed the AFDC-U and Home Relief grant levels on the same explanatory variables. The results, which are presented in Appendix A, are similar although not as pronounced as for AFDC. Although the welfare rights movement is, for the most part, an AFDC movement, its impact appears to have spread to other types of assistance as well.

Finally, the linear form of the model, in all cases, provides better explanation of the grant level. That there appear to be constant returns to welfare rights activities is an important finding. It implies that, during the period considered, welfare rights organizations were relatively uninhibited in securing higher grant levels for their members in those districts where they were active. This may have been a result of the small size of their membership relative to the total caseload. Or, it may have been a result of a generally receptive attitude toward welfare rights activities by many caseworkers and other welfare administration officials authorized to distribute special grants.

Summary

Our analysis suggests that the city's welfare rights organizations did have an impact on the grant level during the first half of 1968, the period just prior to the termination of most types of special grants. Moreover, the nature of this impact varied during the period with changes in welfare rights tactics. From January through April welfare rights organizations placed greater emphasis on securing, through collective action, increased grants for individual members. During this period, there was a statistically significant relationship between the grant level and the percentage of the AFDC caseload belonging to welfare rights organizations. In May the welfare rights organizations began a militant campaign of demonstrations at the various welfare centers and other city offices designed to dramatize their demands and to build popular support for retention of the special grant. In May the grant level varied significantly with demonstrations but not with membership. However, from June through August the grant level was

[i]Experimentation with various nonlinear forms of the equation also failed to yield significant coefficients for these months.

[j]The variables included in the equation explain between 59 and 79 percent of the total variance in grant levels during the first five months of 1968 (see Table 15-1). However, this finding is deceptive. By far the largest percentage of total variance is explained by family size which, one might take for granted, should influence the family's welfare check. In contrast, the two variables representing welfare rights activities together account for no more than 3 percent of total variance each month. This might be cause for concern were our objective to explain variation in the grant level. Rather, it is to determine whether welfare rights organizations have influenced the grant level and, if so, how. For this purpose, explanation of total variance is not very important.

functionally related to neither measure of welfare rights activity, despite the continuance at high levels of both organization membership and the number of demonstrations.[k] The reason, we suspect, is that the city-wide campaign of demonstrations helped to publicize the availability of special grants to non-members and to erode the reluctance of welfare center officials to authorize these grants. For this reason, during the last three months a much larger proportion of the city's caseload was able to share in the special grants than had previously been the case.

Although there is a statistically significant relationship between the grant level and welfare rights activity for the first five months of 1968, the average increase in the total grant attributable to welfare rights activity is quite small. This is due largely to the fact that welfare rights organizations represent a small fraction of the welfare population. However, if one assumes that all or most of the increase in the grant level associated with membership accrued to members, which is reasonable, the return to welfare rights membership would be substantial. It is no surprise, therefore, that early 1968 was a period of rapid growth in the membership of these organizations. The welfare rights movement was able to provide a clear and tangible benefit to its members.

[k]This was true even when various lags were introduced into the equation.

16 Acceptances, Applications, and Closings

We now turn to our central task, an effort to determine by use of regression techniques whether there is a statistically significant relationship between the three decision variables and welfare rights activity. Once again, the description of our model and the discussion of some of the problems of estimation incurred in developing it are relegated to Appendix A. In this chapter, we concentrate on the results.

The Acceptance Rate

It is widely believed that welfare rights organizations have affected the caseload by fighting for, or encouraging, higher acceptance rates.[1] We are inclined to doubt this because, again, the welfare rights movement has been recipient-oriented. The local welfare rights groups, at least, have not been primarily concerned with admissions standards.[a] Still, it is useful to test this belief with some analytical rigor.[b]

The results are what might be expected. For most months there is a positive relationship between the AFDC acceptance rate and the several measures of welfare rights activity, but in no month is this relationship statistically significant.[c] Nor is there evidence that, at any time during the two-year period, welfare rights activities affected acceptance rates for AFDC-U and Home Relief.

It is still possible, however, that the welfare rights movement, as a whole, by instituting court action and advocating reforms by the state and city government, may have been partly responsible for the steady increase in acceptance rates during the second half of the 1960s. We have no way of testing this hypothesis with our analysis. Rather, our study suggests only that the activities

---

[a]However, the NWRO has. Any effect that the NWRO has had on these standards would, presumably, be across the board and would not be relevant to our analysis of variation in acceptance rates between welfare districts.

[b]If for no other reason, we should do this to make certain that our applications and closings rate equations, discussed in Appendix A, are properly specified. In these equations, we treat the acceptance rate as an exogenous, independent variable. We can do this only if it is unrelated to welfare rights activity. If, instead, the two variables are functionally related, a simultaneous equations model would be required.

[c]During the 24 months between January 1967 and December 1968, the maximum value of a coefficient divided by its standard error (t-value) is 1.47, which, at 29 degrees of freedom, allows considerably less than 90 percent confidence that the estimate differs significantly from zero. For most months, the standard error is greater than the estimated coefficient.

of local welfare rights groups have not influenced acceptance rates. This is not too surprising given the focus of their interests and the nature of their constituencies.

Nor do we find a relationship between the acceptance rate and closings for failure to comply with departmental policy. The acceptance rate does not appear, in other words, to have varied from district to district with the relative stringency of the districts' welfare administrations. In short, the acceptance rate appears to be an exogenous variable, i.e., a variable determined by factors other than those included in our model.

The Applications Rate

We found in Chapter 13 that applications have been the most important of the three decision variables affecting New York City's caseload. Applications increased sharply between 1966 and 1968, the same time that the city's welfare rights movement reached its zenith. It is understandable, therefore, why this growth in applications might be attributed to welfare rights activities. The purpose of this section is to determine whether, in fact, this was the case.

Our analysis of the applications rate is, by far, the most difficult part of this study (see Appendix A). First, we had to estimate the eligible nonrecipient population, or population at risk. Many an analyst has been troubled by this problem. We did the best we could with the data available to us at the time of our analysis (see Appendix C). In addition, there are major problems of estimation using least-squares regression techniques because of simultaneity and the underlying non-linearity of the applications rate model. (For further discussion, see Appendix A.) We have resolved these problems by estimating reduced form coefficients and simulating a nonlinear applications rate equation with a kinked linear equation. Our results are presented in Table 16-1.

Welfare Rights Activity

As expected, there is a discontinuous relationship between the applications rate and welfare rights activity for each month. Given a minimum level of activity in a district, the welfare rights movement has had an impact on the caseload through applications. Below this level, however, one finds no significant relationship between the two.

The results of our analysis of applications rates also reflect the basic change in welfare rights tactics that occurred in May 1968. Between February and May, the AFDC applications rate was positively related to the percentage of AFDC families belonging to welfare rights organizations. The effect of the widespread demonstrations on applications first appears in June. From June through August

Table 16-1

Estimated Parameters of Linear Models Explaining the AFDC Applications Rate in New York City February through August 1968a

Month	Constant Term $(\gamma_0, \gamma_0',$ or $\gamma_0 + \gamma_4\beta_0)$	Coefficients (t-Values in Parentheses)		Grant per Case (γ_4)	Corrected R^2	Sample Size
		WRO Membership $(\gamma_1$ or $\gamma_1 + \gamma_4\beta_2)$	WRO Membership Multiplied by Demonstrations (γ_1')			
February - Direct Estimation						
$M \leqslant 5$	−36.83			0.173 (3.12)	0.31	21
$M > 5$	−36.48	1.173 (3.35)		0.134 (1.94)b	0.61	10
March						
$M \leqslant 5$ Direct Estimation	−40.05			0.186 (2.47)	0.20	21
$M > 5$ Reduced Form	−47.46	1.371 (3.22)		0.220 (2.12)	0.56	10
Structural Form	−57.34	1.167		0.220		
Direct Estimation	−45.53	1.206 (2.83)		0.170 (2.10)	0.56	10
April						
$M \leqslant 5$ Direct Estimation	−20.97			0.102 (2.80)	0.25	21

Table 16-1 (cont.)

		Coefficients (t-Values in Parentheses)				
Month	Constant Term $(\gamma_0, \gamma_0', \text{or } \gamma_0 + \gamma_4\beta_0)$	WRO Membership $(\gamma_1 \text{ or } \gamma_1 + \gamma_4\beta_2)$	WRO Membership Multiplied by Demonstrations (γ_1')	Grant per Case (γ_4)	Corrected R^2	Sample Size
$M \geqslant 5$						
Reduced Form	−47.04	1.225 (2.55)		0.135 (2.30)	0.53	10
Structural Form	−34.72	0.755		0.135		
Direct Estimation	−25.63	0.994 (1.89)[b]		0.096 (2.00)	0.48	10
May[c]						
$M \leqslant 5$						
Direct Estimation	−8.16			0.051[d] (2.66)	0.24	20
$M > 5$						
Reduced Form	−93.18	2.382 (4.80)		0.243[d] (4.49)	0.80	10
Structural Form	−70.99	1.536		0.243[d]		
Direct Estimation	−47.52	1.755 (2.68)		0.155[d] (2.96)	0.66	10
June - Direct Estimation						
$M \cdot D \leqslant 30$	6.39[e]				–	24
$M \cdot D > 30$	−1.14		0.169 (10.42)		0.94	8

July - Direct Estimation				
$M \cdot D \leqslant 30$	6.52[e]		—	22
$M \cdot D > 30$	−8.72	0.164 (3.33)	0.53	10
August - Direct Estimation				
$M \cdot D \leqslant 30$	7.12[e]		—	22
$M \cdot D > 30$	6.40	0.206 (3.97)	0.62	10

[a]Unless otherwise specified only those estimates are included that are significant at the 95 percent confidence level. Initial regressions were recomputed dropping insignificant variables to yield the estimates presented in this table. Fulton and Bushwick districts have been excluded. See Appendix C.

[b]Marginally significant at the 90 percent confidence level.

[c]Nevins district also excluded. See Appendix C.

[d]Grant level lagged one month.

[e]Average applications rate in districts for which $M \cdot D \leqslant 30$.

1968, there is still a positive relationship between the applications rate and welfare rights activity. However, a measure of interaction between membership and demonstrations now provides the best explanation of variance in the dependent variable and, for each of the three months, is highly significant under usual tests of significance.

In short, our results support the hypothesis that, at least during the seven months of 1968 examined in this study, the level of applications in New York City was influenced by welfare rights activity. However, the relationship between the applications rate and welfare rights activity is found in only about one-third of the welfare districts in the city, i.e., those in which welfare rights groups were especially strong;[d] the influence of the welfare rights movement on applications was, in other words, a localized phenomenon. A critical minimum level of welfare rights activity appears to have been necessary in a district before this activity had an influence on the applications rate.

It is also clear that the intensive campaign of demonstrations became the dominant influence on applications during the summer of 1968. However, again, this was true only of those welfare districts in which the welfare rights movement was most active.

We have also experimented with various lags in demonstrations.[e] The unlagged variable, in all instances, offers substantially better explanation of variance in the applications rate. This is an important finding because it suggests not only a strong response by eligible nonrecipients to welfare rights activities, but a high degree of immediacy of this response.

The Grant Level

The applications rate was also related to the grant level during the first four months of the period. However, from June to September, there was no apparent relationship between the two variables.

Because our study examines applications within one welfare jurisdiction, it has, in effect, held welfare eligibility constant. Having accounted for family size, the variation in the grant level between welfare districts that is observed here is due almost entirely to variation in the special grant, and not variation in the basic grant upon which eligibility depends. In other words, in measuring the relationship between the applications rate and the grant level, one is able to measure a true supply response by potential welfare recipients, and not the fact that more individuals are likely to apply for welfare assistance if more are eligible. It would appear from our results that welfare applicants are, indeed, economic women. They do respond positively to higher benefit levels.

---

[d]These districts were concentrated in the Bedford-Stuyvesant area of Brooklyn, Jamaica in Queens, and parts of Manhattan.

[e]In particular, we tried two forms of the lagged variable: demonstrations in the previous month and demonstrations in the current and the previous month combined.

We have also experimented with several lags in grant levels. With one exception, there is little reason to choose between the lagged and unlagged measures. That exception occurred in May. In that month, there is no discernible relationship between the applications rate and the unlagged grant level. There is, however, a significant relationship between this rate and the lagged grant level.

After May 1968, the applications rate bears no relationship to the grant level, lagged or unlagged. There are several possible explanations for this. The more widespread distribution of special grants to the welfare population may have affected cross-sectional variation in the grant level in a way that limits the usefulness of cross-sectional analysis in determining whether and how applications vary with welfare benefits. Or, the city-wide campaign of demonstrations beginning in May 1968 may have helped to break down inhibitions against applying for welfare, even in districts with relatively low grant levels. Whatever the reason, during this period the principal spur to applicants seems to have been welfare rights activity in certain districts and not this activity coupled with the economic incentives created by higher welfare payments.

One of the disadvantages of the linear form is that the regression coefficients are not supply elasticities; nor are the supply elasticities constant for all grant levels.[f] One can, however, make point estimates of elasticities for the four months during which the grant level was a significant explanatory variable.

A rough estimate of the average supply elasticity each month is 5.0 (see Tables 16-2 and 16-3). This estimate is unbelievably high. It implies that, for every 1 percent increase in the average grant level, one can expect a 5 percent increase in the percentage of eligible nonrecipients applying for public assistance. For example, suppose the city's average AFDC grant level during the period, about \$260 a month, were instead, \$286, an increase of 10 percent. One would then expect the percentage of eligible nonrecipients applying for AFDC to increase from about 6.5 percent to 9.8 percent, a jump of 50 percent.[g]

Here, we should warn the reader to exercise more than normal caution in interpreting the results of this type of analysis. The measured response to grant levels is extremely and, we think, unbelievably large.[h] One reason for this, we

---

[f]The elasticity of supply (e) is a familiar concept to economists. It is the percentage change in supply associated with a 1 percent change in price. In this case, the supply elasticity of welfare recipients would be the percentage change in the percentage of eligible nonrecipients applying associated with a 1 percent change in the average grant level:

$$e = \frac{\delta a}{\delta G} \cdot \frac{G}{a}$$

where $\dfrac{\delta a}{\delta G}$ is the estimated coefficient of the grant level variable; G, the average grant level; and a, the average applications rate.

[g]It should be emphasized, however, that this is based on a point elasticity estimate. The more the grant level increases, the more the elasticity would fall and, therefore, the greater the unreliability of a projected response based upon it.

[h]This will become even more apparent later in this chapter and in Chapter 17, when we simulate the effect of increases in the grant level on AFDC applications and the AFDC caseload.

Table 16-2
Estimated Point Elasticities of AFDC Applicant Supply (Percentage)

Month	Estimated Directly		Estimated from Structural Form
	$M \leqslant 5$	$M > 5$	$M > 5$
February	8.5	5.2	NC [b]
March	8.1	6.0	7.7
April	5.0	2.9	4.1
May[a]	2.7	4.1	6.4

[a]Grant level lagged one month.

[b]NC indicates that the estimate is not calculated.

Source: Estimated from coefficients presented in Table 16-1 and means of applications rates and grant levels presented in Table 16-3. Elasticities have been estimated at the means.

Table 16-3
Mean Values of Dependent and Independent Variables per Welfare District

Month	AFDC Applications Rate (%)		Membership[a] (%)	WRO Membership · Demonstrations[b]	AFDC Grant Level	
	$M \leqslant 5$	$M > 5$			$M \leqslant 5$	$M > 5$
February	4.93	6.37	8.48	–	241.28	246.10
March	5.63	7.07	8.48	–	245.67	248.70
April	5.21	9.12	8.48	–	255.95	279.70
May	4.68	10.61	8.48	–	253.55[c]	279.70[c]
June	6.39	11.49	–	74.79	–	–
July	6.52	24.54	–	96.38	–	–
August	7.12	29.02	–	109.91	–	–

[a]Average for districts in which $M > 5$.

[b]Average for districts in which $M \cdot D > 30$.

[c]The grant level is lagged one month. Because Nevins district was dropped in the May regressions, the average lagged grant level for May, for districts where $M \leqslant 5$, differs slightly from the average grant level for April.

Source: Estimated from data discussed in Appendixes B and C and presented in the *Monthly Statistical Report*, published by New York City's Department of Social Services. Averages have been included only for significant-explanatory variables in each month.

suspect, is that applicants are influenced by the grant level others are known to receive and not by the grant level that they, themselves, are likely to get. During the first half of 1968, a relatively small number of welfare families obtained special allotments. One heard stories, probably exaggerated, about recipients coming away from welfare centers with $1,000 checks in their hands. It is quite conceivable that applicants were reacting to stories like these; that they were responding to extraordinarily large special grants given to a relatively few welfare families. Their expected grant level, in other words, probably exceeded their actual grant level by a considerable margin. And, it was their expected, not the actual grant level, that most likely influenced their decision to apply for welfare assistance.

If this supposition is correct, it suggests the existence of a relationship between the grant level and the applications rate, but not the relationship estimated here. One would still expect to find the applications rate to be a function of the average grant level. However, one would also expect this relationship to be exaggerated. Individuals who appear to be responding to a 10 percent increase in the average grant level from, let us say, $244 to $268, may, in fact, be responding to a 50 percent increase in the expected grant level from $400 to $600. If so, a more accurate measure of supply elasticity would be one and not five.

Perhaps all that can or need be said is that the evidence indicates a considerable degree of responsiveness by applicants to changes in the grant level in early 1968. It supports the view, in other words, that the decision to apply for public assistance is, to some extent, a deliberate act influenced by the expected, if not the actual benefits of dependency status. Unfortunately, we are unable to measure with the precision we might like the actual relationship between the applications rate and the expected grant level.

The Acceptance Rate

As expected, there is a positive relationship between the applications and acceptance rates in all seven months. However, except for one of these months, none of the estimated coefficients even approaches usually accepted levels of significance. There is, in other words, no evidence to support the hypothesis that, during the period, applicants were encouraged by a greater willingness on the part of welfare officials to open cases at one center than at another. Nor is this conclusion altered by introducing lags in the acceptance rate on the assumption that it may take some time for changes in welfare center attitudes to be communicated to the low-income community.

Some Extensions of the Analysis

One can use the model to identify the direct and indirect effects of welfare rights groups on applications. The direct effect measures the groups' influence, among other things, because of contact by members with eligible nonrecipients, the publicity generated by demonstrations, and the contribution by welfare rights organizations to a general change in the attitudes of the indigent population. The indirect effect measures their influence on applications because of their influence on the grant level. Estimates of the relative importance of these two effects are presented in Table 16-4.

From February to April 1968, the indirect effect was dominant. Between 70 and 80 percent of the impact of welfare rights groups on applications occurred because of their impact on the grant level and the effect that the grant level then had on applications. However, after May, the welfare rights organizations had only a direct impact on applications. This change is the result of the shift in welfare rights tactics in May 1968 and the absence of any observable relationship between the applications rate and the grant level after that shift.

We can also estimate the actual increase in applications attributable to welfare rights activities and higher grant levels during the period covered by our study.[i] The results are presented in Table 16-5. For example, if welfare rights activity had no influence on applications in March 1968, the average applications rate for the entire city would have been 5.81 percent, rather than 6.10 percent. If there were no increase in the grant level between February and March, the average applications rate would have been 5.41 percent. Together, these two factors raised the March applications rate from 5.12 to 6.10 percent.

These results are converted to numbers of applications in Table 16-6. There were, on the average, 6,715 applications per month during the seven months between February 1 and September 1, 1968. In the absence of welfare rights

Table 16-4

The Direct and Indirect Effects of Welfare Rights Activities on the AFDC Application Rate in New York City. February through May 1968 (Percentages)

Month	Direct Effect	Indirect Effect
February	29.5	70.5
March	27.5	72.5
April	19.9	80.1
May	29.8	79.2

Source: Estimated from data presented in Tables 15-1 and 16-1. The reduced form equations are broken down into their direct and indirect components. The direct component is measured by γ_1; the indirect component by $\gamma_4 \beta_2$. For February, the indirect effect is given by:

$$\frac{\delta a}{\delta M} = \frac{\delta a}{\delta G} \cdot \frac{\delta G}{\delta M}$$

The direct and indirect effects for all districts are approximated by weighting the percentage distributions for the two subgroups by the proportion of districts in each subgroup.

[i]It is tempting to extend our analysis outside this period. In our judgment, however, this use of the applications rate model would not be justified and could result in misleading inferences.

Table 16-5
AFDC Applications Rates Attributable to Welfare Rights Activities and Higher Grant Levels in New York City, February through August 1968 (Percentage)

Month	Average Applications Rate per District	Average Applications Rate Attributable to:	
		Welfare Rights Activity[a]	Higher Grant Levels[b]
February	5.46	0.26	0.00
March	6.10	0.29	0.69
April	6.47	0.48	1.91
May	6.65	1.53	2.10
June	7.60	1.21	–
July	12.15	5.63	–
August	13.96	6.84	–

[a]Assuming as a base no welfare rights activity. Equations for $M \leqslant 5$ and $MD \leqslant 30$ are used for all districts; weighted average grant levels are assumed.

[b]Assuming as a base average grant levels in February and weighting the estimated applications rates for the two sets of districts by the number of observations in each set.

Source: Estimated from data contained in Tables 16-1 and 16-3. We have used directly estimated structural form coefficients.

Table 16-6
AFDC Applications in New York City, February through August 1968

Month	Actual AFDC Applications	Probable AFDC Applications Given Absence of:		
		Welfare Rights Activities	An Increase In Real Grant Levels	Both
February	5,757	5,543	5,757	5,543
March	6,059	5,771	5,373	5,085
April	5,970	5,527	4,207	3,765
May	6,350	4,889	4,345	2,884
June	6,067	5,101	6,067	5,101
July	8,516	4,570	8,516	4,750
August	8,292	4,229	8,292	4,229

Source: Estimated from data contained in Table 16-4 using the ratio:

$$\hat{A} = A \left(\frac{\hat{a}}{a}\right),$$

where A and a are actual applications and applications rates, respectively, and A and $\hat{a}$, probable applications and applications rates extracting the effect of welfare rights activities and higher grant levels.

activities and increased grant levels, there would have been 4,453 applications per month. In other words, these two factors explain about one-third of all applications during the period. Our results also suggest that, had it not been for welfare rights activities and increased benefit levels, applications would have fallen in 1968 from their record level in the two preceding years. Instead, the level of applications reached an all-time high.[j]

The Closings Rate

The third decision variable affecting the AFDC caseload is the closings rate. A certain percentage of AFDC cases is terminated each month. The greater this percentage, the lower the caseload increase.

Closings have risen steadily since 1966. This is understandable. There is continual turnover in the welfare caseload; one would expect closings to increase as the caseload rises. Far more significant has been a secular decrease in the percentage of cases terminated, or the closings rate (see Table 16-7). This

Table 16-7
Monthly AFDC Closings Rate in New York City, January 1966 through September 1970

Month	Year (%)				
	1966	1967	1968	1969	1970
January	2.4	2.2	2.3	2.2	1.9
February	2.8	1.9	2.0	1.7	1.7
March	3.0	2.3	2.2	1.8	1.9
April	2.6	2.1	2.0	2.1	1.8
May	2.8	2.4	2.0	2.0	1.6
June	2.4	1.5	1.4	1.8	1.6
July	2.2	1.5	1.8	1.9	1.6
August	2.4	2.4	1.8	2.0	1.6
September	2.2	2.0	1.7	2.2	1.6
October	2.5	2.3	2.1	2.4	1.2
November	2.3	2.1	1.6	1.8	1.4
December	2.0	1.8	1.6	2.0	1.6

Source: Computed from New York City, Department of Social Services, *Monthly Statistical Report*, various months.

[j]Once again, however, the measured impact of higher grant levels on applications is improbably high for April and May especially. What one observes, we suspect, may be the consequences of an improperly measured independent variable. The reader should therefore interpret these results with caution.

decrease supports the belief that, increasingly, welfare is becoming a way of life; rather than relying on welfare as a short-run expedient, families are, more and more, becoming permanently dependent on public assistance in New York City. In this subsection, we consider some of the reasons why this has happened.

One would expect the closings rate to be related to welfare rights activities; support in fair hearings and other efforts to protect recipients against removal from the welfare rolls have been important objectives of the welfare rights movement in the city. The closings rate may also be a function of the grant level (G) and the stringency of the welfare center administrations (S). The higher the grant level, the lower the number of welfare recipients who will choose to withdraw from dependency status; the more stringent a welfare center administration, the more likely that it will terminate a case.

The closings rate is significantly related to only one of the explanatory variables—the grant level—and then only after April 1968.[k] Welfare rights groups have influenced closings only through their effect on the grant level; they have

Table 16-8
Estimated Parameters of Linear Models Explaining AFDC Closing Rates, February through August 1968[a]

Month	Constant Term	Coefficient for the Grant Level (ϕ_4) (t-value in parentheses)	R^2	Sample Size
February	(b)	(b)		
March	(b)	(b)		
April	4.212	−.008 (−2.88)	0.21	33
May	5.125	−.010 (−3.47)	0.28	33
June	4.591	−.010 (−3.69)	0.30	34
July	6.470	−.015 (−5.76)	0.51	34
August	4.629	−.007 (−2.24)	0.14	34

[a]Unless otherwise specified, only those estimates are included that are significant at the 95 percent confidence level. Initial regressions were recomputed dropping insignificant variables to yield estimates presented in this table.

[b]No discernible relationship.

Source: Analysis discussed in text. Coefficients for the grant level are estimated directly.

[k]See Table 16-8. Because we found no significant relationship between the closings rate and welfare rights activity, we have estimated directly structural form coefficients for the grant level, ignoring the welfare rights variables.

had no observable direct impact on the closings rate.[1] Nor is the closings rate related to the measure of administrative stringency in any of the seven months covered by the analysis.

Our finding that the closings rate has been a function of the grant level is consistent with the results of our analysis of applications. It suggests, moreover, that welfare recipient behavior is economic; that welfare families respond rationally to price incentives created by the welfare system. As the payment rises, the supply of welfare recipients also rises. This is not only true at intake, but at termination as well.

It is dangerous to try to use this type of analysis to predict welfare recipient behavior outside the period covered by the study. Despite this warning, in Table 16-9 we present estimates of what closings might have been were there no increase in the actual grant level since 1966. (These estimates are computed from data presented in Tables 16-8 and 16-10.) Assuming the actual grant level to have remained unchanged, the average closings rate would have been 2.68 percent between April and August 1968.[m] This was only slightly above the actual rate during the same months of 1966.[n] It would appear, in other words, that a number of recipients have chosen to remain on welfare for longer periods of time because it has become more remunerative to do so. Most of the decrease

Table 16-9
The Estimated Impact of Higher Grant Levels on AFDC Closings Rates and the Average Level of AFDC Closings in New York City, April through August 1968

Month	Closing Rates (%)		Closings (no.)	
	Actual	At the Grant Level in Force in mid-1966[a]	Actual	At the Grant Level in Force in mid-1966[a]
April	1.98	2.36	2,840	3,385
May	2.07	2.80	2,925	3,956
June	1.52	2.27	2,164	3,232
July	1.90	2.99	2,849	4,483
August	1.88	3.00	3,869	4,578

[a]The average grant level, in 1968 dollars, was approximately $232 in mid-1966.

Source: Estimated from data presented in Tables 16-8 and 16-10. Case closings are taken from the *Monthly Statistical Report*, various months. Estimates of actual closings rates are unweighted averages per district. For this reason, they differ slightly from average closings rates for each month presented in Table 16-7.

[1]This is true regardless of the form of the equation and of the welfare rights variable and whether or not the sample is segmented by level of welfare rights activity in each district.

[m]In making this projection, we use the closings rate equations presented in Table 16-8. We assume, as a base period, the comparable five months of 1966. At that time, the average grant level, *at 1968 prices*, was about $232.

[n]See Table 16-7. The average closings rate during the same five months of 1966 was 2.48.

Table 16-10
Mean Values of AFDC Closings Rates and AFDC Grant Levels per Welfare District[a]

Month	Closings Rates (%)	Grant Levels (Dollars)
April	1.98	266.12
May	2.07	304.15
June	1.52	298.32
July	1.90	295.24
August	1.88	372.62

[a]Mean values are unweighted averages per month per district.

Source: Estimated from data presented in the *Monthly Statistical Report*, various months.

in the closings rate between 1966 and 1968 can be attributed to the increase in actual grant levels during that period.

Finally, in Table 16-11 we estimate supply elasticities from the closings rate equation. The impact of the grant level on closings, while not small, is considerably smaller than its impact on applications. A 1 percent increase in the grant level yields between a 1.1 and 2.3 percent decrease in the percentage of AFDC cases closed during the five months of 1968.[o]

Here, we do not obtain unbelievably large closings elasticities. These results tend to confirm our suspicions about the applications rate elasticities. In 1968, at least, applicants appear to have responded to expected grant levels that were considerably higher than actual grant levels. However, closings involve existing welfare recipients who, most likely, would respond to actual grant levels when terminating their dependency status. Existing welfare recipients have, presumably, reasonably perfect knowledge about the grant levels they receive. The actual grant level would seem, therefore, a more appropriate measure of the independent variable in our analysis of closings than in our analysis of applications.

Whatever, our analysis of both applications and the closings rate strongly suggest that the city's poor are economically rational. For much of the period covered by our analysis the poor responded positively to higher grant levels both in applying for, and terminating, their welfare status.

[o]For a comparison with elasticities of applicant supply, see Table 16-2.

Table 16-11
Estimated Point Estimates of AFDC Closings Rate Elasticities (Percentage)

Month	Elasticity
April	−1.1
May	−1.5
June	−2.0
July	−2.3
August	−1.4

Source: Estimated from coefficients presented in Table 16-8 and means of closings rates and grant levels presented in Table 16-10. Elasticities have been estimated at the means using the formula:

$$e = \frac{dk}{dG} \cdot \frac{G}{k}.$$

The elasticities are negative. To obtain the more conventional positive elasticity of supply, one might prefer to compute an elasticity of nonclosings. For our purposes, however, this would be a needless refinement.

17

Some Explanations for the Caseload Increase in 1968

Until now, we have disaggregated our analysis of the caseload increase by examining acceptance rates, applications rates, and closings rates separately. Now we put the pieces back together again; we try to determine the effect that each of the explanatory variables has had on the overall AFDC caseload increase.

The Simulation Model

To do this, we simulate what the city's AFDC rolls would have been had there been no change in each of the explanatory variables. Our simulation covers the seven months between February and August 1968, the period spanned by our analysis of applications and closings. Extension of the simulation outside this period would not be justified because of the highly volatile nature of the welfare system and welfare rights movement at the time covered by our study.

The reader is referred, once again, to the basic equation representing the caseload increase (see Chapter 13):

$$\dot{C} = raN - kC. \tag{17.1}$$

We now know that in early 1968 the acceptance rate (r) was an exogenous variable and the applications rate (a) and the closings rate (k) were determined, in part, by welfare rights activities and the grant level. Substituting the estimated forms of the equations for the applications and closings rates into Equation (17.1), one can then determine for each month during the seven-month period what the caseload increase should have been, given actual levels of welfare rights activity, the grant level, and the acceptance rate, and what it would have been had these levels been different.[a] In Table 17-1 we present the resulting equations explaining the caseload increase as a function of five variables—the acceptance rate, welfare rights activity, the average grant level during each month, the eligible nonrecipient population, and the AFDC caseload at the beginning of each month.

The simulation is by no means an easy exercise. Both the eligible nonrecipient population (N) and the AFDC caseload (C) will change each month with changes in each of the explanatory variables. If, for the sake of argument, there

---

[a]In doing this, we assume that the caseload increase in any given month is a function of the eligible nonrecipient population and caseload at the beginning of the month.

Table 17-1

Models Explaining the AFDC Caseload Increase, February through August 1968

February

$$\dot{C} = (-0.3683 + 0.00173G)rN - 0.020C \qquad (M \leqslant 5)$$

$$\dot{C} = (-0.3648 + 0.01173M + 0.00134G)rN - 0.020C \qquad (M > 5)$$

March

$$\dot{C} = (-0.4005 + 0.00186G)rN - 0.022C \qquad (M \leqslant 5)$$

$$\dot{C} = (-0.4553 + 0.01206M + 0.00170G)rN - 0.022C \qquad (M > 5)$$

April

$$\dot{C} = (-0.2097 + 0.00102G)rN - (0.04212 - 0.00008G)C \qquad (M \leqslant 5)$$

$$\dot{C} = (-0.2563 + 0.00994M + 0.00096G)rN - (0.04212 - 0.00008G)C \quad (M > 5)$$

May[a]

$$\dot{C} = (-0.08163 + 0.00051G)rN - (0.05125 - 0.00010G)C \qquad (M \leqslant 5)$$

$$\dot{C} = (-0.4752 + 0.01755M + 0.00155G)rN - (0.05125 - 0.0001G)C \quad (M > 5)$$

June

$$\dot{C} = 0.06388rN - (0.04591 - 0.00010G)C \qquad (MD \leqslant 30)$$

$$\dot{C} = (-0.01145 + 0.00169MD)rN - (0.04591 - 0.00010G)C \qquad (MD > 30)$$

July

$$\dot{C} = 0.06517rN - (0.06470 - 0.00015G)C \qquad (MD \leqslant 30)$$

$$\dot{C} = (0.08721 + 0.00164MD)rN - (0.06470 - 0.00015G)C \qquad (MD > 30)$$

August

$$\dot{C} = 0.07115rN - (0.04629 - 0.00007G)C \qquad (MD \leqslant 30)$$

$$\dot{C} = (0.06398 + 0.00206MD)rN - (0.04629 - 0.00007G)C \qquad (MD > 30)$$

[a]Grant level lagged one month.

Source: Estimated by substituting Equations (A.4), (A.5), and (A.8) in Appendix A, whose parameters are presented in Tables 16-1 and 16-8, into Equation (17.1). Where relevant, coefficients have been divided by 100 in order to present applications and closing rates as proportions rather than percentages. Directly estimated coefficients of the applications rate equations are used for March, April, and May. Where the relationship between a decision and an explanatory variable is insignificant, the average applications or closings rate is used for that month.

were no welfare rights activities after February 1, 1968, case openings would be lower. The eligible nonrecipient population would, in succeeding months, increase relative to the AFDC caseload. However, this adjustment in N and C, resulting from the absence of welfare rights activities, would generate a secondary and opposite effect. The increase in the population at risk would lead to a higher level of admissions while the reduction in the caseload would lead to a lower level of closings. Both would serve to increase the caseload. These secondary effects must be considered if our simulation is to be done properly.

To do this, we conduct the simulation month by month, taking care that adjusted and not actual values of N and C are used each succeeding month during the period. For example, let us assume once again that there were no welfare rights activities after February 1, 1968. The population at risk on March 1 would have been 119,990 rather than 119,964; the AFDC caseload 140,498, rather than 140,524. The divergence between the estimated and actual values of N and C would be still greater on April 1, and so on throughout the seven-month period. These higher estimates of the population at risk and lower estimates of the caseload must be used in the simulation in each succeeding month.

Another difficulty emerges in our estimation of N, the population at risk. We must have a measure of the number of eligible nonrecipient families in New York City. In Appendix C, we note that the measures of the population at risk upon which our analysis of applications rests are rough approximations derived from the very limited information available about the distribution of low-income families in the city. How, then, can a reasonably accurate estimate be obtained?

In all truth, it cannot. However, we approximate the eligible nonrecipient population for the city as a whole by the simple expedient of solving for N in the equations presented in Table 17-1. To do this, we substitute into the equation for February the actual values of the caseload on February 1, as well as the actual caseload increase, the acceptance rate, the membership rate, and grant level during February. The result of this computation is presented in Table 17-2.

Table 17-2

Approximation of the AFDC Caseload, Eligible Nonrecipient Families, and the Eligible Population in New York City, on February 1, 1968 (Number of Families)

| Item | Districts Where the Percentage of the AFDC Caseload Belonging to WRO Equaled: | | |
	Five Percent or Less[a]	More than 5 Percent[b]	Total for City
Caseload (C)	96,111	42,411	138.552[a]
Eligible Nonrecipient Families (N)	98,295	23,615	121,910
Total Number of Families Eligible for AFDC (C + N)	194,406	66,056	260,462

[a]Includes welfare centers serving a specialized clientele such as veterans.

[b]Includes Lower Manhattan, Gramercy, Amsterdam, and St. Nicholas districts in Manhattan, Borough Hall, Fulton, Bushwick, Clinton, Bay Ridge, Prospect, and Fort Greene districts in Brooklyn, and Jamaica district in Queens.

Source: Estimated from data contained in Tables 16-3 and 16-10 as well as the *Monthly Statistical Report*, using equations for February presented in Table 17-1.

This estimate of the population at risk provides the basis upon which the simulation is built.[b]

The Simulation Results

Our estimation of what the caseload increase might have been under different circumstances is a complex calculation requiring several assumptions.[c] The results are presented in Table 17-3.

Comparison of the Actual with the Estimated Caseload Increase

We start by assuming no change in the explanatory variables from what they actually were during each of the seven months. Our purpose is to test the predictive reliability of the model.

The simulated growth in the caseload over the seven-month period is roughly consistent with the growth that actually took place.[d] This finding is very

[b]One can make other estimates of the eligible nonrecipient population by choosing other months of the period. The February estimate has an advantage, however; it is in the middle of the range of possible estimates and, for this reason, gives one greater confidence that it is a reasonably accurate starting point. (Estimates of the city's eligible population ($N + C$) vary between 249,000 and 286,000 families during the seven-month period, depending on which month is chosen.) The reader should bear in mind that the results of our simulation depend, to some extent, on the initial estimate of the eligible population assumed. For this reason, these results should be treated as no more than rough approximations of what would have happened to the city's welfare rolls under different circumstances.

[c]We assume that the total number of eligible families remained constant at 260,462 families throughout the seven-month period. (See Table 17-2.) This means that each monthly increase in the welfare caseload was matched by a corresponding decrease in the number of eligible nonrecipient families. It also implies no change in the eligible nonrecipient population because of migration, desertion, or changes in eligibility rules. In addition, several problems arise because of the existence of two separate sets of regression equations for each month, depending on the strength of welfare rights organizations in particular districts. In the later months, there was some change in the composition of districts covered by each of the two sets of equations. This requires a rather complicated and tedious reassignment of the caseload and eligible nonrecipient population between each set each month. Also with one exception, both sets of equations must be treated separately in the simulation. The exception occurs in estimating what the caseload increase would have been in the absence of welfare rights activity. Then, we use only those equations for districts with little or no welfare rights activity, i.e., for districts where $M \leqslant 5$ and $MD \leqslant 30$.

[d]See columns 2 and 3, Table 17-3. Two discrepancies should be noted. (1) The estimated increase in the AFDC caseload exceeds the actual increase for the entire seven-month period by about 8 percent. (2) There is noticeable oscillation between the estimated and actual increase from one month to the next. In February, April, June, and August, the estimated caseload increase is greater than the actual increase; in March, May, and July, it is less than the actual increase. Both discrepancies can be explained, in part, by another, thus far unstated assumption of the simulation exercise. It has been assumed, implicitly, that an application in a particular month is acted upon by welfare officials in that month. In fact, there is usually some delay and, consequently, some carry-over of cases pending from one month to the next. One cannot expect, therefore, a precise month-to-month correspondence between the actual and estimated caseload increase.

Table 17-3

Simulated Changes in New York City's AFDC Caseload, February through August 1968 (Net Increase in Cases)

Month	Actual Increase in the Caseload	Estimated Increase in the Caseload[a]	Estimated Increase Assuming:					
			No Welfare Rights Activity[b] (no.)	(%)	No Increase in Grant Levels[c] (no.)	(%)	No Increase in Acceptance Rates[d] (no.)	(%)
February	1972	1974	1946	98.6	1974	100.0	1974	100.0
March	2639	2416	2336	96.7	1725	71.4	2197	90.9
April	2217	2616	2526	96.6	762	29.1	2325	88.9
May	3346	2370	1742	73.5	353	14.9	2078	87.7
June	2256	4262	3450	80.9	3925	92.1	3860	90.6
July	5596	5294	2736	51.7	5094	96.2	4976	94.0
August	4698	5675	3033	53.4	4946	87.2	5269	92.8
Total	22724	24607	17769	72.2	18779	76.3	22679	92.2

[a]Assuming actual levels of welfare rights activity, grant levels, and acceptance rates for each of the seven months presented in Tables 16-3 and 16-10. Average acceptance rates have been estimated for both sets of welfare districts.

[b]Assuming both M and MD = 0. This computation measures the direct effects of welfare rights activity only.

[c]Assuming February grant levels indicated in Table 16-3. The effect of higher grant levels on the caseload increase includes the indirect effect of welfare rights activity.

[d]Assuming an average acceptance rate of 74.8 percent for districts with little or no welfare rights activity and 74.5 percent for districts with substantial activity.

Source: Estimated from equations presented in Table 17-1 by means of the simulation discussed in the text.

encouraging, indeed. At this point, we feel like mechanics who, having disassembled an engine, have succeeded in putting it back together again.

The Direct Impact of Welfare Rights
Activities

If there had been no welfare rights activities during the seven-month period, the growth in New York City's AFDC caseload would have been 72 percent of what it actually was. Virtually all of the direct impact of the welfare rights movement on the caseload occurred after May, when the city's welfare rights organizations switched their tactics to more militant confrontation with the city's welfare administration. This was particularly true in July and August. During these two months, our analysis suggests that the welfare rights organizations accounted for one-half of the city's caseload increase.

Our analysis suggests, in other words, that both sides may be right in the controversy over whether or not the welfare rights movement has had an influence on New York City's caseload. It all depends on the period one is talking about. During the intensive campaign of demonstrations by the welfare rights organizations, from May through September of 1968, the movement appears to have had a significant effect on growth in the city's caseload; it was, it would seem, primarily responsible for an abnormal bulge in applications that occurred at that time.

This does not mean, however, that the welfare rights movement had little impact on the city's caseload prior to May 1968. To the contrary, because the movement influenced the grant level, it also had an indirect effect on applications and closings. This indirect effect, however, is not measured by the simulation results presented in Table 17-3. For this reason, our results understate the overall influence of the movement on the city's welfare rolls.

The Impact of Higher Grant Levels

The simulation suggests that about 24 percent of the caseload increase during the seven-month period can be explained by rising grant levels. However, most of the effect of higher grant levels occurs during April and May and is a result of the fact that, during these months, we estimated a substantial relationship between the benefit level and applications and a significant although less substantial relationship between the benefit level and closings. Once again, we suspect that the importance of the grant level has been exaggerated to some unknown extent by use of actual rather than expected grants in the applications rate equation (see Chapter 16). The grant level was probably related to the caseload during the period through its influence on applications. We doubt, however, that it bore as strong a relationship as is indicated by our analysis.

After May, roughly 8 percent of the caseload increase could be attributed to higher grant levels. This was because higher grant levels also affected closings which, in turn, affected the caseload. One consequence of the rise in benefit levels appears to have been some encouragement given to a slowdown in the turnover of welfare recipients. As a result, the caseload grew more rapidly than it would have otherwise.

The Impact of Higher Acceptance Rates

Approximately 8 percent of the increase in the AFDC caseload during the seven-month period was the result of higher acceptance rates.[e] Increased acceptances had only a direct effect on the caseload; there is no evidence that

---

[e]By coincidence, this percentage is nearly identical to that estimated in the analysis of the caseload increase over the five years between 1966 and 1970. See Table 13-3.

liberalized acceptances also influenced applications and closings. Of the three variables, liberalized acceptances is, once again, the least important. The claim that a more generous welfare administration has been the sole or even the principal reason for the rise in the city's caseload is an exaggeration. The rise in acceptance rates has been only one reason, and a relatively unimportant one at that, for growth in welfare dependency in New York City.

The Impact of the Welfare Rights
Movement on the Proportion of Eligible
Families on Welfare

Despite an approximately threefold increase in New York City's caseload during the first eight years of the 1960s, our estimates in Table 17-2 suggest that almost one-half of the eligible families in the city were not receiving AFDC in early 1968. Cloward and Piven, in a celebrated article, found the same percentage of eligibles outside the city's welfare system in 1960.[1] Our results suggest, in other words, that the growth in the city's welfare caseload prior to February did little more than keep pace with the growth in the city's indigent families.

What happened after February appears to have been a very different matter. From February 1 until September 1, 1968, New York City's AFDC caseload rose by 17 percent. At the same time, the eligible population in the city appears to have remained more or less constant.[f] Because of this, according to our simulation, the percentage of eligible families on AFDC rose from 53 percent on February 1 to nearly 62 percent on September 1. The extraordinary increase in the caseload in early 1968 seems, at last, to have made a significant dent in the proportion of eligible families receiving assistance in the city. As we have seen, this dent can be credited in large part to the welfare rights movement and, in particular, the direct effect of welfare rights organizations on applications and their indirect effect on applications and closings through the grant level.

[f]Using the same method to calculate the number of families eligible for AFDC ($C + N$), there was little apparent change over the seven-month period. For example, the estimate for August 1 is 254,885, which is slightly lower than the 260,461 estimate for February 1.

18 Conclusions

To talk meaningfully about the impact of welfare rights activities in New York City, one should first express the change in the caseload as a function of three decision variables—the acceptance rate, the applications rate, and the closings rate. The determinants of each of these variables should then be examined separately. In doing this, we concentrate on AFDC, the most controversial and rapidly growing category of assistance. We also focus on the first eight months of 1968, the period in which the city's welfare rights movement attained its greatest strength and the city's AFDC caseload grew most rapidly.

When we estimate the individual and cumulative effects of changes in the three decision variables, increased applications and, to a lesser extent, the lower closings rate have clearly been most responsible for growth in the city's AFDC caseload during the latter half of the 1960s. Far less important has been the higher acceptance rate. This finding calls into question the frequent assertion that liberal policies and lax administration by the city have been major contributors to the unprecedented growth in the city's caseload in recent years.

During the first eight months of 1968, welfare rights organizations influenced the overall grant level in their efforts to obtain higher special grants for their members. Moreover, the nature of their influence varied over time with changes in their tactics. Although the measured impact of welfare rights groups on the average grant level was small, the impact on the grant received by members appears to have been substantial. It is no surprise, then, that this was a period of rapid growth in the groups' membership.

The acceptance rate has risen since 1966. Although this increase has had a direct impact on the city's AFDC caseload, it has not had an indirect impact by encouraging applications or closings. Nor do our results support the frequent assertion that welfare rights activities have been at least partly responsible for the recent increase in acceptance rates.

The extraordinary level of applications in 1968 was the result of at least two factors. First, applications increased with the grant level. More applicants were attracted to welfare assistance the more remunerative this assistance was. In other words, welfare applicant behavior is economically rational. Our analysis also indicates that welfare rights activities had a major influence on the level of applications in 1968. The impact of these activities was both direct and indirect. Welfare rights organizations encouraged applicants, first, by the information and publicity resulting from their demonstrations and, second, by their influence on the grant level which, in turn, encouraged applications. The indirect effect was

181

strongest prior to the change in tactics toward militant confrontation with the welfare administration in May 1968. The direct effect was strongest after this change.

Finally, local welfare rights groups do not appear to have influenced the level of closings, even though one of their important activities has been to demand fair hearings and, otherwise, protest termination of assistance to member families. However, closings have been affected by the grant level in a way consistent with the relationship between the grant level and applications. The higher the grant level in a district, the lower the percentage of AFDC cases closed. This, too, suggests economic rationality on the part of welfare recipients.

The welfare rights groups emerge from our study as highly effective organizations during the period which we have studied. They were able to provide their membership with higher grant levels. This was a major benefit to the membership that, while it lasted, provided a private good, to use Olson's terminology, that helped to ensure to the organizations a rapid rate of growth and considerable influence on the city's welfare system. At the same time, these organizations helped to bring many eligible nonrecipients into the system by encouraging new applicants. Again using Olson's terminology, this was a by-product of their activities that did not benefit the membership directly. (Indeed, it may even have hurt the membership in the long run by strengthening opposition to the special grant and the welfare system as a whole.) Welfare rights activities provided a social good by assisting a larger percentage of families eligible for public assistance under the law to obtain it. The welfare rights movement provided, in other words, both private benefits to the membership and public benefits to the poverty population as a whole.

However, the foundation upon which the movement was built in the city was fragile. It depended upon the continuation of special grants which, in turn, depended on the mood of the state legislature. The successful exploitation of special grants by the welfare rights movement was largely responsible for termination of these grants. The strategy around which the welfare rights movement built its organization in the city was, in other words, self-defeating.

It is not clear, however, that the long-run effects of this strategy have, on balance, been injurious to the welfare population. Although the average benefit level in New York City, in real dollars, fell immediately after the abandonment of the special grant, it is probable that the benefit level would have been reduced anyway as the economy worsened and, consequently, the state's budgetary problems intensified. At the least, monies are now being distributed more equitably among welfare recipients than they were under the system of special grants.

Also it is not clear that the net effects of this strategy have been injurious to the welfare rights organizations themselves, as some critics within the movement have alleged. Had there been no special grant, the movement in New York City might have been much weaker today than it now is. The special grant was, in a sense, a once-and-for-all opportunity for the movement, available at the right time and in the right place.

If, however, welfare rights organizations are to continue to grow, they will have to find some substitute possessing the essential attributes of the special grant. This substitute must provide a clearly private benefit to the membership. The movement could, perhaps, discover some other means of attracting membership. Some leaders of the movement have suggested, for example, working toward a closed shop with welfare rights groups acting as sole bargaining agents with the city. This, however, seems like wishful thinking given the temper of the times and the comparatively powerless position of the welfare poor.

Another significant finding of the study is that low-income families are economically rational. Actual and potential welfare recipients respond to changes in the grant level both in applying for, and in terminating, their welfare status. The evidence suggests, in other words, that welfare recipients are aware of what is in their own self-interest and act accordingly.

Although economists have recognized this pattern of behavior since Adam Smith, others have not. There is a tendency, particularly among some welfare administrators, to think that low-income families require more than normal supervision because they do not act in ways consistent with their own self-interest. Low-income families may require some guidance in understanding the complex maze of welfare regulations that has been established by society and some organizational backing to push their way through this maze. However, probably no one knows better what is in his self-interest than the person himself. Our findings offer some evidence in support of this view.

Another bit of evidence is the speed with which the low-income population appears to respond to changes in incentives. Throughout, we have experimented with various time lags. With one exception (the May 1968 applications rate equation), there is no evidence that a lagged variable provides as good an explanation of the grant level or caseload increase as an unlagged variable. Applicants typically respond to current, not past grant levels. They also respond to this month's and not last month's demonstrations. All things considered, this suggests surprisingly good communication within the low-income community.

Finally, our study suggests some measure of eccentricity by local welfare centers. Prior to May 1968, different attitudes at different welfare centers seem to have been a factor in the distribution of special grants. The acceptance rate also varied substantially from one welfare center to another. This raises questions about whether standards were being applied equitably in determining need and eligibility and, if the system is not being administered equitably, whether it should be replaced by another that does not place a premium on the particular part of the city in which the recipient happens to live.

We have attempted to examine as best we can the impact of the welfare rights movement on New York City's welfare system. Much of the past discussion of the movement's impact has been descriptive and little more than informed opinion; there has been a dearth of hard analysis of what the movement has accomplished. We do not, for one moment, think that our study has fully satisfied the need for quantitative anlaysis of welfare rights activities. There is still much that can and should be done both on the city and the nation. Our study is, rather, more a beginning toward providing the analytical rigor that an understanding of protest activity and the welfare system requires. Even if we have succeeded only in pointing out some of the directions that studies of the welfare rights movement and rising caseloads might take, or some of the pitfalls they should avoid, we have succeeded in fulfilling a principal objective of our work.

Appendixes

Appendix A: A Model of Welfare Dependency in New York City

Specification of the Model

In this appendix, we develop a simple model for determining whether welfare rights activities, increases in the grant level, and changes in the attitude of the welfare administration have been responsible for the recent growth in New York City's AFDC caseload. Following the direction begun in Chapters 12 and 13, our model begins with the difference equation:

$$\dot{C} = raN - kC, \tag{A.1}$$

which expresses the change in the caseload ($\dot{C}$) as a function, among other things, of the caseload (C) and the eligible nonrecipient population (N). The model consists of three basic equations representing the three decision variables: the acceptance rate (r), the applications rate (a), and the closings rate (k). In particular:

$$r = f(W,S)$$
$$a = f(W,S,G)$$
$$k = f(W,S,G),$$

where W = welfare rights activity,

   S = the stringency of the welfare administration, and

   G = the grant level.

The exact form of the equations will be discussed later.

Several points should be stressed at the outset. First, we could construct a far more elaborate model with additional variables and equations. However, throughout, we are motivated by an interest in answering one fundamental question: What have welfare rights activities accomplished in New York City? While it would be informative to include in the model variables representing migration, family instability, and other factors that may have contributed to the rise in New York City's welfare caseload, we are precluded from this by the nonexistence of usable data. A more elaborate model would, for this reason, be of little more than academic interest.

Second, we estimate the size and significance of the effect of each of the explanatory variables on the decision variables by means of the familiar statistical tool, least-squares multiple regression analysis. For those readers not familiar with this method of analysis, it is a way of estimating whether and how several independent variables, operating at the same time, influence a particular dependent variable.[1] In our study, the three explanatory variables (W, S, and G) are independent variables; the three decision variables (r, a, and k) are dependent variables.

We should also note that a number of assumptions are made in applying this method of analysis to the question we have posed. Whenever possible, each of these assumptions is spelled out and its implications discussed fully. It should be stressed, however, that the analysis indicates only the most likely relationship between the change in the caseload and the various explanatory variables such as welfare rights activity. Our results appear more precise than they actually are.

We must choose between using cross-sectional and time-series data. Time-series analysis, with the year or month serving as the unit of observation, was ruled out because the data cover too short a period of time. Most usable data are available only for a few months of 1968. Moreover, during that period there were, each month, fundamental changes in the administration of public assistance and welfare rights tactics that are difficult to account for in the specification of a time-series model. For this reason, we rely on cross-sectional data, with the welfare district serving as the unit of observation.[a] There are problems with drawing time-series inferences from cross-sectional analysis. However, these problems are minor when compared to the difficulties generated by a time-series model.[2]

In this study, we estimate the parameters of regression equations explaining each of the three decision variables for each of the first eight months of 1968. This was the period in which the welfare rights movement achieved its maximum strength. It was also the period in which it underwent a basic change in tactics from relatively nonmilitant advocacy of member interests at particular welfare centers to militant demonstrations at most centers throughout the city. Our method of analysis is, essentially, comparative statics. By comparing the regression results for each month, it should be possible to determine not only whether welfare rights organizations have influenced the caseload, but also whether their impact has changed over time, for example, with changes in welfare rights tactics.

Finally, the model, as it is now specified, suffers from the problem of simultaneity. Not all independent variables are exogenous to the model. This problem arises in two ways. First, the acceptance rate is assumed to be a function of welfare rights activity. It may also affect the level of applications along with welfare rights activity. There is, in other words, a strong likelihood of multicollinearity or intercorrelation of two of the independent variables.[b]

[a]During 1968 there were more than thirty welfare districts in New York City, a sample size that is not overly large but, nevertheless, is adequate for our purposes.

[b]Multicollinearity results in biased estimates of standard errors and unreliable tests of significance for regression coefficients.

Second, both the applications rate and the closings rate are assumed to be a function of welfare rights activities and the grant level. Yet we know that welfare rights organizations focused their energies on obtaining higher grant levels for their members. It would not be surprising to find that the grant level is itself a function of these activities. Once again, the model as it is now stated runs a considerable risk of intercorrelation between two of the independent variables.

This problem can be resolved, in part, by introducing another equation into the model, an equation explaining the grant level; in particular:

$$G = f(W,S,F),$$

where F is family size. This equation states, simply, that the grant level will vary from district to district with welfare rights activities, differences in the stringency of the welfare administration, and variation in average family size. We now have a model consisting of four equations. The two equations representing the grant level and the acceptance rate can be estimated directly using normal least-squares regression techniques. The remaining two equations, however, must be estimated indirectly by first substituting the grant level and acceptance rate equations into the applications and closings rate equations and then estimating reduced form coefficients. In the following sections, we consider the exact forms these equations will take.

The Grant Level Equation

The grant level is expressed as a function of several variables representing welfare rights activity, as well as measures of administrative stringency and family size. The parameters of this equation are then estimated and their statistical significance tested using cross-sectional regression analysis.

We start by assuming a linear equation having the form:

$$G = \beta_0 + \beta_1 I + \beta_2 M + \beta_3 D + \beta_4 S + \beta_5 F + E, \qquad (A.2)$$

where G = average grant per AFDC case;

I = a dummy variable, where $I = 1$ for districts in which membership in welfare rights organizations is known to have been underestimated, and zero otherwise;

M = membership in welfare rights organizations in a district as a percentage of the district's AFDC caseload;

D = demonstrations in the current month or, alternatively, demonstrations in the current month plus demonstrations in the previous month;

S = one of the two proxies for the relative stringency of welfare center administrations, the rejection rate $(1 - r)$ or the percent-

age of closings due to failure of the recipient to comply with
departmental policy;

F = family size; and

E = the error term.

We use the AFDC grant per case as a measure of the grant level. This measure includes the basic as well as the special grant. For this reason, one would expect the grant level to vary from district to district with family size as well as welfare rights activities and the attitudes of welfare center administrations. It may also vary with other factors such as the age structure of families, the level of rents, and supplemental income from employment. We are unable to include these other factors in the equation.

The grant level is assumed to be positively related to the level of welfare rights activity in a district. We have two basic measures of this activity: membership in local welfare rights organizations as a percentage of the district caseload (M) and, after April 1968, the number of demonstrations held at each welfare center (D). Where possible, we have supplemented membership data for organizations affiliated with the NWRO with data for nonaffiliated organizations. We do not have membership estimates for all of these organizations. We do know, however, which are excluded, the districts in which they have operated, and when they were active. To test whether omission of these groups is a serious shortcoming of our analysis, we have included a dummy variable (I) in the model for welfare districts in which these excluded groups operated. We would expect the coefficient of the dummy variable to be positive.

The average grant level may also vary from district to district with the attitudes of welfare center officials. Some districts are reputed to have center directors, unit supervisors, and caseworkers who are unresponsive to the interests of welfare families and to pressures by welfare rights organizations. Other districts are thought to have administrators who are openly sympathetic with welfare families and the activities of the welfare rights organizations. We use two proxies for administrative stringency: the rejection rate and closings for failure to comply with departmental policy as a percentage of total closings. Problems may arise if one or both of these proxies is, itself, affected by welfare rights activity.[c] We would expect the grant level to be negatively related to closings for failure to comply with departmental policy and positively related to the acceptance rate.

Under law, the basic grant increases with the number of persons in a family. Family size varies from one part of the city to another, with welfare districts in Manhattan tending, as a rule, to have smaller families than districts elsewhere in the city. Therefore, one would also expect the grant level to vary between districts.

---

[c]We test for this possibility later. It is sufficient to say here that there is no apparent relationship between the two proxies and any of the measures of welfare rights activity.

The results of our analysis of grant levels are presented in Chapter 15 (see Table 15-1). It will suffice to say here that there is a statistically significant relationship between the grant level and welfare rights activity, one of the surrogates for administrative stringency, and family size, and that the nature of this relationship varies over time with changes in welfare rights tactics. In the remainder of this section we discuss some extensions of the analysis to determine, among other things, whether several of the assumptions we have made affect our results.

Extension of the Analysis to an
Earlier Time Period

We first estimate whether welfare rights organizations influenced the average grant level prior to 1968. Using 1967 membership data, we find no statistically significant relationship between the AFDC grant level and membership until the last month of 1967 and, then, this relationship is only marginally significant. Using 1968 membership data to analyze 1967 grant levels, we arrive at essentially the same conclusion. However, because the 1967 membership data are poor[d] and the 1968 data are not really applicable to 1967 grant levels, it is probably unwarranted to draw any conclusions from these results.

As expected, the grant per case was positively related to family size in 1967. However, we failed to find the expected relationship between the grant level and either measure of administrative stringency. In fact, for several months in 1967, the grant level was significantly related to the rejection rate, but with the wrong sign.

Extension of the Analysis to Other
Categories of Assistance

Although most members of welfare rights organizations are AFDC mothers, it would be useful to know also whether these organizations have influenced the grant level for categories of assistance other than AFDC. To this end, we have estimated the parameters of a parallel set of regressions for AFDC-U and Home Relief covering the five months between April and August 1968. Our results are reproduced in Table A-1.

There is a similarity between the results for AFDC-U and Home Relief, presented in Table A-1, and the results for AFDC, presented in Table 15-1. In

[d]There was a larger number of groups for which we had no 1967 membership data. Perhaps more serious, there was less certainty among informants about which groups were active or inactive in 1967, and, if active, in which districts. Because of frequent boundary changes, neighborhood groups would often find themselves working in several different welfare districts at different points in time.

Table A-1
Estimated Parameters of Linear Models Examining AFDC-U Home Relief Grants per Case, April through August 1968

Month	Constant Term	Demonstrations	WRO Membership	Closings for Noncompliance with Departmental Policy	Average Family Size	Corrected R^2	Sample Size
			Coefficients (t-Values in Parentheses)[a]				
AFDC-U							
April	−36.140		2.339 (1.88)[b]	−3.978 (−2.40)	63.051 (3.94)	0.60	33
May	66.716	3.574 (4.16)			42.259 (2.46)	0.56	33
June	c	c	c	c	c	c	
July	144.867				35.251 (2.06)	0.12	34
August	153.185				51.104 (2.37)	0.15	34
Home Relief							
April	89.056		1.813 (2.87)	−2.109 (2.46)	23.001 (4.16)	0.53	33
May	97.908	1.375 (4.01)			16.757 (3.58)	0.58	33
June	106.768				19.411 (3.20)	0.24	34
July	110.127				19.655 (3.17)	0.24	34
August	134.183				27.407 (4.17)	0.35	34

[a]Unless otherwise specified, only those estimates are included that are significant at the 95 percent confidence level. Initial regressions were recomputed dropping insignificant variables to yield estimates presented in this table.
[b]Marginally significant at the 90 percent confidence level.
[c]No discernible relationship.

April, membership is significant; in May, demonstrations; and in June through August, neither variable. However, the impact of welfare rights activities on the AFDC-U and Home Relief grant level is almost invariably smaller than their impact on the AFDC grant level. The welfare rights movement is predominantly an AFDC activity.

Tests of the Assumption of Linearity

Two of the three independent variables may be subject to diminishing returns. There is a point beyond which demonstrations and demands for special grants by welfare rights members will begin to lose effectiveness and may actually become counterproductive. Also, in New York State, basic grant levels increase with family size, but at a decreasing rate. Both factors suggest some nonlinear form of the equation.

We have experimented with several forms. Almost invariably, the simple linear form given by Equation (A.2) provides the best fit of the regression to the data. It is clearly preferred for the welfare rights variables; it is marginally better for family size. This choice of a linear relationship on the basis of goodness of fit is a critical juncture in our study. For reasons that will become apparent later, it establishes the form of equations that must be assumed in our subsequent study of applications and closings.

Tests of the Interaction between
Membership and Demonstrations

Finally, we estimate the parameters of an alternative form of the grant level equation:

$$G = \beta_0' + \beta_1' (D \cdot M) + \beta_2' (D \cdot I) + \beta_3' S + \beta_4' F + E,$$

where $D \cdot M =$ an estimate of the membership's participation in demonstrations each district each month, and,

$\quad\quad D \cdot I =$ a dummy variable to adjust participation for underestimation of membership in some districts.

This form permits us to test whether the interaction between membership and demonstrations has had an impact on the grant level or, conversely, whether it is more appropriate to treat each of these variables independently. Use of the interaction variable as a measure of welfare rights activity in all months explains less variance in the grant level than when the two measures are treated as separate independent variables. This supports our hypothesis that the two variables, membership and demonstrations, reflect two distinct sets of tactics employed by the welfare rights organizations at different points in time.

The Acceptance Rate Equation

The acceptance rate equation is straightforward and requires little explanation. The linear form is

$$r = \delta_0 + \delta_1 M + \delta_2 D + \delta_3 S + E,\qquad\qquad\text{(A.3)}$$

where r, M, D, and S represent, as before, the acceptance rate, the membership variable, demonstrations, and closings for failure to comply with departmental policy.[e] Once again, we have used cross-sectional analysis, with the welfare district serving as the unit of observation. Our analysis covers each of the 24 months of 1967 and 1968.

In none of these months is there a significant relationship between the acceptance rate and any of the explanatory variables. The acceptance rate can, in other words, be treated as an exogenous variable. This finding holds regardless of the form of the equation or the lag in demonstrations assumed. It also holds when we regress the applications rate on the interaction variable ($M \cdot D$) rather than regressing it on membership and demonstrations separately, and for AFDC-U and Home Relief as well as AFDC.

The Applications Rate Equation

We encounter three basic problems in our analysis of applications: measurement of the "population at risk," the existence of simultaneity, and specification of the applications rate equation.

Measurement of the Population at Risk

To determine the applications rate, one must first estimate the size of the eligible nonrecipient population (N), the pool from which applicants are drawn. Unfortunately, there are only a few rough and widely divergent estimates of this pool, and none of these estimates is given at the district level. For this reason, we have had to develop our own estimates for each month and welfare dis-

---

[e]We also experimented with the dummy variable accounting for possible underestimation of membership in some welfare districts. As in the analysis of grant levels, however, the coefficient of the dummy variable proved, in all instances, to be insignificant.

trict.[f] These estimates are discussed at length in Appendix C. We deflate applications in each month and district by the population at risk. Our dependent variable is the applications rate (a), the percentage of eligible nonrecipients applying for assistance. Because of the difficulties of estimating the population at risk, we have had to restrict our analysis of applications to AFDC and to the seven months between February and August 1968.[g]

The Problem of Simultaneity

We again employ cross-sectional regression analysis, using the welfare district as the unit of observation. We assume, first, that the applications rate bears a linear relationship with three independent variables: welfare rights activity, the acceptance rate, and the grant level. Treating the two measures of welfare rights activity as separate independent variables, this relationship has the form:

$$a = \gamma_0 + \gamma_1 M + \gamma_2 D + \gamma_3 r + \gamma_4 G + E, \tag{A.4}$$

where a = the applications rate,
  M = membership in welfare rights organizations in a district as a percentage of the district's AFDC caseload,
  D = demonstrations,
  r = acceptances as a percentage of applications acted upon,
  G = the average grant per case, and
  E = the error term.

Assuming that the two measures of welfare rights activity interact with each other, the equation would have the form:

$$a = \gamma_0' + \gamma_1' (M \cdot D) + \gamma_2' r + \gamma_3' G + E, \tag{A.5}$$

where, as before, $M \cdot D$ is an estimate of the participation of the membership in demonstrations in each district each month.

[f]We are indebted to Joan Wohlstetter of The New York City-Rand Institute for making these estimates. They necessarily rest on many heroic assumptions. Where possible, these assumptions have been tested. For most purposes, the biases resulting from them should not seriously affect the validity of our conclusions. When these biases have an effect, this has been noted and, where possible, our analysis modified to account for them.

[g]Some of these difficulties arise from the fact that welfare district boundaries are changed frequently. There were, for example, changes in boundaries at both the beginning and the end of the seven-month period, and once in the middle, in June 1968. The eligible nonrecipient population is estimated by aggregating health areas to obtain welfare districts. This is a tedious job made substantially more difficult by the frequent boundary changes. See Appendix C.

One problem with this specification of the model is readily apparent. We have included welfare rights activity and the grant level in the same equation even though it is known from Chapter 15 that, in some months, the grant level was itself a function of welfare rights activity. In other words, in the form in which the equation is now expressed, we are confronted with the simultaneous determination of grant levels and the applications rate and possible intercorrelation between of the independent variables. This problem should not arise, however, from the inclusion of welfare rights activity and the acceptance rate in the same equation. We have established in Chapter 16 that these two variables are unrelated.

Once again, the grant level equation has the form:[h]

$$G = \beta_0 + \beta_2 M + \beta_3 D + \beta_4 S + \beta_5 F + E. \tag{A.2}$$

By substituting Equation (A.2) into Equation (A.4), we can remove the grant level from the applications rate model by expressing it as a function of other variables:

$$a = (\gamma_0 + \gamma_4\beta_0) + (\gamma_1 + \gamma_4\beta_2)M$$
$$+ (\gamma_2 + \gamma_4\beta_3)D + \gamma_3 r + \gamma_4\beta_4 S + \gamma_4\beta_5 F. \tag{A.6}$$

Equation (A.6) is, in effect, a "reduced form" in which the various independent variables are not related to each other. However, we are now faced with still another problem. One cannot estimate the parameters of the "structural" equation [Equation (A.4)] from the reduced form because γ_4 is overidentified. To resolve this problem, we have forced γ_4 to assume a unique value by rewriting Equation (A.6):

$$a = (\gamma_0 + \gamma_4\beta_0) + (\gamma_1 + \gamma_4\beta_2)M$$
$$+ (\gamma_2 + \gamma_4\beta_3)D + \gamma_3 r + \gamma_4(\beta_4 W + \beta_5 F). \tag{A.7}$$

We have already estimated the betas (see Table 15-1); the gammas are now fully identifiable once the parameters of Equation (A.7) are determined.

This indirect method of estimation is necessary to the extent that intercorrelation results in biased estimates of the standard error and misleading tests of significance. One may find, for example, that welfare rights organizations have not influenced applications in a particular month when, in fact, they have, simply because there is a strong relationship between welfare rights activity and the grant level. Estimation of the reduced form equation protects against this risk.

The reduced form also permits one to determine much more from the data. It

[h]Because it was insignificant, we have dropped the dummy variable from Equation (A.2).

is now possible, for example, to separate the direct effect of welfare rights membership on the applications rate (given by γ_1) from the indirect effect (given by $\gamma_4\beta_2$). One can, in this way, determine whether in any one month the primary influence of welfare rights organizations on applications has been through their mobilization of the poverty population, perhaps by the publicity generated by their activities, or through their influence on the grant level and the encouragement that this, in turn, has given to applicants.

Specification of the Applications
Rate Equation

Each independent variable is measured the same way as in the grant level equation. We have also experimented with time lags for demonstrations, the acceptance rate, and the grant level, in the expectation that (1) there may be some delay between the individual's decision to apply for welfare assistance and his actually doing so, and/or that (2) his decision to apply for welfare assistance may, itself, be based on out-of-date information.

We also assume that the applications rate is a function of the acceptance rate. Applicants may be discouraged by welfare center administrations that turn away relatively large numbers of families requesting assistance. The acceptance rate is, in other words, a measure of the probability of success of an applicant. The higher this probability, the more likely that an applicant will apply for public support.

The applications rate should also vary directly with the average grant level in a district. The supply of welfare recipients should act like the supply of labor or a commodity—the higher the price, the greater the number of applicants making themselves available to society.

The problem of specification arises with the welfare rights variable. It would appear from scatter diagrams and experimentation with the data that a simple linear relationship between the applications rate and welfare rights activity is inappropriate. In districts that have had relatively intensive activity one finds, as expected, an apparent positive relationship with the applications rate. However, in districts that have had little welfare rights activity, there is little apparent relationship between the two variables. The evidence suggests, in other words, that a critical minimum level of welfare rights activity is necessary in a district if this activity is to have an influence on applications.[i]

Under normal circumstances, this might call for a nonlinear form of the equation such as quadratic, indicating increasing returns to welfare rights

[i]Figure A-1 represents a typical scatter diagram. For districts with relatively little welfare rights activity, there seems to be little or no relationship between the applications rate and the welfare rights variables. For districts with relatively high levels of activity, however, there is an apparent relationship. In some months, a step function is suggested, like that indicated in the figure; in other months, it is not.

membership. The problem, however, is that a nonlinear form would make the solution of the system of equations all but impossible. In effect, a linear form of the applications rate model is dictated by the fact that we have already found the grant level equation to have that form.

As an alternative, we break the linear model into two parts in the expectation that applicants will be highly responsive to welfare rights activity once a critical minimum level of activity is reached. In this way, we can simulate a stepped or kinked linear relationship between the two variables. This is the nearest expedient to a nonlinear form which permits an easily soluble system of equations.

A problem still arises, however, with the choice of the appropriate break points in the stepped or kinked relationship. Scatter diagrams suggest that the appropriate points are somewhere around $M' = 5$ and $(MD)' = 30$. Experimentation in the regression analysis with different break points generally confirms this. We should stress, however, that our results are quite sensitive to which points are chosen.

The estimated parameters of the applications rate equations are presented in Table 16-1. Once again, we have excluded those variables that initially prove insignificant by rerunning the regressions without them. In addition to the reduced form coefficients, we present two estimates of structural form coefficients for three of the seven months. One is determined algebraically from the reduced form coefficients; the other, directly by means of regression analysis. We have not included the reduced form equation for February in Table 16-1, even though there was a weak relationship between the grant level and welfare

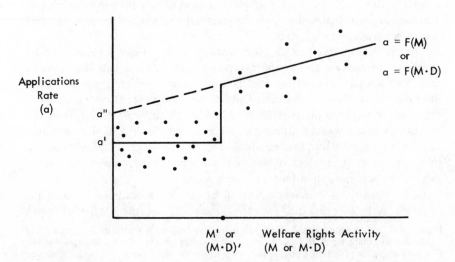

Figure A-1. The Relationship between the Applications Rate and Welfare Rights Activity in New York City

rights activity that month (see Table 15-1). It is clear from our analysis of applications in February that this relationship was too weak to have mattered.

The Closings Rate Equation

To determine which factors have influenced the closings rate, we again use cross-sectional regression analysis, with the welfare district serving as the unit of observation. We also restrict our analysis to the seven months between February and August 1968. The form of the equation explaining the closings rate (k) is similar to that for applications:

$$k = \phi_0 + \phi_1 M + \phi_2 D + \phi_3 S + \phi_4 G + E. \tag{A.8}$$

We are again faced with a problem of simultaneity arising from the fact that two of the independent variables—the grant level and welfare rights activity—are related in certain months. The treatment of this problem parallels its treatment in the section concerning the applications rate. We must first substitute the grant level equation [Equation (A.2)] into the closings rate equation [Equation (A.8)] and then estimate reduced form coefficients. The reduced form of the equation can be written:

$$k = (\phi_0 + \phi_4 \beta_0) + (\phi_1 + \phi_4 \beta_2)M + (\phi_2 + \phi_4 \beta_3)D \tag{A.9}$$
$$+ (\phi_3 + \phi_4 \beta_4)S + \phi_4 \beta_5 F.$$

Each coefficient is fully identifiable. We must first estimate the reduced form coefficients and then determine the structural form coefficients algebraically from the reduced form coefficients.

No other major problems are encountered in the analysis of closings. Our conclusions are, once again, presented in Chapter 16.

Appendix B: Measurement of Independent Variables

In Appendix A, the decision variables are expressed as a function of four independent variables. The parameters of these equations are then estimated and their statistical significance tested using least-squares multiple regression analysis. The purpose of this appendix is to explain how the four independent variables included in these equations have been measured.

The Grant Level

Measurement of the grant level requires several difficult choices. First, we deflate the grant level by the number of cases rather than the number of persons in each district. The grant per case, or family welfare income, is the relevant measure of the explanatory variable included in our analysis of applications and closings. This much is clear.

A more fundamental difficulty arises from the need to choose between the special and the total grant measure. Because only the special grant could be influenced directly by welfare rights activity and welfare center officials in New York City, choice of the special grant is preferred. However, our decision to use cross-sectional analysis and the nonavailability of suitable data dictate otherwise. The only published data on special grants by month and by welfare district are for clothing allowance and household furnishings. Until August 1968, these data were reported each month in the Department of Social Services' *Monthly Statistical Report*. They were deficient on two counts. First, there were many other types of special grants. Second, the published data on special grants do not distinguish between different categories of assistance. For this reason, one of our objectives—to determine whether the predominance in welfare rights organizations of AFDC mothers affected differentially grant levels for AFDC and other categories of assistance—would be impossible were we to use these data. We have unpublished data on all types of special grants for each category of public assistance. However, these data are available for the city as a whole and not by welfare district, and they therefore are not suitable for cross-sectional analysis.

We resolved this dilemma by utilizing published statistics on the total grant per case. The total grant per case (or the grant per family) is the basic grant supplemented by the special grant. Because at any one point in time the basic grant is, in theory, constant for a family of given size and composition, use of the total grant in cross-sectional analysis should do little violence to the hypothesis we are attempting to test. By holding family size constant, most of

201

the variation in the total grant between districts should result from variation in the special grant.[a]

We are primarily interested in assessing the reasons for higher grant levels for AFDC recipients. However, we also analyze grant levels for two other categories of assistance—AFDC-U and Home Relief—which, along with AFDC, support about 75 percent of the city's caseload and 90 percent of its welfare recipients.

Data on total grants per case, by month, welfare district, and category of assistance, are readily available in the *Monthly Statistical Report* and are therefore not reproduced here. We include only those welfare centers in our analysis that function in defined geographic areas. Several other centers now serve or used to serve a special clientele such as nonresidents and veterans. During the time covered by our study, these other centers handled less than 5 percent of all AFDC recipients and for the most part were not the object of welfare rights activities in the city. They can be safely ignored.

Welfare Rights Activity

We use two basic measures of welfare rights activity, membership in welfare rights and related organizations and recorded demonstrations in each district each month.

Table B-1

Membership in Welfare Rights and Other Welfare-oriented Community Organizations, by Welfare District, 1967 and 1968

		1967		1968	
Welfare District	Borough	Estimated Membership	AFDC Caseload in June	Estimated Membership	AFDC Caseload in June
Lower Manhattan	Manhattan	151	2,416	250	2,927
Gramercy	Manhattan	173	2,368	208	2,218
Waverly	Manhattan	a	a	24	1,131
Yorkville	Manhattan	68	1,659	94	1,865
East End	Manhattan	75	3,333	142	4,199
Amsterdam	Manhattan	174	1,433	96	1,543
St. Nicholas	Manhattan	265	2,319	385	3,296
Hamilton	Manhattan	b	b	16	2,220
Harlem	Manhattan	109	4,819	97	4,670

[a]The basic grant may vary from district to district to the extent that employment of welfare recipients and, therefore, income supplementation by the welfare system varies. However, in 1967 only about 5 percent of AFDC mothers also received some income from employment. For this reason, we are not overly concerned with exclusion of this variable from our analysis. See Durbin, p. 92.

Table B-1 (cont.)

Welfare District	Borough	1967 Estimated Membership	1967 AFDC Caseload in June	1968 Estimated Membership	1968 AFDC Caseload in June
Dyckman	Manhattan	0	4,052	83	3,778
Melrose	Bronx	32	7,162	333	8,952
Tremont	Bronx	8	5,064	132	7,147
Kingsbridge	Bronx and Manhattan	16	5,386	213	7,465
Concourse	Bronx	2	3,937	21	5,544
Mott Haven	Bronx	0	2,401	0	3,111
Fordham	Bronx	10	3,413	17	4,589
Soundview	Bronx	17	3,950	10	5,478
Queens	Queens	100	6,416	79	5,274
Jamaica	Queens	c	c	299	3,977
Borough Hall	Brooklyn	104	5,845	385	4,948
Fulton	Brooklyn	141	4,827	432	4,656
Clinton	Brooklyn	273	5,390	480	7,143
Wyckoff	Brooklyn	63	4,073	54	3,518
Greenwood	Brooklyn	0	3,164	0	3,988
Bushwick	Brooklyn	221	4,251	315	5,067
Linden	Brooklyn	0	4,263	213	5,896
Prospect	Brooklyn	91	3,761	261	4,846
Bay Ridge	Brooklyn	138	3,035	199	3,701
Brownsville	Brooklyn and Queens	0	2,485	13	3,366
Nevins	Brooklyn	d	d	175	4,838
Livingstone	Brooklyn	e	e	85	3,844
Fort Greene	Brooklyn	249	3,393	654	4,047
Williamsburg	Brooklyn	66	4,071	106	5,030
Richmond	Richmond	0	1,015	0	1,327
Total		2,546	109,701	5,871	145,599

aWaverly district was created in February 1968.

bHamilton district was created in June 1968.

cJamaica district was created in July 1967.

dNevins district was created in October 1967.

eLivingston district was created in November 1967.

Source: Group membership data were obtained from the office of the National Welfare Rights Organization, Washington, D.C., and various New York City welfare rights and community action groups. The AFDC caseload is obtained from New York City, Department of Social Services, *Monthly Statistical Report*, June 1967 and 1968.

Membership

The dues-paying membership in each New York City group affiliated with the National Welfare Rights Organization has been obtained from NWRO files. The membership data used in our study cover two years, 1967 and 1968. These data have been supplemented by information on community action and other local groups not affiliated with the NWRO but involved in the welfare rights movement. On the basis of discussions with local welfare rights organizations, we have also determined in which districts the various groups have operated and whether they were active or inactive during the year. By aggregating membership data for active groups only, we have been able to construct estimates of the membership in welfare rights and related organizations by welfare district. These estimates are presented in Table B-1.

We were faced with a problem in aggregating the membership data for individual organizations. Some organizations have been active in more than one welfare district. Should the membership of these organizations be assigned in full to each of the districts in which they have operated or be apportioned to each by some standard such as the districts' welfare caseload? The first method of estimating membership by district assumes, implicitly, that welfare rights members have come in contact with, or have been active on behalf of, a relatively wide cross-section of the city's welfare population; the second, that welfare rights members have been primarily concerned with their own or local interests. In estimating the grant level equation, the second measure provides the best fit of the regression to the data. Accordingly, we use this measure in all subsequent analysis.

Membership data are reported annually to the NWRO some time early in the summer. For this reason, in making the second estimate of district membership, we have selected the June AFDC caseload as the basis on which to apportion individual groups' membership to the districts in which they have been active. This raises still another problem: all welfare rights members are not AFDC mothers. However, most are; AFDC mothers account for more than 90 percent of New York City's welfare rights membership. For this reason, this is probably not too serious a problem.

The total membership in the city's welfare rights organizations is indicated by the sum of district memberships presented in Table B-1. Despite the fact that membership more than doubled between 1967 and 1968, it still amounted to only a little more than 4 percent of the city's AFDC caseload in the latter year. Clearly, the movement has represented a small, although extremely vocal minority of the city's welfare population.

One might expect welfare rights organization membership to vary from district to district with the AFDC caseload. However, the correlation between the AFDC caseload and welfare rights membership, although positive, is not significant.[b] Even so, we deflate membership in each district by the caseload.

[b]The simple correlation coefficient between WRO membership and the June 1968 AFDC caseload is 0.34.

Our first index of welfare rights activity is therefore a relative rather than an absolute measure. Because there is only one estimate of membership for each year, we have had to make the further assumption that the percentage of the caseload belonging to welfare rights organizations in June remained more or less constant for all other months of the year.

Finally, our estimates understate to some unknown extent the actual number of individuals active in the welfare rights movement. Some welfare recipients have been involved in welfare rights activities but have not paid dues to the NWRO. We know of the existence of some welfare-oriented community organizations not affiliated with the NWRO, whether they were active or inactive in either year, and in which districts they operated. However, we do not know the membership of these organizations. The districts in which membership is underestimated because some unaffiliated groups are excluded are:

Lower Manhattan	Dyckman
Gramercy	Melrose
Yorkville	Tremont
East End	Fordham
Amsterdam	Soundview
St. Nicholas	Jamaica
Harlem	

In our model we try to account for this underestimation by inserting a dummy variable for these districts. The dummy or shift variable will help to determine whether this underestimation of the effect of welfare rights membership is statistically significant.

Demonstrations

We also have data on the number of demonstrations at each of the city's welfare centers from April 1968, one month before the welfare rights organizations shifted to more militant confrontation with the welfare center administrations, through March 1969 (see Table B-2).

The data on demonstrations suffer from several deficiencies. First, they give no indication of the intensity of each demonstration, the number of persons involved, or who was involved. In effect, use of these data assumes that each demonstration had more or less the same intensity and, therefore, that a simple tabulation of the number of demonstrations is meaningful. Second, they give no indication of the intent of each demonstration. We know that most of the demonstrations were meant to secure higher benefit levels. However, some may have been staged to protest the treatment of a recipient or the closing of a case. Use of the data on demonstrations in the grant level model, for example, must assume that each demonstration, or at least a constant proportion of demonstrations in a district, was intended to secure higher grant levels.

Table B-2

Number of Reported Demonstrations at New York City Welfare Centers, April 1968 through March 1969

Welfare District	April	May	Jun	Jul	Aug	Sept	Oct	Nov	Dec	Jan	Feb	March
				1968						1969		
Lower Manhattan	2	5	6	6	4	4	0	0	0	0	0	0
Gramercy	1	2	1	4	3	2	0	0	0	0	0	0
Yorkville	1	1	0	3	1	1	0	0	0	0	0	0
East End	0	4	1	0	4	5	0	0	0	0	0	0
Amsterdam	0	1	8	2	0	1	0	0	0	0	0	0
St. Nicholas	0	1	2	1	0	2	1	1	1	1	1	0
Harlem	0	0	3	13	16	0	0	0	2	1	0	0
Dyckman	0	0	5	1	3	0	0	0	1	0	0	0
Melrose	0	13	4	0	10	0	0	0	3	0	0	0
Tremont	0	9	1	3	4	0	2	0	2	0	0	0
Kingsbridge	0	24	9	2	11	1	0	0	4	0	0	0
Concourse	0	3	7	0	0	1	2	0	0	0	0	0
Mott Haven	0	2	2	2	3	0	0	0	0	0	0	0
Fordham	0	2	2	0	2	0	0	0	0	0	0	0
Soundview	0	3	8	5	1	0	0	0	0	0	0	0
Queens	1	1	2	7	11	8	2	1	0	0	0	0
Borough Hall	2	8	2	4	7	0	0	0	4	0	0	0
Fulton	0	12	16	7	14	8	0	1	3	1	0	0
Jamaica	0	2	0	16	11	16	6	1	1	1	0	0
Clinton	3	20	9	10	23	6	1	2	1	0	0	0
Wyckoff	0	5	14	16	4	1	0	0	0	0	0	0
Greenwood	0	0	2	0	0	0	0	0	0	0	0	0
Bushwick	1	4	6	13	25	12	4	4	1	0	0	0
Linden	3	13	13	15	17	10	1	0	8	1	0	0
Prospect	2	6	8	12	14	5	1	0	1	2	1	0
Bay Ridge	0	9	6	7	1	2	0	0	0	1	0	0
Nevins	1	16	11	13	9	6	1	1	1	1	0	0
Livingston	1	1	8	2	3	0	0	0	1	0	0	0
Brownsville	0	6	6	5	8	1	2	0	0	0	0	0
Fort Greene	0	6	17	28	33	19	5	4	11	4	0	0
Williamsburg	0	2	7	3	0	0	0	0	0	0	0	0
Richmond	0	0	0	2	2	0	0	0	0	0	0	0
Waverly	0	0	0	7	0	2	0	0	0	0	0	0
Hamilton	(a)	(a)	8	0	0	0	0	0	1	0	0	0
Crotona	(a)	(a)	(a)	(a)	(a)	0	0	0	3	0	0	0
Bergen	(a)	(a)	(a)	(a)	(a)	(a)	0	0	2	2	0	1

Table B-2 (cont.)

Welfare District	1968								1969		
	April	May	Jun	Jul	Aug	Sept	Oct	Nov	Dec	Jan	Feb	March
Willis	(a)	(a)	(a)	(a)	(a)	(a)	(a)	(a)	9	1	5	1
Other	0	7	5	4	3	0	0	0	0	0	0	0
Total	18	188	172	217	213	113	28	15	60	16	7	2

aThe center was not in existence.
Source: City-Wide Coordinating Committee.

We also vary the use of the demonstrations data. First, one might expect some lag between a demonstration and the resulting increase in grant levels and the caseload. A lag of a full month seems excessive. Therefore we have also simulated a lag of one-half month by regressing each dependent variable in a month against demonstrations in that and the preceding month. In addition, as a crude measure of the intensity of a demonstration, we have regressed each dependent variable on demonstrations times membership per caseload in a district. The resulting statistic, which we call the "interaction variable," is a rough measure of the number of demonstrations by women in a district each month.

Administrative Stringency

We use two proxies for administrative stringency: the rejection rate and the percentage of Home Relief closings due to failure to comply with departmental policy.

Rejection Rate

The percentage of applicants accepted at intake and after review by each welfare center is published in the *Monthly Statistical Report*. This rate is available for each category of assistance, each month, and each district. The rejection rate is merely one minus the acceptance rate.

*Home Relief Closings for Failure
to Comply with Departmental Policy*

Data on reasons for closing cases are also published in the *Monthly Statistical Report*, but, unfortunately, only for Home Relief. Among these reasons is a category, "failure to comply with departmental policy." A decision is made by the caseworker, the unit director, or some other welfare official to close a case for this reason as a punitive measure against a welfare recipient. It is therefore a potentially useful proxy for the general level of stringency at the various welfare centers. Because the data on the two measures of stringency are readily available in the *Monthly Statistical Report*, we do not reproduce them here.

Family Size

The *Monthly Statistical Report* also contains data on the number of persons per case for each month, welfare district, and category of assistance. Once again, data obtained from this source are readily available and therefore not reproduced in this study.[c]

---

[c]A complete series of the *Monthly Statistical Report* is available at the New York Public Library and the city's Human Resources Administration, the parent agency for the Department of Social Services.

Appendix C: Families
Eligible for AFDC in
New York City[a]

To analyze AFDC applications to each welfare center, we first deflate applications by the number of eligible families not on welfare residing in the district served by the center.[b] The purpose of this appendix is to explain how the number of eligible nonrecipients in each district each month has been estimated.

Method of Analysis

The AFDC applications rate (a) in a particular district is given by the expression:

$$a = \frac{A}{c'\left(\frac{RP}{F}\right) - C} \qquad (C.1)$$

where A = AFDC applications in the district,
$\quad c'$ = the ratio of AFDC cases to the total caseload in the district,
$\quad C$ = the AFDC caseload,
$\quad R$ = the proportion of the district's population whose family income falls below the welfare eligibility level,
$\quad P$ = the district's population, and
$\quad F$ = average family size in the district.

With two exceptions, all the data necessary to estimate the applications rate are available on a district-by-district basis in the Department of Social Service's *Monthly Statistical Report*. The exceptions are the proportion of a district's population for which family income falls below the welfare eligibility level (R) and the welfare district's population (P). These statistics must be obtained from information generated outside the welfare system.

It is no easy matter to estimate the proportion of the poor to the total population, particularly by welfare district. The most recent small-area data indicating the distribution of incomes in New York City, available at the time of

---

[a]This appendix is based in part on the work of Joan Wohlstetter of The New York City-Rand Institute. Several pages have been written by Miss Wohlstetter.

[b]Throughout this study, we use the word "welfare center" to refer to the actual office having jurisdiction over a geographical area, which we call the "welfare district." New York City's Department of Social Services now uses the term "social service center" to refer to both.

this study, were collected in 1966 and refer to children enrolled in the school lunch program, not to the total population.[1] These data are by health area. Despite some difficulties, discussed below, the health area data have been aggregated to obtain welfare district estimates of the proportion of elementary school children participating in the school lunch program. We use this statistic (L) as a surrogate for the proportion of the people living in a welfare district who are eligible for welfare assistance (R).

Intercensal small-area population estimates are equally difficult to obtain. One study has estimated the number of people residing in city planning areas in 1965 and 1970.[c] To measure population by city planning areas in 1968, the year on which this study focuses, it is assumed that the 1968 population in each area was equal to the average of the population estimates for 1965 and 1970. City planning area population estimates are then aggregated to obtain welfare district estimates. The estimates of the proportion of children enrolled in the school lunch program (L) and the low-income population for each welfare district (LP) are presented in Table C-1.

Table C-1

Estimates of New York City's Low-Income Population and the Proportion of Elementary School Children Enrolled in the Free Lunch Program, by Welfare Center, 1968

Welfare Center	Number of Low-Income Residents	Proportion of Children Enrolled in Free Lunch Program
Lower Manhattan	59,467	0.525
Gramercy	64,512	0.424
Yorkville	128,528	0.364
East End	60,730	0.686
Amsterdam	65,299	0.535
St. Nicholas	64,718[a]	0.550[b]
Harlem	75,211[a]	0.680[b]
Dyckman	106,196[a]	0.584[b]
Melrose	98,225	0.507
Tremont	76,646	0.224
Kingsbridge	136,703	0.383
Concourse	54,464	0.410
Mott Haven	35,244	0.580
Fordham	79,105	0.233
Soundview	65,664	0.249
Queens	164,166	0.099

[c]Unpublished tables prepared by the CONSAD Research Corporation for the New York City Planning Commission. Most city-planning areas are identical to health areas; a few planning areas contain more than one health area.

Table C-1 (cont.)

Welfare Center	Number of Low-Income Residents	Proportion of Children Enrolled in Free Lunch Program
Borough Hall	38,478[c]	0.389[d]
Fulton	31,004	0.446
Jamaica	30,799	0.142
Clinton	67,622	0.481
Wyckoff	77,757	0.504
Greenwood	90,453	0.152
Bushwick	33,779[c]	0.345[d]
Linden	61,508	0.155
Prospect	70,879	0.346
Bay Ridge	61,887	0.175
Nevins	37,202[c]	0.422[d]
Livingston	40,404	0.403
Brownsville	49,941	0.326
Fort Greene	31,582	0.409
Williamsburg	63,542	0.454
Richmond	56,762	0.209
Waverly	102,062	0.456
Hamilton	79,764[e]	0.596[e]
Total	2,280,549	NC

[a]Estimates are for boundaries in existence between February and May 1968. In June, there were several district boundary changes. From June to August, the following district low-income populations are estimated: St. Nicholas, 54,134; Harlem, 61,034; and Dyckman, 64,863.

[b]Estimates are for boundaries in existence between February and May 1968. In June, there were several district boundary changes. From June to August, the following district poverty ratios are estimated: St. Nicholas, 0.638; Harlem, 0.667; and Dyckman, 0.648.

[c]Boundary changes in June 1968 affected three districts in Brooklyn. Because the Department of Social Services had no record of what the new boundaries were after June, their former boundaries are assumed in estimating the low-income population of these districts.

[d]Boundary changes in June 1968 affected three districts in Brooklyn. Because the Department of Social Services had no record of what the new boundaries were after June, their former boundaries are assumed in estimating the poverty ratios of these districts.

[e]Hamilton district was created in June 1968.

NC = not calculated.

Sources: Number of low-income residents estimated from data developed by the CONSAD Research Corporation for the New York City Planning Commission. Unless otherwise specified, estimates are for boundaries in existence between February and August 1968. The proportion of children is estimated from Nora Piore and Sandra Sokal, *Disadvantaged Children in the Neighborhoods of New York City*, Urban Medical Economics Research Report, New York City, Health Services Administration, August 1968.

The low-income population divided by the average family size provides a measure of poor families. The number of poor families is multiplied by the proportion of welfare families receiving AFDC, giving a rough measure of the number of poor families eligible for AFDC. We then subtract from this the actual number of families already receiving AFDC to determine the number of eligible nonrecipient families by district. Needless to say, these estimates of the eligible nonrecipient population are extremely rough and should be treated only as approximate measures of the pool from which welfare applicants are drawn in each district.

Problems with the Analysis

Estimating the eligible nonrecipient population by welfare district is a complex calculation based on a number of assumptions. Each of these assumptions must be examined to determine its implications for the analysis. This is the major purpose of this appendix.

Problems with Welfare District Boundaries

The conversion of data from a health area to a welfare district basis raises several problems. First, welfare district boundaries do not coincide with health area boundaries. Health areas are much smaller than welfare districts[d] and can therefore be aggregated to approximate welfare districts. Where boundaries overlap, health areas have been split between welfare districts by allocating the number of school children, school lunch program participants, and inhabitants according to the approximate proportion of the health area's land space located in the district.

Second, welfare district boundaries have not been constant over time. There were, in fact, boundary changes in at least five of the twelve months of 1968.[e] In most instances, these boundary changes were the result of the creation of new welfare centers from several existing centers. Boundary changes typically do not affect all districts simultaneously. However, they are frequent enough that, in any one year, most districts are likely to have been involved in at least one change. For this reason, it is dangerous to compare district welfare data over time. It is quite possible that one might be comparing two entirely different areas of the city.[f]

[d]In early 1968 there were over 500 health areas, compared to between 31 and 34 welfare districts.

[e]February, June, September, October, and December.

[f]St. Nicholas district is a good case in point. During 1968 the area designated by this name actually shifted from the Upper West Side to central Harlem. See Figures C-1 and C-2.

The mapping of welfare districts and the assignment of health areas to districts is a long and tedious process. It is primarily for this reason that we have restricted our study of applications to the seven months between February and August 1968, a period during which there was only one set of boundary changes. These changes occurred in June and affected several districts in Manhattan and Brooklyn.

Maps showing welfare district boundaries in early 1968 are presented in Figures C-1 through C-6. The names of these districts can be misleading because districts often are not located in neighborhoods of the same name. For example, in 1968 the Williamsburg district covered Greenpoint, while the area known as Williamsburg was in the Wyckoff welfare district. The Brownsville welfare district did not contain Brownsville at all. Instead, it covered part of East New York and Far Rockaway. There were many other anomalies in the designation of welfare districts, all resulting from the frequent boundary changes affecting New York City's welfare districts.

Problems with School Lunch Data

Use of the school lunch data is based on the assumption that the proportion of children receiving free lunches (L) approximates the proportion of the low-income families in a welfare district (R). There are a number of reasons why this may not be so. This is, perhaps, the major limitation of our analysis of applications.

Incomplete Enrollment in the Free Lunch Program. Not all eligible children may be enrolled in the free lunch program. To the extent that this is the case, the low-income population would be underestimated by this measure.

With the exception of welfare recipients, who are automatically enrolled, there is no standard procedure for informing parents about the school lunch program. Discretion is left to the principal and to other community sources of information. Consequently, there is likely to be a greater proportion of children enrolled in neighborhoods with active community action groups and heavy concentrations of welfare recipients. However, the school lunch program is thought to have reached most eligible children and, for this reason, this problem is likely to be minor.[2]

Attendance at Schools Outside Neighborhoods of Residence. The health area in which a particular school is located may not be the same as the area the school serves.[3] There may be attendance at schools in one health area by children living in another. However, this is also likely to involve nearby health areas falling within the same welfare district. The Bureau of Pupil Transportation estimates that, under the open enrollment plan, only about 10 percent of public

Figure C-1. Manhattan, February through May 1968

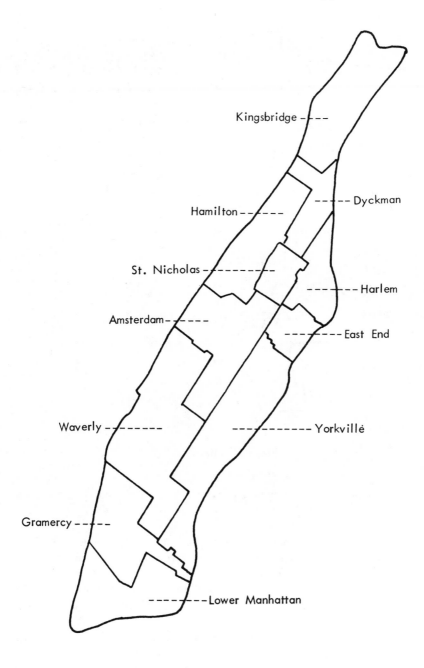

Figure C-2. Manhattan, June through August 1968

Figure C-3. Bronx

elementary school children attend schools relatively distant from their neighborhoods. This, too, should not be a serious limitation of our study.

Underestimation of Elementary School Enrollment. All public and most Catholic elementary schools participate in the free lunch program. With the exception of a few Greek Orthodox and Protestant elementary schools, non-Catholic private schools do not participate. In general, schools that do not participate serve relatively affluent segments of the city's population and account for less than 5 percent of total elementary school enrollment in the city.[g] Even so, if their student body is drawn from a few neighborhoods, the estimates of the poverty ratio could be substantially overstated and the estimates of the applications rate understated for welfare centers serving these neighborhoods.

---

[g]Information provided by the Board of Education.

Figure C-4. Queens

Available information on private school enrollment gives us the location of the school rather than the residence of students. As a result, we have had to make guesses as to which districts are likely to have substantial enrollment in non-Catholic private schools. These are: Yorkville, which covers most of the high-income areas of the East Side; Gramercy, which contains Greenwich Village; St. Nicholas, which until June 1968 covered the area around Columbia University; Hamilton, which after June 1968 contained this area; and Amsterdam, which covers much of the West Side. We have experimented with dummy

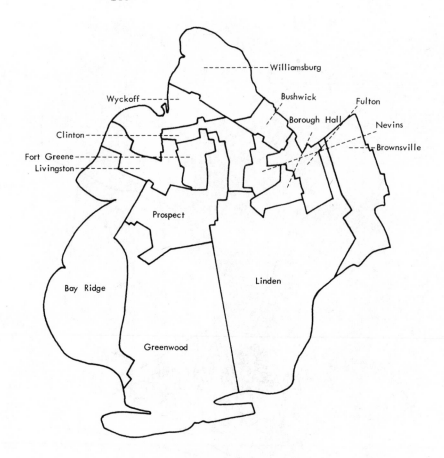

Figure C-5. Brooklyn

variables for these five districts in the applications rate equation in the expectation that they would account for any underestimation of the dependent variable resulting from incomplete measurement of total school enrollment in these districts. However, in no instance are their estimated coefficients significant with the right sign.[h] This finding suggests that underestimation of elementary school enrollment in some districts is not a serious problem.

Differences in Time. A far more serious problem with our measure of the poverty population arises from the fact that the school lunch data are for 1966,[i] while all other data are for 1968. There is no way of knowing how much the

[h]In some months, they were significant with *wrong* sign.

[i]School registration figures are for March 1966 and school lunch program figures for October 1966.

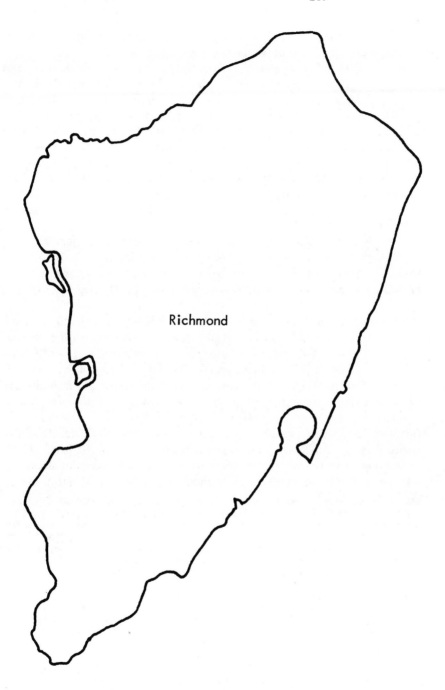

Figure C-6. Richmond

city's welfare districts may have changed during this period. There are indications, however, that some of the districts were substantially transformed.

When application rates were calculated for the city's welfare districts, rates for two districts were extraordinarily high for all months and, in some months, actually exceeded 100 percent. The districts are Fulton and Bushwick, both in Brooklyn. Upon investigation, it was found that, between 1966 and 1968, there was, in fact, a significant change in the socioeconomic character of these districts.[j] Were one to use the 1966 school lunch data to estimate the 1968 poverty population, it would bias upward estimates of the applications rate for these districts and, parenthetically, measures of the effectiveness of welfare rights groups. To avoid problems from this bias, we have chosen, instead, to drop both districts from our analysis, even though both have had quite active welfare rights organizations.

For one month, May 1968, Nevins district also registered an unusually high applications rate. We suspect an error in reporting or printing by the Department of Social Services that we are unable to correct without further information. For this reason, we have also dropped Nevins district from the May regressions.

Differences between Income Eligibility Levels. Finally, we come to the most serious problem of all. The income eligibility level for the free lunch program is not the same as the eligibility level for welfare assistance (see Table C-3). To enroll its children in the free lunch program in 1966, a family of five could not earn more than $5,096. Since the program has been administered generously and bears relatively little stigma, certainly in comparison to welfare, the actual income eligibility figure may have been somewhat higher. Between January and October 1968, the annual basic welfare allowance for an AFDC family of five ranged between $3,006 and $4,038, depending on the age of the oldest child.[k] In addition, the welfare family receives free medical care, a laundry allowance, and special grants. In an apartment without central heating, it might also be

---

[j]One outgrowth of The New York City-Rand Institute's work for New York City's Fire Department has been the suggestion that the increased incidence of fires in an area of the city might serve as an indicator of its social and economic deterioration. Data on fire neighborhoods have been aggregated over welfare districts in the same way that data for health and city planning areas have been aggregated. The data do, indeed, indicate that Fulton and Bushwick districts have had the highest increase in fire incidence. (See Table C-2.) They also indicate a relatively high increase in fire incidence in the Brooklyn portion of Brownsville district, another welfare district in which there has tended to be an abnormally large applications rate.

A second measure of social and economic change in an area of the city is increased juvenile delinquency. Again, the highest rate of increase has occurred in Fulton, Bushwick, and, to a lesser extent, the Brooklyn portions of Brownsville district. However, there was also a relatively large increase in Greenwood district, an area of the city that has not had an especially high rate of applications for public assistance. (Again, see Table C-2.)

[k]In general, the allowance is the same as the income eligibility level for a family with income from no other sources. However, the income eligibility level would be higher for an AFDC family participating in the work incentive program. This is probably a minor problem since only a few AFDC families have actually participated in this program.

Table C-2

Increase in Fire Incidence and Juvenile Delinquency in Brooklyn Welfare Districts, 1966-1968 (Ratio of the 1968 to the 1966 Rate)

Brooklyn Welfare Districts	Fire Alarms	Juvenile Delinquency
Fulton	1.84	1.40
Bushwick	1.69	1.50
Brownsville	1.69	1.34
Clinton	1.56	1.20
Williamsburg	1.54	1.05
Prospect	1.48	1.24
Livingston	1.48	1.17
Bay Ridge	1.48	1.14
Wyckoff	1.46	1.03
Fort Greene	1.45	1.24
Borough Hall	1.45	1.07
Nevins	1.40	1.11
Greenwood	1.36	1.48
Linden	1.23	1.25
Average	1.46	1.24

Source: Data on fire incidence are based on unpublished statistics collected by the city's Fire Department and have been obtained from Edward Blum, former head of The New York City-Rand Institute's fire project. Data on juvenile delinquency are based on unpublished data provided by the New York City Youth Board and obtained from Robert Yin of The Rand Corporation, Washington, D.C.

given an allowance for heating, although, at the same time, it would presumably pay, and therefore receive less for, rent. However, these special allowances do not enter into the determination of whether or not the family is eligible for welfare assistance.

The welfare eligibility income level is well below the school lunch program eligibility level. For this reason, use of the school lunch data would tend to bias the applications rate downward. It is essential that we consider what this bias is likely to do to our analysis of applications.

Ideally, we should use the measure of the dependent variable, a, given by Equation (C.1). In fact, we have used a^*, where

$$a^* = \frac{A}{c'\left(\dfrac{LP}{F}\right) - C}, \tag{C.2}$$

Table C-3

Eligibility Levels for the School Lunch Program and AFDC Assistance in New York City (Dollars of Annual Income)

Type of Assistance	Family Size (Number of Members)					
	2	3	4	5	6	7
School Lunch Program[a]	3,120	3,900	4,524	5,096	5,720	6,344
AFDC Assistance[b]						
Minimum allowance[c]	1,940	2,430	2,718	3,006	3,353	3,713
Maximum allowance	2,228	2,982	3,510	4,038	4,601	5,057

[a]Effective September 1, 1965. The eligibility level measures gross or before-tax income.

[b]Effective January 1, 1968 to October 1, 1968. The welfare assistance level includes payments for food, clothing, personal incidental purchases, household supplies, school, utilities, sales taxes, and "typical" shelter. Variation between the minimum and maximum level depends on the age of children.

[c]The minimum payment level is for families in which all children were under six years of age. For this reason, minimum payment standards for large families are more hypothetical than real.

Source: Welfare data have been taken from New York City, Department of Social Services, Forms W-634 and M-197, January 1968; lunch program data, from Priore and Sokal.

and where L is the school lunch ratio. The problem arises because $L > R$ and, therefore, $a > a^*$.

If one can assume that the percentage of error in the poverty ratio is constant for each district, then

$$L = kR. \tag{C.3}$$

If one can assume, also, that the percentage of error in the dependent variable is constant for each district, then,

$$a = (1 + g)a^*. \tag{C.4}$$

Then, from Equations (C.1) through (C.4),

$$FC = \frac{1 + g - k}{gk} (LP) = g'(LP). \tag{C.5}$$

If $g > 0$, then use of L as a measure of R will result in a bias in both estimates of regression coefficients and their standard errors. However, because the formulas for both are linear and homogeneous with respect to the dependent variable, the usual tests of the coefficients' significance are unbiased. In other words, while we may not be able to estimate the true coefficient or its standard error, the t-statistics given by the ratio of the two should be unaffected.[1]

We must demonstrate that this in fact is the case. To do so, we must first demonstrate that Equation (C.4) is, itself, linear and homogeneous—that is, that FC/LP is a constant. Using data for April 1968, we have regressed FC on LP to estimate the coefficient, g'. This estimate is positive and significant, as expected, while the constant term is not significantly different from zero.[m]

It is useful to have at least a rough estimate of g, the bias in the dependent variable resulting from the use of L instead of R. However, to obtain this, we must first estimate k, which in turn requires that we know R, the statistic we do not have.

As a first approximation of the proportion of families eligible for welfare, we use 1960 census data on the proportion of families with incomes less than $3,000 (see Table C-4). This income level was nearly equal to the minimum welfare eligibility level for a family of five in 1968 and almost certainly understates the eligible population. As a second approximation, we use the proportion of families in 1960 with incomes less than $5,000, an amount only slightly below the 1968 eligibility level for the school lunch program. The true eligibility level for welfare recipients should fall within this range.

For the proportion of families with incomes less than $3,000, k is 1.93.[n] For the proportion of families with incomes less than $5,000, k is 1.06.[o] These results support our assumptions of linearity and homogeneity. They also imply that the proportion of the city's families with incomes less than $5,000 actually increased slightly, by about 6 percent, between 1960 and 1966. However, most of the differences between R and L appear to be a result of the different income

---

[1] Using standard notation, where each X_i is an independent variable and $a = Y$, the dependent variable:

$$B = (X'X)^{-1}X'Y \text{ and } B^* = (X'X)^{-1}X'Y^*,$$

where

$$Y = (1 + g) Y^*.$$

Therefore,

$$B = (1 + g) B^*.$$

Also

$$S_{X \cdot Y} = \sigma^2 (X'X)^{-1},$$

where

$$\sigma^2 = Y'Y - B'X'Y.$$

Similarly,

$$\sigma^{*2} = Y^{*'}Y^* - B^{*'}X'Y^*.$$

Therefore,

$$S_{Y \cdot X} = (1 + g) S_{Y^* \cdot X}.$$

[m] The coefficient $g' = 1.65$ with a standard error of 0.54. The constant term is 21,664 with a standard error of 21,604.

[n] The standard error of the estimate is 0.159, indicating a high level of significance. The estimated constant term is 0.00002 with a standard error of 0.175.

[o] The coefficient is again highly significant, with a standard error of 0.100. The estimated constant term is -0.081; the standard error of the constant term, 0.247.

Table C-4

The Incidence of Low-Income Residents in New York City Welfare Districts, 1960 (Proportion of the Welfare District Population)

Welfare District (April 1968 Boundaries)	Annual Family Income Less than	
	$3,000	$5,000
Lower Manhattan	0.311	0.631
Gramercy	0.234	0.475
Yorkville	0.132	0.300
East End	0.364	0.708
Amsterdam	0.247	0.457
St. Nicholas	0.268	0.531
Harlem	0.347	0.683
Dyckman	0.275	0.589
Melrose	0.237	0.551
Tremont	0.139	0.367
Kingsbridge	0.160	0.388
Concourse	0.171	0.395
Mott Haven	0.235	0.528
Fordham	0.132	0.313
Soundview	0.132	0.336
Queens	0.082	0.226
Borough Hall	0.278	0.602
Fulton	0.193	0.451
Jamaica	0.085	0.232
Clinton	0.253	0.566
Wyckoff	0.260	0.563
Greenwood	0.133	0.309
Bushwick	0.164	0.422
Linden	0.108	0.285
Prospect	0.161	0.368
Bay Ridge	0.133	0.331
Nevins	0.249	0.574
Livingston	0.229	0.460
Brownsville	0.159	0.381
Fort Greene	0.238	0.509
Williamsburg	0.190	0.459
Richmond	0.096	0.247
Waverly	0.201	0.395

Source: *1960 Census*. We are indebted to Elizabeth Durbin, who provided us with the census tapes and assisted in their interpretation.

levels used to determine eligibility for the welfare and the school lunch programs, and not the larger proportion of low-income families in the city's population.

If k were equal to 1.93, g would equal 1.25. In other words, the actual applications rate would be more than double the estimated rate used in our analysis. However, this represents an upper limit to the bias inherent in our method of estimating the applications rate, both because of the slight increase in the number of low-income families in the city during the early 1960s and, more important, the unduly large disparity between income eligibility levels assumed in our use of the 1960 census data. Setting k equal to 1.06, g would be 0.23. Clearly, there is a rather broad range within which the actual bias lies.

For some purposes, underestimation of the applications rate is a serious problem. However, we are primarily concerned with whether there is a statistically significant relationship between this rate and the various explanatory variables. This appendix demonstrates that, although the regression coefficients and their standard errors may be biased, the usual tests of significance are not. Our results should, however, be used with this limitation clearly in mind.

Problems with Welfare District
Population Estimates

The population estimates for welfare districts are straightforward and require little discussion. They are simply aggregates of CONSAD's city-planning-area population estimates based on essentially the same assignment of health areas to welfare districts used to compute school lunch ratios for each district.[P] CONSAD's estimates are very rough. However, the weaknesses of these estimates lie in their breakdown of the city's population by specific characteristics such as race and age. Persons familiar with the CONSAD data are generally agreed that the basic population estimates are reasonably accurate.

Comparison with Other Estimates
of the Population at Risk

In spite of all these problems with the data, our estimates of the eligible welfare population approximate estimates made by others. On the basis of our calculations, the total poverty population (LP) for the entire city works out to be 2.28 million (see Table C-1). Dividing by k equal to 1.93 to adjust for a more appropriate welfare income eligibility level, an alternative estimate of the poverty population (RP) is 1.18 million. The first estimate is almost certainly

PPlanning and health areas are, with a few exceptions, coterminous.

too high; the second, too low. Another study puts the eligible population at 1.64 million in 1969, about midway within the range estimated here.[4] A third study places the eligible population at 1.04 million in 1968, somewhat below this range.[5] However, this second estimate is too low. There were in 1968, 1.05 million welfare recipients in the city and, by definition, all 1.05 million must have had family incomes at or below the welfare eligibility level unless a sizable number of recipients were ineligible or enrolled in special programs for the partially employed in which higher than eligibility level incomes were permitted.

Notes

Notes

Chapter 1
Introduction

1. The number of recipients each month is published in city of New York, Department of Social Services, Division of Statistics, *Monthly Statistical Report*, various months, 1960 and 1970. The 1960 estimate used in this calculation is the average monthly caseload for all twelve months of the year; the 1970 estimate, the average for the first eight months of the year. Population data are obtained from the *1960 Census* and preliminary reports of the *1970 Census*.

2. Committee on Ways and Means, U.S. House of Representatives, *Report on Findings of a Special Review of Aid to Families with Dependent Children in New York City* (Washington, D.C.: U.S. Government Printing Office, September 24, 1969).

3. Again, population estimates are taken from the *1960 Census* and preliminary reports of the *1970 Census*. The 1960 estimate of the national welfare population has been made, in part, from data contained in the Social Security Administration's *Social Security Bulletin* for that year. However, federal data for 1960 do not include General Assistance (or, in New York City, Home Relief) recipients, who are entirely state and locally supported. As an estimate of the total number of General Assistance recipients in the nation we have assumed the average of HEW's estimates of recipients of General Assistance in June and December of that year. These data are obtained from U.S. Department of Health, Education, and Welfare, Social and Rehabilitation Service, Assistance Payments Administration, *Trend Report: Graphic Presentation of Public Assistance and Related Data*, (Washington, D.C.: U.S. Government Printing Office, 1966). The number of recipients in 1970 is estimated from data for January through July 1970, contained in U.S. Department of Health, Education, and Welfare, Social and Rehabilitation Service, National Center for Social Statistics, *Public Assistance Statistics*, NCSS Report A-2, (Washington, D.C.: U.S. Government Printing Office, 1970). See also the *Social Security Bulletin*. The 1970 federal data include General Assistance recipients. Data for both years exclude recipients in Guam, Puerto Rico, and the Virgin Islands.

4. *Monthly Statistical Report*, various months.

Chapter 2
Theories of Protest and Organizational
Activity

1. One obvious example is labor. The union-sponsored strike is, by and large, an instrument of middle-class labor. For a review of interest groups in the United

States and their use of protest, see Samuel I. Eldersveld, "American Interest Groups: A Survey of Research and Some Implications for Theory and Method," in Henry W. Ehrmann (ed.), *Interest Groups on Four Continents* (Pittsburgh, Pa.: The University of Pittsburgh Press, 2nd printing, 1960), pp. 173-96.

2. Sidney Verba, "Democratic Participation," *The Annals of the American Academy of Political and Social Science* 363 (September 1967): 53-78.

3. For a discussion of the politics and administration of welfare prior to the mid-1960s, see Gilbert Steiner, *Social Insecurity: The Politics of Welfare* (Chicago, Ill.: Rand McNally, 1966), Ch. 1.

4. Samuel Lubell, *The Hidden Crisis in American Politics*, (New York: W.W. Norton and Company, 1970), pp. 42-43 and 221-222.

5. Amitai Etzioni, "Demonstration Democracy," Paper prepared for the Task Force on Demonstrations, Protests, and Group Violence of the President's National Commission on the Causes and Prevention of Violence, Washington, D.C., November 18, 1968, p. 1.

6. Ibid., p. 4.

7. Ibid., pp. 5-7. However, Etzioni allows that blacks and students probably participate with a higher degree of frequency than other groups.

8. Donald Matthews and James Prothro, *Negroes and the New Southern Politics*, (New York: Harcourt, Brace and World, 1966); Ruth Searles and J. Allen Williams, Jr., "Negro College Students' Participation in Sit-ins," *Social Forces* 40 (March 1962): 215-22; John Orbell, "Protest Participation among Southern Negro College Students," *American Political Science Review* 61 (June 1967): 446-56; Martin Oppenheimer, "The Genesis of the Southern Negro Student Movement," Ph.D. dissertation, University of Pennsylvania, 1963.

9. The classic work is still James Q. Wilson's *Negro Politics, The Search for Leadership* (Glencoe, Ill.: The Free Press, 1960). For studies of specific southern communities, see Daniel Thompson, *The Negro Leadership Class* (Englewood Cliffs, N.J.: Prentice-Hall, Inc., 1963); Margaret Elaine Burgess, *Negro Leadership in a Southern City* (Chapel Hill, N.C.: University of North Carolina Press, 1962); Jack L. Walker, "Protest and Negotiation: A Case Study of Negro Leadership in Atlanta, Georgia," *Midwest Journal of Political Science* (May 7, 1963), pp. 99-124; Jack L. Walker, *Sit-ins in Atlanta: A Study in the Negro Protest* (New York: Eagleton Institute Case Studies, No. 34, 1964); Jack L. Walker, "The Functions of Disunity: Negro Leadership in a Southern City," *Journal of Negro Education* 32 (Summer 1963): 227-36; William E. Wright, *Memphis Politics: A Study in Racial Bloc Voting* (New York: Eagleton Institute Case Studies, No. 27, 1962); Charles Hamilton, *Minority Politics in Black Belt Alabama* (New York: Eagleton Institute Case Studies, No. 19, 1960).

10. John H. Strange, "The Negro in Philadelphia Politics, 1963-65," Ph.D. dissertation, Princeton University, 1966; and William R. Keech, *The Impact of Negro Voting: The Role of the Vote in the Quest for Equality* (Chicago, Ill.: Rand McNally, 1968). The latter study examines black politics in Durham, North Carolina, and Tuskegee, Alabama.

11. Charles Hamilton, "Conflict, Race and System Transformation in the United States," *Journal of International Affairs* 23 (1969): 106-118; Dwaine Marvick, "The Political Socialization of the American Negro," *The Annals of the American Academy of Political and Social Science* 361 (September 1965): 112-27.

12. Gunnar Myrdal, *An American Dilemma*, 2nd ed. (New York: Harper and Row, Inc., 1962), pp. 474-505.

13. See Robert Dahl, *A Preface to a Democratic Theory* (Chicago, Ill.: University of Chicago Press, 1962), esp. Ch. 5.

14. John H. Strange found in Philadelphia that blacks did not benefit from the political system to any great extent and have achieved no major changes in their political, economic, and social status through the operations of the political system. Strange, pp. 132-98. Dahl's findings in New Haven differ. Dahl notes that, "in comparison to Whites, therefore, Negroes find no greater obstacles to achieving their goals through political action but very much greater difficulties through activities in the private socio-economic sphere." Dahl, p. 294. See also Keech's study. Theodore Lowi has suggested that pluralism in the American political process may have resulted in the exclusion of blacks from most benefits of society. See Theodore J. Lowi, *The End of Liberalism: Ideology, Policy, and the Crisis of Public Authority* (New York: Norton, 1969).

15. Exhaustive studies have been prepared by two presidential commissions on protest and violence. See, for example, Kerner Commission, *Report of the National Advisory Commission on Civil Disorders* (Washington, D.C.: U.S. Government Printing Office, 1968); *Supplemental Studies for the National Advisory Commission on Civil Disorders*, Washington, D.C., 1968; and *Violence in America: Historical and Comparative Perspectives*, vols. I and II. See also National Commission on the Causes and Prevention of Violence, *Report*, (Washington, D.C.: U.S. Government Printing Office, June 1969). Other studies include Jerome H. Skolnick, *The Politics of Protest*, (New York: Simon and Schuster, 1969); Albert Gollin, *The Demography of Protest: A Statistical Profile of Participants in the Poor People's Campaign*, (Washington, D.C.: Bureau of Social Science Research, 1969); Albert Gollin, "Poor People's Campaign and the March on Washington," Paper presented at the American Association for Public Opinion Research, May 1969; and Urban Research Corporation, *The Tenants' Rights Movement*, Chicago, Illinois, 1969. For a study of university student protest, see Columbia University, *Crisis at Columbia: Report of the Fact-Finding Commission Appointed to Investigate the Disturbances at Columbia University in April and May, 1968* (New York: Vintage Books, 1968). For two perceptive explorations of recent protest literature and the study of political science, see Strange, esp. Ch. I, pp. 4-45, and Michael Lipsky, "Protest and Power in City Politics: A Study of Rent Strikes and Housing in New York City," Ph.D. dissertation, Princeton University, 1967, pp. 1-25.

16. James Q. Wilson, "The Strategy of Protest: Problems of Negro Civic Action," *Journal of Conflict Resolution* 3 (September 1961): 291-303.

17. Wallace Sayre and Herbert Kaufman, *Governing New York City* (New York: Norton, 1965).

18. David B. Truman, *The Governmental Process* (New York: Knopf, 1963). Other general studies that explore the role of nongovernmental groups in the political process are: James Coleman, *Community Conflict*, (Glencoe, Ill.: The Free Press, 1957); Edward C. Banfield and James Q. Wilson, *City Politics*, (Cambridge, Mass.: Harvard University Press, 1963); Robert Dahl, *Who Governs?* (New Haven, Conn.: Yale University Press, 1961); Martin Meyerson and Edward C. Banfield, *Politics, Planning and the Public Interest* (Glencoe, Ill.: The Free Press, 1955).

19. Michael Lipsky, "Protest as a Political Resource," *American Political Science Review* 62 (December 1968): 144-58.

20. Mancur Olson, *The Logic of Collective Action: Public Goods and the Theory of Groups*, (Cambridge, Mass.: Harvard University Press, 1965).

21. Wilson, pp. 291-93.

22. Ibid., p. 291.

23. Ibid., p. 298.

24. Banfield and Wilson, pp. 294-303. The inability of the black lower classes to engage in significant political and organizational activity, and the constraints placed on black civic life by the gap between the middle and lower classes, has been noted elsewhere. See E.U. Essien-Udom, *Black Nationalism, A Search for Identity in America* (Chicago, Ill.: University of Chicago Press, 1962), pp. 298-340. For more general accounts of the inability of the lower classes to participate widely in political life, see Seymour M. Lipset, *Political Man*, (Garden City, N.Y.: Doubleday and Company, Inc., 1960), pp. 97-130; Robert E. Lane, *Political Life: Why People Get Involved in Politics* (Glencoe, Ill.: The Free Press, 1959), pp. 220-255.

25. Michael Lipsky, "Protest as a Political Resource," *American Political Science Review*, pp. 144-58; see also, Michael Lipsky, "Rent Strikes: Poor Man's Weapon," *Transaction* 6, no. 4 (February 1969): 10-15.

26. Lipsky, "Protest as a Political Resource," *American Political Science Review*, pp. 144-45.

27. Donald Von Eschen, Jerome Kirk, and Maurice Pinnard, "The Conditions of Direct Action in a Democratic Society," *Western Political Quarterly* 22 (June 1969): 309-325.

28. Ibid., pp. 322-25.

29. Olson, p. 7.

Chapter 3
The Origins of Welfare Protest Activity
in America

1. Committee on Finance, U.S. Congress, Senate, *Hearings, Social Security Amendments of 1967*, 90th Cong., 1st sess., 1967, pp. 1464-66. Beulah Sanders,

the second vice president of the National Welfare Rights Organization and chairman of the New York City-Wide Coordinating Committee of Welfare Rights Groups.

2. Joint Economic Committee, Subcommittee on Fiscal Policy, U.S. Congress, *Hearings, Income Maintenance Programs*, 90th Cong., 2nd sess., 1968, pp. 75-76.

3. Virginia C. Searles, "Cuyahoga County Relief Administration Clients as Members of the Unemployment Council," master's thesis, Western Reserve University, Cleveland, Ohio, May 1935, p. 5.

4. Helen Seymour, "When Clients Organize," A study sponsored by the American Public Welfare Association, Chicago, Illinois, December 1937, pp. 4-12. See, also, Alice Brophy and George Hallowitz, "Pressure Groups and the Relief Administration in New York City," master's thesis, New York School of Social Work, April 1937, pp. 6-12; also, see James Dumpson, "The Administration of Public Assistance and Its Relationship to Pressure Groups, paper, December 1938, files of ex-commissioner of welfare in New York City.

5. Abraham Holtzman, *The Townsend Movement* (New York: Bookman Associates, 1963).

6. For further discussion, see Jean H. Rothman, "Welfare Rights in the 1930s and 1960s," master's thesis, New York University, 1969.

7. Dwaine Marvick, "The Political Socialization of the American Negro," *The Annals of the American Academy of Political and Social Science* 361 (September 1965).

8. Karl Deutsch, "Social Mobilization and Political Development," *American Political Science Review* 55, no. 3 (September 1961).

9. Donald Von Eschen, Jerome Kirk, and Maurice Pinard, "The Disintegration of the Negro Non-Violent Movement," *Journal of Peace Research* no. 3 (1969): 129.

10. Ibid., pp. 129-31.

11. Allen J. Matusow, "From Civil Rights to Black Power: The Case of SNCC, 1960-1966," in Barton J. Bernstein and Allen J. Matusow (eds.), *Twentieth Century America: Recent Interpretations* (New York: Harcourt and Brace, 1969), pp. 531-39.

12. Michael Harrington, *The Other America* (New York: Macmillan, 1962).

13. See Mollie Orshansky, "Children of the Poor," *Social Security Bulletin* 26, no. 7 (July 1963); "Who's Who among the Poor: A Demographic View of Poverty," *Social Security Bulletin* 28, no. 7 (July 1965): 3-32; "Recounting the Poor: A Five Year Review," *Social Security Bulletin* 29, no. 4 (April 1966): 20-37; and "More about the Poor in 1964," *Social Security Bulletin* 29, no. 5, May 1966, pp. 3-38. See also Department of Health, Education, and Welfare, *Growing Up Poor*, (Washington, D.C.: Welfare Administration, 1966); and *Low-Income Life Styles* (Washington, D.C.: Welfare Administration, 1968).

14. Claude Brown, *Manchild in the Promised Land*, (New York: Macmillan, 1965; Malcolm Little, *The Autobiography of Malcolm X*, Grove Press, New York, 1965).

234

15. John Kenneth Galbraith, *The Affluent Society*, (Boston, Mass.: Houghton Mifflin, 1958), esp. Ch. 23.

16. Arthur Schlesinger, Jr., *The Age of Roosevelt: The Coming of the New Deal*, (Boston, Mass.: Houghton Mifflin, 1959).

17. Harrington, p. 9.

18. Galbraith, p. 323.

19. Harrington, p. 15.

20. John C. Donovan, *The Politics of Poverty* (New York: Pegasus, 1967); also see Brian Smith, "The Role of the Poor in the Poverty Program: The Origin and Development of Maximum Feasible Participation," master's thesis, Department of Political Science, Columbia University, 1966.

21. Peter Marris and Martin Rein, *Dilemmas of Social Reform*, (London: Routledge and K. Paul, 1967), pp. 15-16. The following account draws on this source, esp. Ch. I.

22. Ibid., p. 19.

23. Paul N. Ylvisaker, "A Foundation Approach to City Problems," paper presented at the 29th Annual National Conference, National Association of Housing and Development, October 1963.

24. See, John E. Moore, "Controlling Delinquency," in Frederic N. Cleaveland and Associates, *Congress and Urban Problems*, (Washington, D.C.: The Brookings Institution, 1969); Donovan, particularly Ch. 4; and Daniel P. Moynihan, *Maximum Feasible Misunderstanding*, (New York: Free Press, 1969), esp. Ch. 4, pp. 61-74.

25. Cited in Herbert Krosney, *Beyond Welfare: Poverty in the Supercity* (New York: Holt, Rinehart and Winston, 1966), p. 9.

26. Marris and Rein, p. 24; also, see the President's Committee on Juvenile Delinquency, *Report to the President* (Washington, D.C.: U.S. Government Printing Office, 1962).

27. Marris and Rein, pp. 29-31.

28. Cited in Krosney, p. 12.

29. Moynihan, *Maximum Feasible Misunderstanding*, p. 42.

30. U.S. Government Accounting Office, *Review of Economic Opportunity Programs*, Report to the Congress of the United States, 91st Cong., 1st sess., 1969.

31. Ibid., p. 30.

32. Ibid., p. 41.

33. Ibid., p. 173.

34. Ibid., p. 131. For research on the neighborhood centers, see Robert Perlman and David Jones, *Neighborhood Service Centers*, Office of Juvenile Delinquency, Welfare Administration, U.S. Department of Health, Education, and Welfare, 1967; see also Kirschner Associates, *A Description and Evaluation of Neighborhood Centers*, Report for the Office of Economic Opportunity, December 1966; "An Evaluation of the Thirteen Neighborhood Service Pro-

grams," A study of the Neighborhood Center Pilot Program, prepared for the Executive Office of the President, Bureau of the Budget, vols. I and II, April 1969.

35. Sar Levitan, *The Great Society's Poor Law: A New Approach to Poverty*, (Baltimore, Md.: Johns Hopkins Press, 1969), p. 123.

36. Jerome E. Carlin, "Store Front Lawyers in San Francisco," *Transaction 7*, no. 6 (April 1970). The following discussion is based largely on this article.

37. Levitan, p. 188. According to Levitan, "during fiscal 1967, OEO pumped more than two million dollars into law schools for research, changes in curricula, and various projects dealing with the poor. Forty law schools instituted courses on law and poverty attended by some 2000 students during the 1965-66 and 1966-67 academic years."

38. Ibid., p. 184.

39. Carlin, p. 67.

40. Frances Fox Piven, "Conceptual Themes in the Evolution of Mobilization for Youth," Paper prepared for the Columbia University School of Social Work-Mobilization for Youth Training Institute on Urban Community Development Projects: Selected Aspects of the Mobilization for Youth Experience, April 27-May 1, 1964. The paper is included in the Mobilization for Youth Training Papers, vol. 8, School of Social Work, Columbia University, New York, May 17, 1965.

41. Robert Merton, *Social Theory and Social Structure* (Glencoe, Ill.: The Free Press, 1949), esp. Ch. 5.

42. Richard Cloward and Lloyd Ohlin, *Delinquency and Opportunity* (Glencoe, Ill.: The Free Press, 1960), p. 211.

43. Multiproblem families were defined as families suffering from a variety of health and welfare problems and chronically dependent upon community services, although apathetic toward social welfare agencies.

44. Gordon Brown, *The Multi-Problem Dilemma* (Metuchen, N.J.: Scarecrow Press, 1968), p. 7. For other recent studies which support, generally, the same conclusions, see Henry J. Meyer, Edgar F. Borgatta, and Wyatt C. Jones, *Girls at Vocational High, An Experiment in Social Work Intervention* (New York: Russell Sage Foundation, 1965); also see Jacob Wayne Wrightstone et al., *Evaluation of the Higher Horizons Program for Underprivileged Children*, New York City Board of Education, New York, 1964; Herbert Hyman, Charles Wright, and Terrence Hopkins, *Applications of Methods of Evaluation: Four Studies of the Encampment of Citizenship* (Berkeley, Calif: University of California Press, 1962); Jonas Muller, Jerome Tobis, and Howard Kelman, "The Rehabilitation of Nursing Home Residents," *American Journal of Public Health* 53, no. 2 (February 1963); New York City Youth Board, *An Experiment in the Use of the Blueck Social Prediction Table as a Prognosticator of Potential Delinquency*, City of New York, October 1961; and Edwin Powers and Helen Witmer, *An Experiment in the Prevention of Delinquency—The Cambridge-Somerville Youth Study* (New York: Columbia University Press, 1951).

45. For bibliographical sources on these studies, see Gordon Brown, pp. 152-61.

46. Charles Silberman, *Crisis in Black and White* (New York: Random House, 1964), esp. Ch. 10.

47. Ibid., p. 313.

48. Ibid., p. 315.

49. Cited in Harlem Youth Opportunities Unlimited (HARYOU), *Youth in the Ghetto: A Study of the Consequences of Powerlessness and a Blueprint for Change*, New York, 1964, p. 3.

50. Ibid., pp. 332-33.

51. U.S. Department of Labor, Office of Policy Planning and Research, *The Negro Family, The Case for National Action* (Washington, D.C.: U.S. Government Printing Office, 1965), p. 3.

52. Bayard Rustin, "From Protest to Politics: The Future of the Civil Rights Movement," *Commentary* 39, no. 2 (February 1965): 25-31.

53. Maryland State Department of Public Welfare, "A Report on Caseload Increase in the Aid to Families with Dependent Children Program, 1960-66," Research Report, No. 2, Government of Maryland, July 1967.

54. Ibid., p. 36.

55. Cited in *The New York Times*, April 5, 1970.

56. Nathan Glazer, "Negroes and Jews: The New Challenge to Pluralism," *Commentary* 38, no. 6 (December 1964): 34.

57. James Q. Wilson, "The Negro in Politics," *Daedalus* 94, no. 4 (Fall 1965): 964-65.

58. For other commentary which supports this view, see Frances Fox Piven, "The Great Society as Political Strategy," *Columbia Forum* (Summer 1970), pp. 17-22; Richard A. Cloward and Frances Fox Piven, "How the Federal Government Caused the Welfare Crisis," *Social Policy* (May-June 1971), pp. 40-49; also see Krosney, p. 3.

Chapter 4
The National Welfare Rights Organization

1. See Anatole Shaffer, "Welfare Rights Organization: Friend or Foe?" *Social Work Practice* (New York: Columbia University Press, 1967), p. 229.

2. Ibid.

3. Joseph Paull, "Recipients Aroused: The New Welfare Rights Movement," *Social Work* 12, no. 2, 1967, pp. 101-106.

4. The following were some of the early welfare rights organizations: the Oakland Welfare Rights Organization; in Boston, the Mothers for Adequate Welfare; and in Los Angeles, the ADC Mothers Anonymous. (Interviews, March 21, 1969, and February 23, 1969.)

5. Richard Cloward and Frances Fox Piven, "Low Income Peoples and the Political Process," Paper prepared for the Training Institute Program on Urban Community Development Projects: Selected Aspects of the Moblization for Youth Experience, April 27-May 1, 1964. The paper is included in the Mobilization for Youth Training Department Papers, vol. 4 (New York: School of Social Work, Columbia University, April 1964).

6. Cloward and Piven, *Social Policy*, pp. 46-47.

7. *The New York Times*, June 5, 1966; see, also, *The Washington Post*, June 9, 1966.

8. PRAC, "Prospectus for the Establishment of an Anti-Poverty Civil Rights Action Center," May 1, 1966, pp. 2-3.

9. Press release of the Ohio Steering Committee for Adequate Welfare, Mimeographed June 15, 1966, Cleveland, Ohio. Organizations supporting the walk included the National Association of Social Workers, the Ohio AFL-CIO, Americans for Democratic Action, The Ohio Council of Churches, Students for a Democratic Society, and local welfare unions. See also *National Guardian*, July 9, 1966.

10. AFDC recipients were receiving only 70 percent of these standards. *National Guardian*, July 9, 1966.

11. Richard Cloward and Frances Fox Piven, "The Birth of a Movement," *The Nation* 204, no. 19 (May 8, 1967): 582.

12. New York, Washington, Boston, New Haven, Newark, Trenton, Philadelphia, Pittsburgh, Baltimore, Syracuse, Chicago, Louisville, Kansas City, Los Angeles, and San Francisco. National Welfare Rights Organization, "Summary Report: Welfare Action Meeting," mimeographed, Chicago, Ill., May 27, 1966, pp. 1-4; see also *National Observer*, July 4, 1966.

13. National Welfare Rights Organization, "Summary Report of National Welfare Rights Meeting," mimeographed, August 6-7, 1966.

14. National Welfare Rights Organization, *Summary Report*, p. 2.

15. National Welfare Rights Organization, "A Brief History of the National Welfare Rights Organization," *NOW!* February 9, 1968. The following discussion is based largely on this article. *NOW!* is the NWRO's official publication.

16. National Welfare Rights Organization, "NWRO National Constitution," mimeographed, Washington, D.C., August 25, 1967.

17. For every 25 to 49 members a group is allowed one delegate and one alternate; for 50 to 99 members, two delegates and two alternates; for 100 to 199 members, three delegates and three alternates; for each additional 100 members one more delegate and alternate. See National Welfare Rights Organization, "How NWRO Works," *NOW!* February 14, 1969.

18. National Welfare Rights Organization, "Goals of the National Welfare Rights Organization," *NOW!* undated.

19. Ibid.

20. National Welfare Rights Organization, "Mother Power," *NOW!* Washington, D.C., June 6, 1968.

21. "Bayonets against Mothers in Madison," *The Welfare Fighter* (October 1969), p. 1.

22. "Total Victory in Nevada," *The Welfare Fighter* (April-May 1971), p. 5.

23. Ibid., p. 5.

24. Ibid., p. 5.

25. Cloward and Piven, *Social Policy*, pp. 48-49.

26. The NWRO publishes guidelines on how to organize around individual problems and to start a local WRO. See National Welfare Rights Organization, "How To Start a WRO," *NOW!* March 25, 1968.

27. See National Welfare Rights Organization, "Rights You Should Know," *NOW!* March 11, 1968; see also *The Massachusetts Welfare Rights Organization Handbook*, pamphlet published by the Massachusetts WRO, Cambridge, Massachusetts, June 1969; and *Know Your Rights*, pamphlet published by the Detroit Metropolitan WRO, Detroit, Michigan, undated.

28. Cloward and Piven, *Social Policy*, p. 47.

29. "Credit Given by Montgomery Ward," *The Welfare Fighter*, December 1969, p. 1; see also, "A Nation-Wide Credit Campaign: Negotiate Now with Sears," NWRO Action Leadership Packet, No. 3, Washington, D.C., undated; "NWRO Launches Sears Boycott," in *WROs in Action*, April 1969.

30. For the position of the NWRO, see National Welfare Rights Organization, "The Welfare WIP Program and You," *NOW!* June 17, 1968; see also "Questions and Answers about the New Anti-Welfare Law," *NOW!* February 21, 1968, and "President Johnson Signs Anti-Welfare Bill into Law," *NOW!* February 2, 1968; "NWRO Battles Welfare Rights Enemy Number One: Wilbur Mills," *NOW* June 17, 1968; finally, see "The 1967 Anti-Welfare Social Security Amendments Law," *NOW!* December 29, 1967.

31. *The Washington Post*, May 25, 1968; see also *The Washington Evening Star*, May 28, 1968.

32. The NWRO came under attack from the large Philadelphia WRO for accepting the contract with the Department of Labor. See *The New York Times*, May 29, 1969.

33. Cloward and Piven, *Social Policy*, p. 49.

34. The NWRO has now acquired many of the characteristics of formal organizations. Its goals, especially, serve as a source of legitimacy and justification for the activities of the organization. See, Amitai Etzioni, *Modern Organizations* (Englewood Cliffs, N.J.: Prentice-Hall, 1964), p. 5.

35. Cloward and Piven, *Social Policy*, p. 48.

Chapter 5
The Emergence of Local Welfare Rights
Activity in New York City

1. For example, see Robert E. Lane, *Political Life: Why People Get Involved in Politics* (Glencoe, Ill.: Free Press, 1959), esp. Ch. 16, pp. 220-234.

2. Seymour Lipset, *Political Man* (Garden City, N.Y.: Doubleday, 1960), p. 110.

3. Ibid., p. 109.

4. For a sample of this literature, see Richard M. Elman, *The Poorhouse State: The American Way of Life on Public Assistance* (New York: Pantheon, 1966); Edgar May, *The Wasted Americans* (New York: Harper, 1969); Sol Yurick, *The Bag* (New York: Simon and Schuster, 1968); Julius Horwitz, *The Inhabitants* (New York: World, 1960); and, finally, Piri Thomas, *Down These Mean Streets* (New York: Knopf, 1967).

5. Lawrence Podell, *Families on Welfare in New York City* (New York: The Center for the Study of Urban Problems, City University of New York, 1968). The following account draws on this source. Since 1966 large numbers have been added to the welfare rolls in New York City. To some extent, this may affect the current applicability of Podell's findings.

6. Olvin McBarnette, "A Study of Problems Confronting Children of Welfare Recipients Attending New York City Public Schools," Paper submitted to the New York City Human Resources Administration, September 1968, p. 8. The following discussion draws from this source.

7. Ibid., pp. 17-18.

8. Ibid., pp. 18-19.

9. Ibid., pp. 24-25. For other studies that support the view that, regardless of race, socioeconomic status, or family head, students of AFDC families have greater problems than those from nonassisted families, see Perry Levinson, "The Next Generation: A Study of Children in AFDC Families," *Welfare in Review* 7, no. 2 (March-April 1969): 1-9; see also, Thomas S. Lagner et al. "Psychiatric Impairment in Welfare and Non-Welfare Children," *Welfare in Review* 7, no. 2 (March-April 1969): 10-21.

10. Louis Harris and Associates, "Transition Neighborhoods in New York City: The People's View of Their Housing Environment," Survey conducted for the Vera Institute of Justice, New York City, December 1969.

11. "Worst buildings" were defined as those having five or more of the following characteristics: no elevator in the building; an elevator, but not in working condition; some mail boxes broken or open; front door not locked; no buzzer system; halls dimly lit; halls dirty or paint peeling; and, compared to the condition of the other buildings on the block, overall, a worse than average condition of the building. Ibid., p. 9.

12. George Sternlieb, *The Urban Housing Dilemma: The Dynamics of New York City's Rent Controlled Housing*, report submitted to the New York City Housing and Development Administration, May 1970.

13. I.S. Lowry, *Rental Housing in New York City: Confronting the Crisis*, vol. I, RM-6190-NYC, The New York City-Rand Institute, February 1970, p. 23.

14. Ibid., pp. 14-15.

15. *The New York Times*, December 19, 1966; New York City Housing Authority, "Annual Statistics on New York City Public Housing Families, 1967-68," Statistics Division, New York City, 1968.

16. Chairman of the City Housing Authority, cited in *The New York Times*, January 26, 1971.

17. U.S. Government, Department of Health, Education, and Welfare, *The Role of Public Welfare in Housing*, Report to the House Committee on Ways and Means and the Senate Committee on Finance (Washington, D.C.: U.S. Government Printing Office, January 1969), p. 8.

18. Ibid., p. 11.

19. Ibid., pp. 11-12.

20. See, Richard Pomeroy, Robert LeJeune, and Lawrence Podell, *Studies in the Use of Health Services by Families on Welfare: Utilization by Publicly-Assisted Families*, The Center for the Study of Urban Problems, City University of New York, New York, 1969, p. 95.

21. Black respondents are more likely to make use of medical services and less likely to present themselves as sick than Puerto Rican respondents. See Robert LeJeune, "Illness Behavior among the Urban Poor," doctoral dissertation, Columbia University, New York, 1968.

22. Lawrence Podell, *Studies in the Use of Health Services by Families on Welfare: Population Comparisons* (New York: The Center for the Study of Urban Problems, City University of New York, 1969), pp. 65-68.

23. David Caplovitz, *The Poor Pay More* (New York: Free Press, 1967), pp. 21, 50-73.

24. Richard Cloward and Frances Fox Piven, *Regulating the Poor: The Functions of Public Welfare* (New York: Pantheon, 1971), esp. Chs. 4 and 5, pp. 123-82.

25. Two accounts focus on East Harlem: Patricia Cayo Sexton, *Spanish Harlem: Anatomy of Poverty* (New York: Harper, 1965); see also New York City Housing and Development Administration, *The East Harlem Triangle: A Sociological and Economic Study*, vols. I and II, Report for HDA submitted by the Social Dynamics Corporation, May 1968. For a classic study of Harlem, see Kenneth B. Clark, *Dark Ghetto: Dilemmas of Social Power* (New York: Harper and Row, 1965). For an account of the Brownsville section of Brooklyn, see James Graham, *The Enemies of the Poor* (New York: Random House, 1970), esp. Chs. 12 and 13, pp. 247-85.

26. Harold Yahr and Richard Pomeroy, *Studies in Public Welfare: Effects of Eligibility Investigation on Welfare Clients* (New York: The Center for the Study of Urban Problems, City University of New York, 1968), pp. 5-6, 53.

27. See Charles Reich, "Individual Rights and Social Welfare: The Emerging Legal Issues," *Yale Law Journal* 74 (1965): 1245-57; Reich, "Midnight Welfare Searches and the Social Security Act," *Yale Law Journal* 72 (1963): 1347-60; also, see, Albert Bendick, "Privacy, Poverty, and the Constitution," in Jacobus TenBroek (ed.), *The Law of the Poor* (San Francisco: Chandler, 1966), pp. 83-118; Robert M. O'Neil, "Unconstitutional Conditions: Welfare Benefits with Strings," in ibid., pp. 119-154.

28. Charles Reich, "The New Property," *Yale Law Journal* 73 (1964): 733.

29. Crane Brinton, *Anatomy of a Revolution* (New York: Vintage, 1965), p. 250.

30. Ibid., p. 250.

31. For a short summary of some of the reforms instituted in New York City, see, John Lindsay, *The City* (New York: Norton, 1970), esp. Ch. 7, pp. 143-73.

32. Sayre and Kaufman, p. xiii.

33. For a good analysis of black attitudes toward education, see David Rogers, *110 Livingston Street* (New York: Random House, 1968).

34. Ibid., pp. 29-30.

35. For one account of this conflict, see Martin Mayer, *The Teacher's Strike, New York, 1968* (New York: Harper and Row, 1969).

36. See, Mary Rabagliati and Ezra Birnbaum, "Organizations of Welfare Clients," in Harold H. Weissman (ed.), *Community Development in the Mobilization for Youth Experience* (New York: Association Press), pp. 102-136.

37. Frances Fox Piven, "Conceptual Themes in the Evolution of Mobilization for Youth," Mobilization for Youth Training Papers (unpaged).

38. Ibid.

39. Mobilization for Youth, "A Proposal for the Prevention and Control of Delinquency by Expanding Opportunities," 1961, p. 126.

40. Ibid., pp. 132-33.

41. *MFY News Bulletin*, Winter 1963.

42. Hettie Jones, "Overview of Services to Individuals and Families," in Harold H. Weissman (ed.), *Individual and Group Services in the Mobilization for Youth Experience* (New York: Association Press, 1969), p. 30.

43. Mobilization for Youth, "A Proposal for the Prevention and Control of Delinquency by Expanding Opportunities," p. 355.

44. Margaret C. Shea, "Helping Stations," Paper presented at the United Neighborhood Houses Fall Conference, New York, Mimeographed, 1964. The paper is included in Mobilization for Youth Papers, School of Social Work, vol. 5 (New York: Columbia University, May 17, 1965).

45. Hettie Jones, "Neighborhood Service Centers," in Harold Weissman (ed.), *Individual and Group Services in the Mobilization for Youth Experience* (New York: Association Press, 1969), pp. 37-38.

46. Sherman Barr, "Poverty on the Lower East Side," Paper prepared for the Columbia University School of Social Work, Mobilization for Youth Training Institute, Program of Urban Community Development Projects: Selected Aspects of the Mobilization for Youth Experience, April 27-May 1, 1964. This paper is included in the Mobilization for Youth Training Papers, vol. 4 (New York: School of Social Work, Columbia University, May 17, 1965).

47. Hettie Jones, "Neighborhood Service Centers," pp. 44-45.

48. Richard A. Cloward and Richard M. Elman, "The Storefront on Stanton Street: Advocacy in the Ghetto," in George A. Braeger and Francis P. Purvell

(eds.), *Community Action against poverty* (New Haven: College and University Press, 1967), pp. 267-68.

49. Edward Sparer, "Poverty, Law, and Social Welfare," Unpublished Mobilization for Youth Training Paper (New York: Mobilization for Youth, January 1964).

50. Michael Appleby, "Overview of Legal Services," in Harold Weissman (ed.), *Justice and the Law in the Mobilization for Youth Experience* (New York: Association Press, 1969), p. 36-37. For a useful summary of MFY legal activity, see Michael Appleby and Henry Hiefetz, "Legal Challenge to Formal and Informal Services of Welfare Rights," in ibid., pp. 88-105.

51. The following discussion is drawn largely from Cloward and Elman, pp. 271-72.

52. Ibid., p. 272.

53. Ibid., pp. 272-73.

54. Hettie Jones, "Neighborhood Service Centers," p. 47.

55. See Mary Rabagliati and Ezra Birnbaum, "Organizations of Welfare Clients," p. 105.

56. Ibid., p. 105.

57. From October 1962 to June 1967 the NSC program served more than 43,000 individuals and 10,500 families. Of these, 70 percent had problems involving the DOSS. Hettie Jones, "Neighborhood Service Centers," p. 53. For further evidence of the overwhelming identification of the clients' problems with the DOSS, see Margaret C. Shea, "MFY Program Report: 1963," MFY Publications, CUSSW Library, and Stephen J. Leeds, "Who Was Reached? An Analysis of the Population Served by Mobilization for Youth, 1962-65," MFY Research and Evaluation Project, CUSSW, undated.

58. One study of political behavior on the Lower East Side concluded that, "in the minds of the residents, welfare, not the anti-poverty program, was the most salient government effort to aid the poor." Stephen Leeds, "The Lower East Side Anti-Poverty Election," unpublished manuscript, New York.

59. This shift conforms broadly to shifts in the entire community development program of MFY. See Harold Weissman, "Overview of the Community Development Program," Harold Weissman (ed.), *Community Development in the Mobilization for Youth Experience* (New York: Association Press, 1969), pp. 23-28.

60. Richard Pious, "Advocates for the Poor: The Legal Service Program in the War on Poverty 1964-69," Ph.D. dissertation, Columbia University, New York, 1970, Ch. 2. Another competing style of operation, theoretically present but not often found in an advocacy situation, is cooperation and accommodation with existing institutions with gentle prodding through persuasion, demonstration projects, and the like toward incremental changes in public policy. This, clearly, was not the style of the emerging welfare rights movement. See George Braeger, "Influencing Institutional Change through a Demonstration Project: The Case of

the Schools," Paper presented at the Training Institute, Columbia University School of Social Work, Mobilization for Youth Workshop Session on Effecting Institutional Change, April 27-May 1, 1964. Paper is included in the Mobilization for Youth Training Papers, vol. 4, School of Social Work, Columbia University, undated.

61. An excellent historical review of the relationship between MFY and the formation of welfare rights groups on the Lower East Side is contained in a memorandum from Bertram Beck, executive director, to the Executive Committee of the Board and Executive Staff, "Subject: Problem in the Organization of Welfare Clients," November 17, 1966.

62. Frank Espada's group, as well as others in Brooklyn, typify those which Sayre and Kaufman characterize as participating only intermittently in the governmental process, and then only in relation to decisions that directly affect some vital interests. See Sayre and Kaufman, pp. 78-80.

63. Interview, April 9, 1969.

64. Interview, October 2, 1968.

65. Graham, *The Enemies of the Poor*, p. 266.

66. Ibid., pp. 269-70.

67. Ibid., p. 271.

68. In complaining about the lack of church participation outside Brooklyn, one commentator has noted: "Except for the Catholic sponsored CUSA of Brooklyn, I could find no systematic participation in or support of the welfare rights movement in the city. The backbone of this Catholic support are [sic] priests, . . . and others who assist and work with local groups in and out of the CUSA storefront network throughout Crown Heights, Bedford-Stuyvesant, Brownsville, East New York, and Bushwick. . . . This involvement on the part of the church in Brooklyn has been a major contributing factor to Brooklyn's being (with the likely exception of MFY on the LES) the best organized area of New York City's welfare rights movement." See Charles P. Gillet, "The Church and the Welfare Crisis in New York," Unpublished paper, City-Wide files, New York, undated.

69. Graham, *The Enemies of the Poor*, pp. 165-166.

70. Interview, April 15, 1968.

71. Graham, *The Enemies of the Poor*, p. 165; also see Gillet, p. 7.

72. Joseph Lyford, *The Airtight Cage* (New York: Harper and Row, 1966), pp. 117-34.

73. Interview, January 17, 1969.

74. Interview, January 10, 1969.

75. Memo from Rick Cotton to David Grossman, Assistant Director, Bureau of the Budget, "Subject: Welfare Activities of CAP Programs," mimeographed, 1967. This memorandum was made public and was widely distributed.

76. CDA Evaluation Unit, "Evaluation of the Bushwick Neighborhood Coordinating Council," mimeographed New York: Community Development Administration Evaluation Unit, June 1967.

Chapter 6
The City-Wide Coordinating Committee
of Welfare Groups

1. Richard A. Cloward and Richard M. Elman, "Advocacy in the Ghetto," *Transaction*, December 1966, p. 27.

2. *The New York Times*, June 30, 1966; *The Guardian*, June 30, 1966.

3. Lillian Rubin, "Maximum Feasible Participation: The Origins, Implementation, and Present Status," *Annals of the American Academy of Political and Social Science* (September 1969), pp. 14-29.

4. Ibid., p. 28.

5. For example, Moynihan has noted that "no Negro was involved in any significant way in planning the Economic Opportunity Act of 1964. This is not a pleasant matter to discuss, but it is an important one that demands more open acknowledgement." See Daniel P. Moynihan, "The Professors and the Poor," *Commentary* (August 1968), pp. 22-23.

6. This phenomenon has been discussed by Robert Dahl, *Who Governs?* (New Haven, Conn.: Yale University Press, 1961), pp. 227-28.

7. The project was submitted to OEO as a two-year test of the feasibility of organizing the poor into a politically self-assertive segment of the community. Jules Witcover and Erwin Knoll, "Politics and the Poor: Shriver's Second Thought," *Reporter* (December 30, 1965), p. 24.

8. Ibid.

9. See, "People's War Council News," Convention Special, No. 4, mimeographed (New York: People's War Council Pamphlet, January 25, 1966).

10. Witcover and Knoll, p. 24.

11. Cited in Metropolitan Applied Research Center, *A Relevant War against Poverty: A Study of Community Action Programs and Observable Social Change*, New York, 1968, p. 154.

12. Witcover and Knoll, p. 23.

13. Ibid., p. 25.

14. In many ways, the War on Poverty is unique in the history of American federalism. It illustrates a basic dilemma: How much localized control is feasible or desirable in federally financed enterprises? See Roger H. Davidson, "The War on Poverty: Experiment in Federalism," *Annals of the American Academy of Political and Social Sciences* September 1969, pp. 1-13. For accounts of the operations of the community action programs within the context of different urban political systems, see Paul Peterson, "Forms of Representation: Participation of the Poor in the Community Action Program," *American Political Science Review* (June 1970), pp. 491-507; see also Paul Peterson, "City Politics and Community Action: The Implementation of Community Action Programs in Three American Cities," Ph.D. dissertation, Division of the Social Sciences, University of Chicago, June 1967.

15. PWCAP, Mimeographed handout, April 22, 1966.

16. Metropolitan Applied Research Center, p. 190.

17. Cited in ibid., pp. 190-91.

18. PWCAP, "Resolutions Passed by the People's Convention for the Total Participation of the Poor," Mimeographed. See also Metropolitan Applied Research Center, pp. 192-193.

19. Ibid., p. 193.

20. Besides Syracuse, other conventions were held in New Jersey, California, and Washington, D.C. See ibid., esp. Ch. 4, pp. 133-204.

21. Ibid., p. 197.

22. Interview, March 11, 1969.

23. Ibid.

24. Mimeographed handout, April 22, 1966.

25. This decision to concentrate on the welfare issue was critical. The common pattern exhibited by most of the other conferences and conventions sponsored by or on behalf of the poor was to focus on many rather than a few areas. See Metropolitan Applied Research Center, p. 197.

26. *The Guardian*, July 19, 1966.

27. Interview, April 9, 1969; see also "Summary Report, Welfare Action Meeting," May 21, 1966, Chicago, Illinois, PRAC files.

28. *The New York Times*, July 1, 1966; also, see *The Guardian*, July 19, 1966; Among the Committee's allies were CUSA, the SSEU, The Hudson Neighborhood Conservation Group, and Social Workers for Civil Rights Action. See City-Wide Committee memorandum, "All Members and Interested Individuals," June 15, 1966, City-Wide files.

29. At the June 30, 1966 demonstration, City-Wide made fifteen specific demands: welfare grants should be brought up to minimum standards; applications for welfare should be changed by allowing people to declare their needs without investigation; the basic welfare allowance should be raised; clients should be allowed to work long enough to get on their feet without making any cuts in their budget; the new July 1 budget should be changed because no real increase in assistance was being made; families should be given a semimonthly grant toward burial life insurance; the inadequacy of the food budget should end; there should be a greater allowance for laundry expenses; carfare should be included in the budget; welfare recipients should be given an equal right to public housing and better housing in general; day-care centers should be opened and made available to welfare recipients so they do not have to take children everywhere they go or leave them alone; recipients with small children should be allowed a telephone; free legal services should be provided to welfare clients; the welfare administration should give people information on education and training programs; and welfare should pay the client's utility bill. City-Wide Coordinating Committee, "Demand for the June 30th Demonstration at City Hall," Mimeographed, City-Wide files.

30. Cited in *The Guardian*, July 19, 1966; see also *The New York Times*, July 1, 1966. Commissioner Ginsberg, on leave from the School of Social Work at Columbia University, was a good friend and professional colleague of Richard Cloward and Frances Piven, both highly influential in the development of the welfare rights movement.

Chapter 7
The Winter Clothing Campaign

1. Rabagliati and Birnbaum have described the influence exerted at this juncture by the MFY staff. To instill confidence in clients to stand up for their rights, without fear of punishment or termination by hostile caseworkers, was one major function of the organizer. A second was to encourage clients to verbalize their feelings (often emotionally) about indignities suffered and, in this way, to have clients share common experiences. Finally, the presence among the MFY staff of lawyers assured clients of the legal basis of their claims. Rabagliati and Birnbaum, pp. 108-108.

2. Interview, February 3, 1969.

3. Cited in Rabagliati and Birnbaum, pp. 109-110. The letter was signed by all recipients, despite the fact that nine of the twenty-one had received partial grants. The recipients decided to stick it out as a group.

4. Among the clients' grievances were requests for special grants for winter clothing, more humane treatment by investigators, and the inclusion in the welfare budget of such items as transportation, school supplies, uniforms, and other miscellaneous items. See Rabagliati and Birnbaum, p. 110.

5. Letter from Commissioner Joseph Louchheim to Mrs. Minita Cortese, CWF, December 7, 1965. The grievance procedure was installed at four welfare centers serving the Lower East Side.

6. Interview, February 3, 1969.

Chapter 8
The Minimum Standards Campaign

1. Rabagliati and Birnbaum, pp. 114-115.

2. Even though the city-wide structure, at this juncture, was relatively weak, many of CWF's members tended to view it as a competitor for recognition, status, and possible resources.

3. Two-page conference program handout, Conference of Welfare Clients, May 21, 1966.

4. The project proposal was prepared by MFY's professional staff. See the CWF proposal, "Joint Children's Cultural Program, Mother's Day Out Program, and Adult Job Training Program," Summer 1966.

5. For an account of this process, see Rabagliati and Birnbaum, pp. 118-122.

6. A basic disagreement over organization and tactics led to Birnbaum assuming staff control of the CWF and Eisman forming the new group. These differences were to have a profound and measurable impact upon the direction of welfare rights activity first in New York City and later in other parts of the nation. See Rabagliati and Birnbaum, p. 122.

7. Ibid.

8. Ibid., pp. 122-23.

9. Rabagliati and Birnbaum state that, although WAGAP's total membership was near 100, it could never muster more than 30 members for a demonstration. Ibid., p. 123.

10. MFY memorandum by Marty Eisman, "The Home Groups," October 6, 1966.

11. Ibid., p. 1.

12. The following account stems largely from these sources: MFY memorandum from Barbara Lounds, community organizer with CWAG, to Dan Morris, assistant executive director for programs, "Welfare Minimum Standard Campaign of CWAG," November 17, 1966; MFY memorandum from Barbara Lounds to Val Coleman, "CWAG," December 15, 1966; and Rabagliati and Birnbaum, pp. 125-28.

13. MFY memorandum from Barbara Lounds to Val Coleman, "Citizens Welfare Action Group," December 5, 1966.

14. "Citizens Welfare Action Group's Proposal for Community Development Submitted to Mobilization for Youth," November 1966.

15. School clothing grants had recently been computerized. Eisman's purpose was to have winter clothing handled in the same way. Memorandum by Martin Eisman, "A Proposal to Flood Selected Welfare Centers," October 5, 1966.

16. Ibid., p. 1.

17. Ibid., pp. 2-3.

18. Richard A. Cloward and Frances Fox Piven, "The Weight of the Poor, A Strategy to End Poverty," *The Nation*, May 2, 1966.

19. Ibid., p. 510.

20. Ibid., p. 516.

21. In fact, Cloward and Piven suggested that one strength of their strategy, and a key to its potential effectiveness, was that it did not require large groups of people to become involved in routinized organizational roles. Ibid., p. 514.

22. Interview, March 20, 1969.

23. In 1966, New York City's Department of Welfare was renamed the Department of Social Services.

24. Rabagliati and Birnbaum, p. 129.

25. Interview, March 20, 1969.

26. Ibid.

27. Emergency Council for Winter Clothing, mimeographed sheet of demands, November 1, 1966.

28. Rabagliati and Birnbaum, p. 129.

29. Telegram sent by the Emergency Council for Winter Clothing to Commissioner Mitchell I. Ginsberg, November 1966.

30. Memo from Ezra Birnbaum to Sherman Barr, "Notes on the Meeting of the Emergency Welfare Council with Commissioner Ginsberg," November 23, 1966.

31. Letter sent from Commissioner of Welfare, Mitchell I. Ginsberg, to local welfare center officials, November 16, 1966. This letter was released to the public by the Department of Social Services.

32. Directive, New York City, Department of Welfare, Informational No. 66-48, November 18, 1966.

33. *The New York Times*, November 20, 1966.

34. Directive from Commissioner Mitchell I. Ginsberg to the New York City welfare department staff, November 18, 1966.

35. Rabagliati and Birnbaum, p. 129.

36. Ibid.

37. Memorandum from Bertram Beck, executive director of MFY, to the Executive Committee of the Board and Executive Staff, "Problems in the Organization of Welfare Clients," November 17, 1966, p. 11.

38. Ibid., pp. 13-14.

39. Ibid., p. 7

Chapter 9
Creation of a City-Wide Movement

1. This chapter draws on a number of interviews with key participants in City-Wide between 1966 and 1968.

2. Memo from Jeanette Washington to Tim Sampson, NWRO, "Notes about the Organizational Problems of City-Wide," City-Wide files, March 13, 1967, p. 1.

3. Ibid., p. 4.

4. Interview, March 11, 1969.

5. Interview, January 13, 1969.

6. Jeanette Washington, p. 1.

7. The following account of the Brooklyn Welfare Action Council draws heavily on a series of interviews with client leaders and staff organizers who were influential in the council's formation.

8. Letter from Rhoda Linton to the various Brooklyn groups, August 2, 1967. This letter stresses the need for group action at the local welfare centers. Letter from Rhoda Linton to the various client groups, August 10, 1967. This letter discusses City-Wide's organizational activities such as the pre-NWRO convention conference of August 19, 1967. BWAC files.

9. The Brooklyn Advisors Forum was also organized at this time. At the first meetings, Richard Cloward and Frances Fox Piven were the guest speakers. Letter from Rhoda Linton to the client group advisors, August 4, 1967. BWAC files.

10. This was partly due to the fact that the welfare department, in response to heavy demands, had designated all clothing as emergency items, thus eliminating home visits and the two-week waiting period. BWAC's organizer claimed that from September 11 through September 15, the campaign helped 2,000 to 3,000 clients get $50,000 in school clothing grants. By September 26, the amount was put at $100,000. Letters to client groups from Rhoda Linton, September 19, 1967 and September 26, 1967. BWAC files.

11. By December, the BWAC-affiliated groups claimed a membership of 2,025. See "BWAC Membership Memorandum," December 5, 1967. BWAC files.

12. The planning committee held its initial session on October 12, 1967. "Report on Minutes on the Planning Session Committee," October 14, 1967. BWAC files.

13. Report of the Minutes of the Planning Committee, October 20, 1967 and October 31, 1967.

14. Article II, "Statement of Purpose," BWAC Constitution, adopted November 9, 1967.

15. Article V, "Officers."

16. Letter from George Wiley to Beulah Sanders, December 27, 1966. NWRO files.

17. Representing the local unions were Victor Gotbaum, Sumner Rosen, Al Viani, Pat Caldwell, Monte Wasch, John Coleman, Lillian Roberts, Sidney Bykofsky, and Michael O'Prey. Representing the clients were George Wiley and Beulah Sanders. "Minutes of the Meeting between Union Officials and the City-Wide Committee of Welfare Rights Groups," July 6, 1967, City-Wide files. A second meeting was held on July 17, 1967.

18. For example, Local 1199 of the Drug and Hospital Employees voted to contribute $50 per month for one year. The Fur, Leather, and Machine Workers' Union contributed $150 to finance a bus to send the New York Delegation to NWRO's founding convention. Local 420 of the American Federation of State, County and Municipal Employees also made periodic contributions.

Chapter 10
The Movement at Its Peak

1. The following discussion draws heavily on interviews with various welfare rights officials in 1968 and 1969. See also Dave Gilman and Ezra Birnbaum, "Report on New York City Minimum Standards-Fair Hearings Campaigns, June-December 1967," December 1967. Because City-Wide was without a staff

director, Gilman and Birnbaum were assigned the task of planning and coordinating the campaign by Beulah Sanders and the City-Wide Executive Board.

2. Gilman and Birnbaum, p. 1.

3. City of New York, Department of Social Services, Procedure 66-26 (Caseworker's notebook), August 19, 1966; see, also, *The New York Times*, August 12, 1966.

4. Chairman of the State Board of Social Welfare, quoted in *The New York Times*, July 22, 1967.

5. See letter from Beulah Sanders to Felix Infausto, secretary of the New York State Board of Social Welfare, July 6, 1967; letter from Felix Infausto to Beulah Sanders, July 13, 1967; and "Summary of Testimony by Beulah Sanders Regarding the State Board of Social Welfare Hearings on Fair Hearing Regulations," Mimeographed press release, July 21, 1967. City-Wide relied heavily on its legal allies for guidance and technical assistance. See "An Analysis of the New Rules Governing Welfare Proposed by the State Board of Social Welfare and the Subject of Public Hearings," Unpublished paper by the Columbia University Center on Social Welfare Policy and Law, New York, July 21, 1967; Bernard E. Harvith, "Procedural Safeguards Increased by Changes in Regulations Governing Fair Hearings Before State Agencies for Categorical Assistance Claimants," New York University Project on Social Welfare Law; December 1967 and testimony by Professor Stanley Zimmerman, legal director, Project on Social Welfare Law, New York University School of Law, at State Board of Social Welfare hearings on proposed rules for fair hearings, July 21, 1967.

6. New York State, State Department of Social Services, *Bulletin No. 128*, February 26, 1968; New York State Board of Social Welfare, Press release, January 16, 1968.

7. This increase in the number of fair hearings requests was recognized by the state as having stemmed from City-Wide's activities. See letter from Virgil J.M. Doyle, Family Services Division, Department of Social Services, New York City Area Office, to Beulah Sanders, November 30, 1967. This letter acknowledged the receipt of 1045 requests, but found that, after duplicates, Home Relief recipients, and unsigned petitions were eliminated, only 839 requests were legitimate.

8. Gilman and Birnbaum, *Report*, p. 5.

9. City-Wide official, quoted in *U.S. News and World Report*, October 30, 1967, p. 37.

10. Gilman and Birnbaum, *Report*, p. 5.

11. See, for example, *New York Daily News*, October 26, 1967.

12. An example was an attempted sit-in at an Arden House conference on welfare problems attended by leading business executives, labor leaders, and educators. The conference was sponsored by Governor Rockefeller. See *New York Daily News*, November 4, 1967.

13. *New York Daily News*, October 25, 26, and 27, 1967.

14. *New York Daily News.* October 25, 1967, p. 2.

15. For example, see *The New York Times* of June 27, 1967, June 30, 1967, August 27, 1967, October 3, 1967, November 4, 1967, and November 22, 1967; *The New York Post*, July 19, 1967 and December 20, 1967; *New York Daily News*, June 30, 1967, October 3, 1967, and November 4, 1967; *The Christian Science Monitor*, June 30, 1967; and *U.S. News and World Report*, October 30, 1967.

16. Since 1966, City-Wide published and distributed to its membership a newsletter, *Tell It Like It Is* (its name was later changed to the *Welfare Fighter*). The Brooklyn Welfare Action Council published its own newsletter, *Knick Nac.* Several local groups also put out newsletters and pamphlets.

Chapter 11
The End of an Era

1. Gilman and Birnbaum, *Report*, p. 6.

2. NWRO, "Report on Welfare Rights Organizations," Conference on Minimum Standards Campaigns, Washington, D.C., January 12-13, 1968.

3. George Wiley, "Draft Memo on the New York Minimum Standard-Fair Hearings Campaign," NWRO files, October 18, 1967, p. 3.

4. Ibid., p. 3.

5. Rhoda Linton, "Leadership Training Project of BWAC," undated BWAC report, p. 1. The Catholic Charities provided funds for both materials and the salaries of instructors.

6. Ibid., p. 4.

7. Ibid., pp. 6-7.

8. Goldberg, quoted in *The New York Times*, May 30, 1968.

9. Ibid.

10. Ibid.

11. *The New York Times*, July 1, 1968.

12. Ibid. See, also, *New York Post*, June 25, 1968, and *The New York Times*, June 26, 1968.

13. The demonstrators, besides seeking better treatment and increased welfare benefits, demanded the elimination of Operation Compass, a program of job counseling for "improperly motivated" clients. *The New York Times*, July 2, 1968.

14. The center was unable to reopen until after a conference between Hulbert James, State Assemblyman Samuel Wright, and Louis Levitt, executive assistant to the commissioner. See *The New York Times*, July 16, 1968.

15. *The New York Times*, July 4, 1968.

16. *The New York Times*, July 15, 1968.

17. *The New York Times*, July 15, 1968.

18. See city of New York, Department of Social Services, Procedure 68-17 (Caseworker's notebook), May 20, 1968.

19. *New York Post*, July 15, 1968.

20. *New York Post*, July 16 and 17, 1968; *New York Post*, August 14, 1968; and *The New York Times*, August 14, 1968.

21. Lawrence Podell, *Families on Welfare in New York City*.

22. *The New York Times*, August 18, 1968.

23. *The New York Times*, June 26, 1968.

24. *New York Post*, June 27, 1968; see also the *New York Daily News*, June 28, 1968.

25. *New York Daily News*, June 27, 1968.

26. *The New York Times*, July 3, 1968; *New York Daily News*, July 3, 1968.

27. *The New York Times*, July 24, 1968. Beulah Sanders' threat was echoed by Joyce Berson, then BWAC Chairman. See *New York Daily News*, June 27, 1968.

28. *The New York Times*, August 27, 1968; *New York Daily News*, August 27, 1968. The flat grant began as a demonstration project under Sec. 1115 of the Federal Social Security Act. See City of New York, Department of Social Services, Procedure 68-65 (Caseworker's notebook), August 27, 1968.

29. *The New York Times*, August 27, 1968.

30. City-Wide's reaction was completely anticipated by the city's Department of Social Services. See City of New York, Department of Social Services, Procedure 68-65 (Caseworker's notebook), August 27, 1968, p. 2.

31. *The New York Times*, August 27, 1968.

32. *The New York Times*, August 28, 1968; *New York Daily News*, August 28, 1968.

33. *The New York Times*, August 30, 1968.

34. At another center, Bushwick in Brooklyn, 300 protestors marched from the intake section to the staff's working quarters, whereupon staff members walked out and stood on the sidewalk as supervisors called the police. *The New York Times*, August 31, 1968.

35. *The New York Times*, August 30, 1968.

36. For example, at the beginning of the second week of demonstrations, Harlem CORE led a demonstration by 300 recipients at the St. Nicholas Center. The center was closed. *The New York Times*, September 4, 5, and 6, 1968.

37. *The New York Times*, September 18, 1968; see also, *New York Daily News*, September 18, 1968.

38. *New York Daily News*, September 19, 1968; *The New York Times*, September 19, 1968.

39. *The New York Times*, September 19, 1968; *New York Daily News*, September 19, 1968.

Chapter 12
The Impact of the Welfare Rights Movement
on the City's Welfare System

1. Edward C. Banfield, "Welfare: A Crisis without 'Solutions'," *The Public Interest* 16 (Summer 1969): 93.

2. Bernard M. Shiffman, and Abraham C. Burstein, "Migration, Residential Mobility and Welfare Policy," Paper prepared for a conference sponsored by the Research Institute on the Social Welfare Consequences of Migration and Residential Movement, San Juan, Puerto Rico, November 2-5, 1969, p. 3.

3. Social Scientists' Committee on Welfare and Social Policy, "Public Welfare in New York City: A Critique of the Podell Report," 1969, p. 15.

4. Cloward and Piven, *Social Policy*, p. 48.

5. Committee on Ways and Means, U.S. House of Representatives, *Report of Findings on a Special Review of Aid to Families with Dependent Children in New York City*, p. 49.

6. Maryland State Department of Public Welfare, pp. 35-37.

7. Lawrence Podell, "The Increase in Public Welfare in New York City," *Public Welfare in Transition: Report of the Joint Legislative Committee To Revise the Social Services Law of New York State*, New York State, Albany, Legislative Document No. 7, 1969, pp. 80-81.

8. Ibid., pp. 80-81.

Chapter 13
Decision Variables Affecting New York
City's Caseload

1. The former Welfare Commissioner, Mitchell Ginsberg, was dubbed "Come-and-Get-It-Ginsberg" by a local newspaper, suggesting what the paper believed to be a primary reason for the city's caseload increase. Lawrence Podell has also argued in this vein. Podell, however, is skeptical that liberalized acceptances were a result of conscious policy by New York City's Department of Social Services. Rather, he seems to favor the notion that they were the unintended consequence of "inexperienced executives, inadequate administrators, or indecisive decision-makers." Podell recognizes, nevertheless, that this variant of the liberalized acceptance thesis needs further research before it can be accepted or rejected as an explanation of the increase in New York City's welfare caseload (Podell, "The Increase in Public Welfare in New York City," pp. 92-93).

Chapter 14
Some Reasons for the Growth in Welfare
Dependency in New York City

1. For example, see Podell, "The Increase in Public Welfare in New York City," p. 80.

2. *Monthly Statistical Report*, various months. For a discussion of changes in New York City's grant levels over time, see Elizabeth Durbin, *Welfare and Employment* (New York: Praeger, 1969), pp. 80-101.

3. This point has been stressed by several writers concerned with the recent growth in the city's caseload. For example, see David M. Gordon, "Income and Welfare in New York City," *The Public Interest, Special Issue, Focus on New York* (Summer 1969), pp. 80-86.

4. For the seminal article on the subject, see C.T. Brehm and T.R. Saving, "The Demand for General Assistance Payments," *American Economic Review* (December 1964), pp. 1002-1018. See also, Bruno Stein and P.S. Albin, "The Demand for General Assistance Payments: Comment," *American Economic Review* (June 1967), pp. 575-85; Brehm and Saving, "The Demand for General Assistance Payments: Reply," *American Economic Review* (June 1967), pp. 585-88; and Leonard J. Hausman, "The Impact of Welfare on the Work Effort of AFDC Mothers," *Technical Papers*, President's Commission on Income Maintenance, U.S. Government Printing Office, Washington, D.C., 1970, pp. 83-100. The underlying theory of labor supply has also been widely discussed in the economics literature. For example, see Marvin Kosters, *Income and Substitution Effects in a Family Labor Supply Model*, The Rand Corporation, P-3339, December 1966; Jacob Mincer, "Labor Force Participation of Married Women," *Aspects of Labor Economics* (Princeton, N.J.: Princeton University Press, 1962), pp. 63-105; Glen G. Cain, *Married Women in the Labor Force*, The University of Chicago Press, Chicago, Illinois, 1966; William G. Bowen and T.A. Finnegan, "Labor Force Participation and Unemployment," Arthur M. Ross (ed.), *Employment Policy and the Labor Market* (Berkeley, Calif.: University of California Press, 1965), pp. 115-61; and Edward D. Kalachek and Fredric Q. Raines, "Labor Supply of Lower Income Workers," *Technical Report*, President's Commission on Income Maintenance, pp. 159-85.

5. This is true of the original study by Brehm and Saving as well as the reformulations by both Stein and Albin and Brehm and Saving. It is also true of other studies done in the spirit of the original Brehm and Saving article. For example, see Hirschel Kasper, "Welfare Payments and Work Incentives: Some Determinants of the Rates of General Assistance Payments," *The Journal of Human Resources* (Winter 1968), pp. 86-110.

6. This problem with existing studies has also been noted by Irwin Garfinkel, "Welfare Programs and Work Effort: A Critique of Existing Studies and a Pessimistic Prognosis," unpublished paper, University of Wisconsin (1970), p. 3.

7. These questions were at the center of the controversy surrounding the Podell Report. For example, see Podell, "The Increase in Public Welfare in New York City," pp. 81-96. See also, Social Scientists' Committee on Welfare and Social Policy, p. 13.

8. Unpublished study by I.N. Fisher of The Rand Corporation.

9. This argument is made by Oscar A. Ornati, *Transportation Needs of the Poor: A Case Study of New York City* (New York: Praeger, 1969), Ch. 4.

10. Committee on Ways and Means, U.S. House of Representatives, p. 59.

11. United States Department of Labor, Office of Policy Planning and Research, *The Negro Family: The Case for National Action* (Washington, D.C.: U.S. Government Printing Office, March 1965).

12. E. Franklin Frazier, *The Negro Family in the United States* (Chicago, Ill.: The University of Chicago Press, 1939).

13. For discussion of this phenomenon, see William A. Johnson, *Changing Patterns of Employment in the New York Metropolitan Area*, The New York City-Rand Institute, R-571-NYC, December 1971.

14. Minority employees accounted for about one-fourth of suburban job growth between 1962 and 1966 (ibid., sec. III).

Chapter 15
The Grant Level

1. For a discussion of the inequitable distribution of special grants, see Anna Berenson Mayer, "Consequences of the Policy of Individual Demonstrated Need," doctoral dissertation, Columbia University School of Social Work, 1968, p. 214.

Chapter 16
Acceptances, Applications, and Closings

1. For example, see Banfield, p. 93. The acceptance rate is defined as the percentage of applications acted upon that is accepted in any one month. An applicant must cross two hurdles. First, his application must pass through intake. Once past intake, it must then be accepted by the caseworker and/or unit director reviewing the case.

Chapter 17
Some Explanations for the Caseload
Increase in 1968

1. Cloward and Piven, "The Weight of the Poor, A Strategy to End Poverty," *The Nation* 202, no. 18 (May 2, 1966): 511.

Appendix A
A Model of Welfare Dependency in
New York City

1. There are many texts that discuss regression analysis. For an excellent introductory discussion of this method of analysis, see Lawrence R. Klein, *An Introduction to Econometrics* (Englewood Cliffs, N.J.: Prentice-Hall, 1962). See also J. Johnston, *Econometric Methods* (New York: McGraw-Hill Book Company, Inc., 1963).

2. We have also experimented with pooling time-series and cross-sectional data by inserting dummy variables for each month. The dummies were used as shift variables for both constant terms and regression coefficients. With a few exceptions, pooling increased substantially the total variance in grant levels, and the dummy variables explained most of the increased variance. In other words, there appears to be little justification for pooling. This is not too surprising given the substantial changes that occurred in welfare rights tactics and the administration of public assistance during the period. We did not have the time or the resources to experiment with other methods of pooling suggested, for example, by Balestra and Nerlove. See Pietro Balestra and Marc Nerlove, "Pooling Cross Section and Time Series Data in the Estimation of a Dynamic Model: The Demand for Natural Gas," *Econometrica* 34, no. 3 (July 1966): 585-612.

Appendix C
Families Eligible for AFDC in New York
City

1. Nora Piore and Sandra Sokal, *Disadvantaged Children in the Neighborhoods of New York City*, Urban Medical Economics Research Report, New York City Health Services Administration, August 1968.

2. Ibid., p. 14.

3. CONSAD Research Corporation, *Population and Housing Stock Small Area Forecasting Models: New York City Technical Report* (New York: CONSAD Research Corporation, June 1967), p. 32.

4. D.M. Fisk, "A Simple Model of the New York City Caseload," unpublished paper, The New York City-Rand Institute, September 1969.

5. Blanche Bernstein, "Welfare in New York City," *City Almanac* 4, no. 5 (February 1970): 5.

Abbreviations Used in the Text

AFDC	— Aid to Families with Dependent Children
AFDC-U	— Aid to Families with Dependent Children with an Unemployed Parent
BWAC	— Brooklyn Welfare Action Council
CAP	— Community Action Program
CATC	— Community Action Training Center
CDA	— Community Development Administration
CDI	— Community Development Incorporated
CFO	— Crusade for Opportunity
City-Wide	— City-Wide Coordinating Committee of Welfare Groups
CORE	— Congress of Racial Equality
CUNY	— City University of New York
CUSA	— Christian and Jews United for Social Action
CUSSW	— Columbia University School of Social Work
CWAG	— Citizens Welfare Action Group
CWF	— Committee of Welfare Families
DOSS	— Department of Social Services
HR	— Home Relief
HRA	— Human Resources Administration
IFC	— Interreligious Foundation for Community Organization
LENA	— Lower East Side Neighborhood Association
MFDP	— Mississippi Freedom Democratic Party
MFY	— Mobilization for Youth
NAACP	— The National Association for the Advancement of Colored People
NAC	— Neighborhood Action Center
NASHCO	— National Self-Help Corporation
NCC	— National Coordinating Committee of Welfare Rights Groups
NIMH	— National Institute of Mental Health
NLADA	— National Legal Aid and Defenders Association
NSC	— Neighborhood Service Center
NWRO	— National Welfare Rights Organization
OEO	— Office of Economic Opportunity
OJD	— Office of Juvenile Delinquency and Youth Development
PCJD	— President's Committee on Juvenile Delinquency
PRAC	— Poverty Rights Action Center
PWCAP	— The People's War Council Against Poverty
PWCAP-NY	— The People's War Council Against Poverty of New York
SCDA	— Syracuse Community Development Association
SCLC	— Southern Christian Leadership Conference

SIF	— Services to Individuals and Families
SNCC	— Student Nonviolent Coordinating Committee
SSEU	— The Social Services Employees Union
TADC	— Temporary Aid to Dependent Children
UWL	— United Welfare League
WAGAP	— Welfare Action Group Against Poverty
WIN	— Work Incentive Program
WRO	— Welfare Rights Organization
WSWRL	— West Side Welfare Recipients League

Bibliography

Bibliography

Appleby, Michael. "Overview of Legal Services." In Harold Weissman (ed.), *Justice and the Law in the Mobilization for Youth Experience.* New York: Association Press, 1969.

Appleby, Michael, and Hiefetz, Henry. "Legal Challenge to Formal and Informal Services of Welfare Rights." In Harold Weissman (ed.), *Justice and the Law in the Mobilization for Youth Experience.* New York: Association Press, 1969.

Banfield, Edward C. "Welfare: A Crisis without 'Solutions.' " *The Public Interest* 16, (Summer 1969).

Banfield, Edward C., and Wilson, James Q. *City Politics.* Cambridge, Mass.: Harvard University Press, 1963.

Barr, Sherman. "Poverty and the Lower East Side," Mobilization for Youth Training Papers, vol. 4. New York: School of Social Work, Columbia University, May 17, 1965.

Bendick, Albert. "Privacy, Poverty, and the Constitution." In Jacobus TenBroek (ed.), *The Law of the Poor.* San Francisco: Chandler, 1966.

Bernstein, B. "Welfare in New York City." *City Almanac* 4, no. 5 (February 1970).

Bowen, William G., and Finnegan, T.A. "Labor Force Participation and Unemployment," Arthur M. Ross (ed.), *Employment Policy and the Labor Market.* Berkeley, California: University of California Press, 1965.

Braeger, George. "Influencing Institutional Change through a Demonstration Project: The Case of the Schools," Mobilization for Youth Training Papers, vol. 4. New York: School of Social Work, Columbia University, undated.

Brehm, C.T., and Saving, T.R. "The Demand for General Assistance Payments." *American Economic Review* 54, no. 6 (December 1964).

Brinton, Crane. *Anatomy of a Revolution.* New York: Vintage, 1965.

Brophy, Alice, and Hallowitz, George. "Pressure Groups and the Relief Administration in New York City." Master's thesis, New York School of Social Work, April 1937.

Brown, Claude. *Manchild in the Promised Land.* New York: Macmillan, 1965.

Brown, Gordon. *The Multi-Problem Dilemma.* Metuchen, New Jersey: Scarecrow Press, 1968.

Burgess, Margaret Elaine. *Negro Leadership in a Southern City,* Chapel Hill, North Carolina: University of North Carolina Press, 1962.

Cain, Glen G. *Married Women in the Labor Force.* Chicago, Ill.: The University of Chicago Press, 1966.

Caplovitz, David. *The Poor Pay More.* New York: Free Press, 1967.

Carlin, Jerome E. "Store Front Lawyers in San Francisco." *Transaction* 7, no. 6 (April 1970).

City of New York, Department of Social Services, Division of Statistics. *Monthly Statistical Report,* various months.

Clark, Kenneth B. *Dark Ghetto: Dilemmas of Social Power.* New York: Harper and Row, 1965.

Cloward, Richard A., and Elman, Richard M. "The Storefront on Stanton Street: Advocacy in the Ghetto." In George A. Braeger and Francis P. Purvell (eds.), *Community Action against Poverty.* New Haven, Conn.: College and University Press, 1967.

Cloward, Richard A., and Ohlin, Lloyd. *Delinquency and Opportunity.* Glencoe, Ill.: The Free Press, 1960.

Cloward, Richard A., and Piven, Frances Fox. "The Birth of a Movement." *The Nation* 204, no. 19 (May 8, 1967).

_____. "How the Federal Government Caused the Welfare Crisis." *Social Policy.* May-June 1971.

_____. "Mobilizing the Poor: How It Can Be Done," Mobilization for Youth Training Papers, vol. 4. New York: School of Social Work, Columbia University, 1965.

_____. *Regulating the Poor: The Functions of Public Welfare.* New York: Pantheon Books, 1971.

_____. "The Weight of the Poor, A Strategy to End Poverty." *The Nation* 202, no. 18 (May 2, 1966).

Coleman, James. *Community Conflict.* Glencoe, Ill.: The Free Press, 1957.

Columbia University. *Crisis at Columbia: Report of the Fact-Finding Commission Appointed to Investigate the Disturbances at Columbia University in April and May, 1968.* New York: Vintage Books, 1968.

Committee on Finance, U.S. Congress, Senate. *Hearings, Social Security Amendments of 1967.* 90th Cong., 1st sess., 1967.

Committee on Ways and Means, U.S. House of Representatives. *Report on Findings of a Special Review of Aid to Families with Dependent Children in New York City.* Washington, D.C.: U.S. Government Printing Office, September 24, 1969.

Comptroller-General of the United States. *Review of Economic Opportunity Programs.* Report to the Congress of the United States, 91st Cong., 1st sess., 1969.

CONSAD Research Corporation. *Population and Housing Stock Small Area Forecasting Models: New York City Technical Report.* New York: CONSAD Research Corporation, June 1967.

Dahl, Robert. *A Preface to a Democratic Theory.* Chicago, Ill.: University of Chicago Press, 1962.

_____. *Who Governs?* New Haven, Conn.: Yale University Press, 1961.

Davidson, R.H. "The War on Poverty: Experiment in Federalism." *Annals of the American Academy of Political and Social Science*, September 1969.

Deutsch, Karl. "Social Mobilization and Political Development," *American Political Science Review* 55, no. 3 (September 1961).

Donovan, John C. *The Politics of Poverty.* New York: Pegasus, 1967.

Durbin, Elizabeth. *Welfare and Employment*. New York: Praeger, 1969.

Eldersveld, Samuel I. "American Interest Groups: A Survey of Research and Some Implications for Theory and Method." In Henry W. Ehrmann (ed.), *Interest Groups on Four Continents*. Pittsburgh, Pa.: The University of Pittsburgh Press, 2d printing, 1960.

Elman, Richard M. *The Poorhouse State: The American Way of Life on Public Assistance*. New York: Pantheon, 1966.

Essien-Udom, E.U. *Black Nationalism, A Search for Identity in America*. Chicago, Ill.: University of Chicago Press, 1962.

Etzioni, Amitai. "Demonstration Democracy." Paper prepared for the Task Force on Demonstrations, Protests, and Group Violence of the President's National Commission on the Causes and Prevention of Violence, Washington, D.C., November 18, 1968.

_____. *Modern Organizations*. Englewood Cliffs, N.J.: Prentice-Hall, Inc., 1964.

Executive Office of the President, Bureau of the Budget. "An Evaluation of the Thirteen Neighborhood Service Programs," A study of the Neighborhood Center Pilot Program," vols. I and II. Washington, D.C., April 1969.

Fisk, D.M. "A Simple Model of the New York City Caseload," unpublished paper, The New York City-Rand Institute, September 1969.

Frazier, E. Franklin. *The Negro Family in the United States*. Chicago, Ill.: The University of Chicago Press, 1939.

Garfinkel, J. "Welfare Programs and Work Effort: A Critique of Existing Studies and a Pessimistic Prognosis." Unpublished paper, University of Wisconsin, circa 1970.

Gell, Frank. *The Black Badge: Confessions of a Caseworker*. New York: Harper and Row, 1969.

Gillet, C.P. "The Church and the Welfare Crisis in New York." Unpublished paper by Committee of Welfare Families, New York, undated.

Glazer, Nathan. "Negroes and Jews: The New Challenge to Pluralism." *Commentary* 38, no. 6 (December 1964).

Gollin, Albert. *The Demography of Protest: A Statistical Profile of Participants in the Poor People's Campaign*. Washington, D.C.: Bureau of Social Science Research, 1969.

_____. "Poor People's Campaign and the March on Washington." Paper presented at the American Association for Public Opinion Research, May 1969.

Gordon, David M. "Income and Welfare in New York City." *The Public Interest, Special Issue, Focus on New York*. Summer 1969, pp. 80-86.

Graham, Hugh D., and Gurr, Ted Robert. *Violence in America: Historical and Comparative Perspectives*, vols. I and II. A Report to the National Commission on the Causes and Prevention of Violence. Washington, D.C.: U.S. Government Printing Office, June 1969.

Graham, James. "Civil Liberties in Welfare Administration." Unpublished report, New York University School of Law, Project on Welfare Law, 1968.

_____ . *The Enemies of the Poor.* New York: Random House, 1970.

Greenberg, David H. *Income Guarantees and the Working Poor in New York City: The Effect of Income Maintenance Programs on the Hours of Work of Male Family Heads.* The New York City-Rand Institute, R-658-NYC, March 1971.

_____ . *The Potential Impact of Family Assistance Plan on New York City,* The New York City-Rand Institute, R-658-NYC (Abridged), 1971.

Hamilton, Charles. "Conflict, Race and System Transformation in the United States." *Journal of International Affairs* 23 (1969).

_____ . *Minority Politics in Black Belt Alabama.* New York: Eagleton Institute Case Studies, 1960.

Handler, Joel. "Controlling Official Behavior in Welfare Administration." In Jacobus TenBroek (ed.), *The Law of the Poor.* San Francisco: Chandler, 1966.

Harrington, Michael. *The Other America.* New York: Macmillan, 1962.

Harris, Lew, and Associates, *Transition Neighborhoods in New York City: The People's View of Their Housing Environment.* Survey conducted for the Vera Institute of Justice, December 1969.

HARYOU (Harlem Youth Opportunities Unlimited). *Youth in the Ghetto: A Study of the Consequences of Powerlessness and a Blueprint for Change.* New York, 1964.

Hausman, Leonard J. "The Impact of Welfare on the Work Effort of AFDC Mothers." *Technical Papers,* President's Commission on Income Maintenance. Washington, D.C.: U.S. Government Printing Office, 1970.

Holtzmann, Abraham. *The Townsend Movement.* New York: Bookman Associates, 1963.

Horwitz, Julius. *The Inhabitants.* New York: World, 1960.

Hyman, Herbert; Wright, Charles; and Hopkins, Terrence. *Applications of Methods of Evaluation: Four Studies of the Encampment of Citizenship.* Berkeley, Calif: University of California Press, 1962.

Johnson, William A. *Changing Patterns of Employment in the New York Metropolitan Area.* The New York City-Rand Institute, R-571-NYC, December 1971.

Joint Economic Committee, Subcommittee on Fiscal Policy, U.S. Congress. *Hearings, Income Maintenance Programs.* 90th Cong., 2d sess., 1968.

Jones, Harry W. "The Role of Law and the Welfare State." *Columbia Law Review* 58 (1958).

Jones, Hettie. "Neighborhood Service Centers." In Harold Weissman (ed.), *Individual and Group Services in the Mobilization for Youth Experience.* New York: Association Press, 1969.

_____ . "Overview of Services to Individuals and Families." In Harold Weissman (ed.), *Individual and Group Services in the Mobilization for Youth Experience*. New York: Association Press, 1969.

Kalachek, E.D., and Raines, F.Q. "Labor Supply of Lower Income Workers." *Technical Report*, President's Commission on Income Maintenance. Washington, D.C.: U.S. Government Printing Office.

Kasper, Hirschel. "Welfare Payments and Work Incentives: Some Determinants of the Rates of General Assistance Payments." *The Journal of Human Resources* (Winter 1968).

Keech, William R. *The Impact of Negro Voting: The Role of the Vote in the Quest for Equality*. Chicago, Ill.: Rand McNally, 1968.

Killian, Lewis, and Grigg, Charles. *Racial Crisis in America, Leadership in Conflict*. Englewood Cliffs, N.J. Prentice-Hall, Inc., 1964.

Kirschner Associates. *A Description and Evaluation of Neighborhood Centers*. Report for the Office of Economic Opportunity, December 1966.

Kosters, Marvin. *Income and Substitution Effects in a Family Labor Supply Model*. The Rand Corporation, P-3339, December 1966.

Krosney, Herbert. *Beyond Welfare: Poverty in the Supercity*, New York: Holt, Rinehart and Winston, 1966.

Lagner, Thomas S. et al. "Psychiatric Impairment in Welfare and Non-Welfare Children." *Welfare in Review* 7, no. 2 (March-April 1969).

Lane, Robert E. *Political Life: Why People Get Involved in Politics*. Glencoe, Ill.: Free Press, 1959.

LeJeune, Robert. "Illness Behaviour among the Urban Poor." Ph.D. dissertation. New York: Columbia University, 1968.

Levine, Robert A. *Poor Ye Need Not Have with You: Lessons from the War on Poverty*. Cambridge, Mass.: MIT Press, 1970.

Levinson, Perry. "The Next Generation: A Study of Children in AFDC Families." *Welfare in Review* 7, no. 2 (March-April 1969).

Levitan, Sar. *The Great Society's Poor Law: A New Approach to Poverty*. Baltimore, Md.: Johns Hopkins Press, 1969.

Lindsay, John. *The City*. New York: W.W. Norton and Company, Inc., 1970.

Lipset, Seymour M. *Political Man*. Garden City, N.Y.: Doubleday, 1960.

Lipsky, Michael. "Protest and Power in City Politics: A Study of Rent Strikes and Housing in New York City." Ph.D. dissertation, Princeton University, 1967.

_____. "Protest as a Political Resource." *American Political Science Review* 62 (December 1968).

_____. "Rent Strikes: Poor Man's Weapon." *Transaction* 6, no. 4 (February 1969).

Little, Malcolm. *The Autobiography of Malcolm X* New York: Grove Press, 1965.

Lowi, Theodore J. *The End of Liberalism: Ideology, Policy, and the Crisis of Public Authority*. New York: Norton, 1969.

Lowry, Ira S. *Rental Housing in New York City: Confronting the Crisis*, Vol. I. RM-6190-NYC, The New York City-Rand Institute, February 1970.

Lubell, Samuel. *The Hidden Crisis in American Politics*. New York: W.W. Norton and Company, 1970.

Lyford, Joseph. *The Airtight Cage*. New York: Harper and Row, 1966.

Marris, Peter, and Rein, Martin. *Dilemmas of Social Reform*. London: Routledge and K. Paul, 1967.

Marvick, Dwaine. "The Political Socialization of the American Negro." *The Annals of the American Academy of Political and Social Science* 361 (September 1965).

Maryland State Department of Public Welfare. "A Report on Caseload Increase in the Aid to Families with Dependent Children Program, 1960-1966." Research Report No. 2, Government of Maryland, July 1967.

Matthews, Donald, and Prothro, James. *Negroes and the New Southern Politics*. New York: Harcourt, Brace, and World, 1966.

Matusow, Allen J. "From Civil Rights to Black Power: The Case of SNCC, 1960-1966." In Barton J. Bernstein and Allen J. Matusow (eds.), *Twentieth Century America: Recent Interpretations*. New York: Harcourt and Brace, 1969.

May, Edgar. *The Wasted Americans*. New York: Harper and Row, 1964.

Mayer, Anna Berenson. "Consequences of the Policy of Individual Demonstrated Need." Ph.D. dissertation. New York: Columbia University School of Social Work, 1968.

Mayer, Martin. *The Teacher's Strike, New York, 1968*, New York: Harper and Row, 1969.

McBarnette, Olvin. "A Study of Problems Confronting Children of Welfare Recipients Attending New York City Public Schools." Paper submitted to the New York City Human Resources Administration, September 1968.

Merton, Robert. *Social Theory and Social Structure*. Glencoe, Ill.: The Free Press, 1949.

Metropolitan Applied Research Center. *A Relevant War against Poverty: A Study of Community Action Programs and Observable Social Change*. New York, 1968.

Meyer, Henry J., and Borgatta, Edgar F. *An Experiment in Mental Patient Rehabilitation*. New York: Russell Sage Foundation, 1959.

Meyer, Henry J.; Borgatta, Edgar F.; and Jones, Wyatt C. *Girls at Vocational High, An Experiment in Social Work Intervention*. New York: Russell Sage Foundation, 1965.

Meyerson, Martin, and Banfield, Edward C. *Politics, Planning and the Public Interest*. Glencoe, Ill.: The Free Press, 1955.

Mincer, Jacob. "Labor Force Participation of Married Women." *Aspects of Labor Economics*, Princeton, N.J.: Princeton University Press, 1962.

Mobilization for Youth. "A Proposal for the Prevention and Control of

Delinquency by Expanding Opportunities." MFY Training Papers, Columbia University School of Social Work Library, 1961.

Moore, John E. "Controlling Delinquency." In Frederic N. Cleaveland and Associates, *Congress and Urban Problems*. Washington, D.C.: The Brookings Institution, 1969.

Moynihan, Daniel P. *Maximum Feasible Misunderstanding*. New York: Free Press, 1969.

_____. "The Professors and the Poor," *Commentary* 46, no. 2 (August 1968).

Muller, Jonas; Tobis, Jerome; and Kelman, Howard. "The Rehabilitation of Nursing Home Residents." *American Journal of Public Health* 53, no. 2 (February 1963).

Myrdal, Gunnar. *An American Dilemma*, 2nd ed., New York: Harper and Row, 1962.

National Commission on the Causes and Prevention of Violence. *Report*. Washington, D.C.: U.S. Government Printing Office, June 1969.

National Welfare Rights Organization. "A Brief History of the National Welfare Rights Organization." *NOW!* Washington, D.C.: NWRO official publication, February 9, 1968.

_____. "Goals of the National Welfare Rights Organization." *NOW!* Washington, D.C.: NWRO official publication, undated.

_____. "How the NWRO Works." *NOW!* Washington, D.C.: NWRO official publication, February 14, 1969.

_____. "How to Start a WRO." *NOW!* Washington, D.C.: NWRO official publication, March 25, 1968.

_____. "Mother Power." *NOW!* Washington, D.C.: NWRO official publication, June 6, 1968.

_____. "The 1967 Anti-Welfare Social Security Amendments Law." *NOW!* Washington, D.C.: NWRO official publication, December 29, 1967.

_____. "NWRO Battles Welfare Rights Enemy Number One: Wilbur Wills." *NOW!* Washington, D.C.: NWRO official publication, June 17, 1968.

_____. "NWRO National Constitution." *NOW!* Washington, D.C.: NWRO official publication, August 25, 1967.

_____. "President Johnson Signs Anti-Welfare Bill into Law." *NOW!* Washington, D.C.: NWRO official publication, February 2, 1968.

_____. "Questions and Answers about the New Anti-Welfare Law." *NOW!* Washington, D.C.: NWRO official publication, February 21, 1968.

_____. "Report on Welfare Rights Organizations," Conference on Minimum Standard Campaigns, January 12-13, 1968.

_____. "Rights You Should Know." *NOW!* Washington, D.C.: NWRO official publication, March 11, 1968.

_____. "Summary Report: Welfare Action Meeting." Mimeographed. Chicago, Ill.: May 21, 1966.

_____. "Summary Report of National Welfare Rights Meeting." Mimeographed. Chicago, Ill.: August 6-7, 1966.

National Welfare Rights Organization. "The Welfare WIP Program and You." *NOW!* Washington, D.C.: NWRO official publication, June 17, 1968.

_____. "Why Is the National Welfare Rights Organization Opposed to the Family Assistance Plan?" *NOW!* Washington, D.C.: NWRO official publication, February 21, 1971.

New York City Housing and Development Administration, *The East Harlem Triangle: A Sociological and Economic Study*, vols. 1 and 2. Report for HDA submitted by the Social Dynamics Corporation, May 1968.

New York City Youth Board. *An Experiment in the Use of the Glueck Social Prediction Table as a Prognosticator of Potential Delinquency.* City of New York, October 1961.

Olson, Mancur, Jr. *The Logic of Collective Action: Public Goods and the Theory of Groups.* Cambridge, Mass.: Harvard University Press, 1965.

O'Neil, Robert M. "Unconstitutional Conditions: Welfare Benefits with Strings." In Jacobus TenBroek (ed.), *The Law of the Poor.* San Francisco: Chandler, 1966, pp. 119-154.

Oppenheimer, Martin. "The Genesis of the Southern Negro Student Movement." Ph.D. dissertation, University of Pennsylvania, 1963.

Orbell, John. "Protest Participation among Southern Negro College Students." *American Political Science Review* 61 (June 1967).

Ornati, Oscar A. *Transportation Needs of the Poor: A Case Study of New York City.* New York: Praeger, 1969.

Orshansky, Mollie. "Children of the Poor." *Social Security Bulletin*, 26, no. 7 (July 1963).

_____. "More about the Poor in 1964." *Social Security Bulletin* 29, no. 5 (May 1966).

_____. "Recounting the Poor: A Five Year Review," *Social Security Bulletin* 29, no. 4 (April 1966).

_____. "Who's Who among the Poor: A Demographic View of Poverty." *Social Security Bulletin* 28, no. 7 (July 1965).

Paull, Joseph. "Recipients Aroused: The New Welfare Rights Movement." *Social Work* 12, no. 2 (1967).

Perlman, Robert, and Jones, David. *Neighborhood Service Centers.* Washington, D.C.: Office of Juvenile Delinquency, Welfare Administration, U.S. Department of Health, Education, and Welfare, 1967.

Peterson, Paul. "City Politics and Community Action: The Implementation of Community Action Programs in Three American Cities." Ph.D. dissertation, Division of the Social Sciences, University of Chicago, 1967.

_____. "Forms of Representation: Participation of the Poor in the Community Action Programs." *American Political Science Review* 64, no. 2 (June 1970).

Piore, Nora, and Sokal, Vandra. *Disadvantaged Children in the Neighborhoods of New York City.* New York: Urban Medical Economics Research Report, New York City Health Services Administration, August 1968.

Pious, Richard. "Advocates for the Poor: The Legal Service Program in the War on Poverty, 1964-69." Ph.D. dissertation, Columbia University, New York, 1970.

Piven, Frances Fox. "Conceptual Themes in the Evolution of Mobilization for Youth." Mobilization for Youth Training Papers, vol. 8. New York: School of Social Work Library, Columbia University, May 17, 1965.

_____. "The Great Society as Political Strategy." *Columbia Forum.* Summer 1970.

Podell, Lawrence. *Families on Welfare in New York City.* New York: The Center for the Study of Urban Problems, City University of New York, 1968.

_____. "The Increase in Public Welfare in Transition: Report of the Joint Legislative Committee to Revise the Social Services Law of New York State." Albany, Legislative Document No. 7, 1969.

_____. *Studies in the Use of Health Services by Families on Welfare: Population Comparisons.* New York: The Center for the Study of Urban Problems, City University of New York, 1969.

Pomeroy, Richard; LeJeune, Robert; and Podell, Lawrence. *Studies in the Use of Health Services by Families in Welfare: Utilization by Publicly Assisted Families.* New York: The Center for the Study of Urban Problems, City University of New York. 1969.

Poverty Rights Action Center. "Prospectus for the Establishment of an Anti-Poverty Civil Rights Center." Mimeographed, May 1, 1966.

Powers, Edwin, and Witmer, Helen. *An Experiment in the Prevention of Delinquency – The Cambridge-Somerville Youth Study.* New York: Columbia University Press, 1951.

President's Committee on Juvenile Delinquency. *Report to the President.* Washington, D.C.: U.S. Government Printing Office, 1962.

Rabagliati, Mary, and Birnbaum, Ezra. "Organizations of Welfare Clients." In Harold H. Weissman (ed.), *Community Development in the Mobilization for Youth Experience.* New York: Association Press.

Reich, Charles. "Individual Rights and Social Welfare: The Emerging Legal Issues." *Yale Law Journal* 74 (1965).

_____. "Midnight Welfare Searches and the Social Security Act." *Yale Law Journal* 72 (1963).

_____. "The New Property." *Yale Law Journal* 73 (1964).

Rogers, David. *110 Livingston Street.* New York: Random House, 1968.

Rothman, Jean H. "Welfare Rights in the 1930's and 1960's," master's thesis, New York University, 1969.

Rubin, Lillian. "Maximum Feasible Participation: The Origins, Implementation, and Present Status." *Annals of the American Academy of Political and Social Science* (September 1969).

Rustin, Bayard. "From Protest to Politics: The Future of the Civil Rights Movement." *Commentary* 39, no. 2 (February 1965).

Sayre, Wallace, and Kaufman, Herbert. *Governing New York City.* New York: Norton, 1965.

Searles, Ruth, and Williams, J. Allen, Jr. "Negro College Students' Participation in Sit-ins." *Social Forces* 40 (March 1962).

Searles, Virginia C. "Cuyahoga County Relief Administration Clients as Members of the Unemployment Council." Master's thesis, Western Reserve University, Cleveland, Ohio, May 1965.

Sexton, Patricia Cayo. *Spanish Harlem: Anatomy of Poverty*. New York: Harper and Row, 1965.

Shaffer, Anatole, "Welfare Rights Organization: Friend or Foe?" *Social Work Practice*. New York: Columbia University Press.

Shea, Margaret C. "Helping Stations." New York: Mobilization for Youth Papers, School of Social Work, Columbia University, 5 (May 17, 1965).

Shiffman, Bernard M. and Burstein, Abraham C. "Migration, Residential Mobility and Welfare Policy." Paper prepared for a conference sponsored by the Research Institute on the Social Welfare Consequences of Migration and Residential Movement, San Juan, Puerto Rico, November 2-5, 1969.

Silberman, Charles. *Crisis in Black and White*. New York: Random House, 1964.

Skolnick, Jerome H. *The Politics of Protest*. New York: Simon and Schuster, 1969.

Smith, Brian. "The Role of the Poor in the Poverty Program: The Origin and Development of Maximum Feasible Participation." Master's thesis, Department of Political Science, Columbia University, 1966.

Social Scientists' Committee on Welfare and Social Policy. "Public Welfare in New York City: A Critique of the Podell Report." 1969, p. 3.

Stein, Bruno, and Albin, P.S. "The Demand for General Assistance Payments: Comments." *American Economic Review* (June 1967).

Steiner, Gilbert. *Social Insecurity: The Politics of Welfare*. Chicago, Ill.: Rand McNally, 1966.

Sternlieb, George. *The Urban Housing Dilemma: The Dynamics of New York City's Rent Controlled Housing*. Report submitted to the New York City Housing and Development Administration, May 1970.

Strange, John H. "The Negro in Philadelphia Politics, 1963-65." Ph.D. dissertation, Princeton University, 1966.

Thomas, Piri. *Down These Mean Streets*. New York: Alfred Knopf, 1967.

Thompson, Daniel. *The Negro Leadership Class*. Englewood Cliffs, N.J.: Prentice-Hall, Inc., 1963.

Truman, David B. *The Governmental Process*. New York: Alfred Knopf, 1963.

Urban Research Corporation. *A Summary of Student Protest, 1969*. Chicago, Ill., 1969.

_____. *The Tenants' Rights Movement*. Chicago, Ill., 1969.

U.S. Bureau of the Census. *1960 Census*. Washington, D.C.: U.S. Government Printing Office, 1961.

_____. *1970 Census*. Washington, D.C.: U.S. Government Printing Office, 1971.

U.S. Congress, Senate, Committee on Finance. *Hearings, Social Security Amendments of 1967*. 90th Cong., 1st sess., 1967.

U.S. Department of Health, Education, and Welfare. *Growing Up Poor*. Washington, D.C.: Welfare Administration, 1966.

_____. *Low-Income Life Styles*. Washington, D.C.: Welfare Administration, 1968.

_____. *Report of Findings of a Special Review of AFDC in New York City*. Report to the House Ways and Means Committee. Washington, D.C.: U.S. Government Printing Office, 1969.

_____. *The Role of Public Welfare in Housing*. Report to the House Committee on Ways and Means and the Senate Committee on Finance. Washington, D.C.: U.S. Government Printing Office, January 1969.

_____. Social and Rehabilitation Service, Assistance Payments Administration, *Trend Report: Graphic Presentation of Public Assistance and Related Data*. Washington, D.C.: U.S. Government Printing Office, 1966.

_____. National Center for Social Statistics, Social and Rehabilitation Service, *Public Assistance Statistics*. NCSS Report A-2, Washington, D.C.: U.S. Government Printing Office, 1970.

_____. Social Rehabilitation Service, Assistance Payments Administration. *Trend Report: Graphic Presentation of Public Assistance and Related Data*. Washington, D.C.: U.S. Government Printing Office, 1966.

U.S. Department of Labor, Office of Policy Planning and Research. *The Negro Family: The Case for National Action*. Washington, D.C.: U.S. Government Printing Office, March 1965.

U.S. Government Accounting Office. *Review of Economic Opportunity Programs*. Report to the Congress of the United States, 91st Cong., 1st sess., 1969.

Verba, Sidney. "Democratic Participation." *The Annals of the American Academy of Political and Social Science* 363 (September 1967).

Von Eschen, Donald; Kirk, Jerome; and Pinnard, Maurice. "The Conditions of Direct Action in a Democratic Society." *Western Political Quarterly* 22 (June 1969).

_____. "The Disintegration of the Negro Non-Violent Movement." *Journal of Peace Research* no. 3 (1969).

Walker, Jack L. "The Functions of Disunity: Negro Leadership in a Southern City." *Journal of Negro Education*. 32 (Summer 1963).

_____. "Protest and Negotiation: A Case Study of Negro Leadership in Atlanta, Georgia." *Midwest Journal of Political Science* 7, no. 2 (May 7, 1963).

_____. *Sit-ins in Atlanta: A Study in the Negro Protest*. New York: Eagleton Institute Case Studies, no. 34, 1964.

Weissman, Harold. "Overview of the Community Development Program." In Harold Weissman (ed.), *Community Development in the Mobilization for Youth Experience*. New York: Association Press, 1969.

Wilson, James Q. *Negro Politics, The Search for Leadership.* Glencoe, Ill.: The Free Press, 1960.

_____ . "The Negro in Politics." *Daedalus* 94, no. 4 (Fall 1965).

_____ . "The Strategy of Protest: Problems of Negro Civic Action." *Journal of Conflict Resolution* 3 (September 1961).

Witcover, J., and Knoll, E. "Politics and the Poor: Shriver's Second Thought." *Reporter*, December 30, 1965.

Wright, William E. *Memphis Politics: A Study in Racial Bloc Voting.* New York: Eagleton Institute Case Studies, no. 27, 1962.

Wrightstone, Jacob Wayne et al. *Evaluation of the Higher Horizons Program for Underprivileged Children.* New York: New York City Board of Education, 1964.

Yahr, Harold, and Pomeroy, Richard. *Studies in Public Welfare: Effects of Eligibility Investigation on Welfare Clients.* New York: The Center for the Study of Urban Problems, City University of New York, 1968.

Ylvisakar, P. "A Foundation Approach to City Problems." Paper presented at the 29th Annual National Conference, National Association of Housing and Development, October 1963.

Yurick, Sol. *The Bag.* New York: Simon and Schuster, 1968.

Index

Index

About the Authors

Larry R. Jackson is associated with Johnson and Marshall, Attorneys and Counsellors at Law, Jacksonville, Florida. He received the B.A. with honors from Morgan State College and the J.D. from Columbia University School of Law. A member of the Florida Bar Association, he is the author of articles which have appeared in the *Afro-American Studies Journal*, the *Journal of Black Studies*, *The Black Politician*, *Black Scholar*, and *Asian Survey*. He is a contributor to Byron Dexter, ed., *The Foreign Affairs Fifty-Year Bibliography: New Evaluations of Significant Books on International Relations, 1920-1970* (New York: Bowker, 1972).

William A. Johnson has been energy adviser to the Secretary of the Treasury, and Assistant Administrator for Policy Analysis and Evaluation, Federal Energy Office. He received the B.A. in economics from Syracuse University (where he was elected to Phi Beta Kappa) and the M.A. and Ph.D. in economics from Harvard University. Dr. Johnson is the author of *The Steel Industry in India* (Cambridge, Mass.: Harvard University Press, 1966) and numerous reports to The Rand Corporation concerning U.S. economic aid programs, military aid and defense planning, and urban problems. More recently he has authored several articles and presented a number of speeches concerning U.S. energy policy.

List of Selected Rand Books

Bagdikian, Ben H. THE INFORMATION MACHINES: THEIR IMPACT ON MEN AND THE MEDIA. New York: Harper and Row, 1971.

Bretz, Rudy. A TAXONOMY OF COMMUNICATION MEDIA. Englewood Cliffs, New Jersey: Educational Technology Publications, 1971.

Bruno, James E. (ed.) EMERGING ISSUES IN EDUCATION: POLICY IMPLICATIONS FOR THE SCHOOLS. Lexington, Mass.: D.C. Heath and Company, 1972.

Dalkey, Norman (ed.) STUDIES IN THE QUALITY OF LIFE: DELPHI AND DECISIONMAKING. Lexington, Mass.: D.C. Heath and Company, 1972.

Davies, Merton E. and Bruce C. Murray. THE VIEW FROM SPACE: PHOTOGRAPHIC EXPLORATION OF THE PLANETS. New York: Columbia University Press, 1971.

DeSalvo, Joseph S. (ed.) PERSPECTIVES ON REGIONAL TRANSPORTATION PLANNING. Lexington, Mass.: D.C. Heath and Company, 1973.

Downs, Anthony. INSIDE BUREAUCRACY. Boston, Mass.: Little, Brown and Company, 1967.

Johnson, William A. THE STEEL INDUSTRY OF INDIA. Cambridge, Mass.: Harvard University Press, 1966.

McCall, John J. INCOME MOBILITY, RACIAL DISCRIMINATION, AND ECONOMIC GROWTH. Lexington, Mass.: D.C. Heath and Company, 1973.

Meyer, John R., Martin Wohl, and John F. Kain. THE URBAN TRANSPORTATION PROBLEM. Cambridge, Mass.: Harvard University Press, 1965.

Novick, David (ed.) CURRENT PRACTICE IN PROGRAM BUDGETING (PPBS): ANALYSIS AND CASE STUDIES COVERING GOVERNMENT AND BUSINESS. New York: Crane, Russak and Co., Inc., 1973.

Novick, David (ed.) PROGRAM BUDGETING: PROGRAM ANALYSIS AND THE FEDERAL BUDGET. Cambridge, Mass.: Harvard University Press, 1965.

Pascal, Anthony H. (ed.) RACIAL DISCRIMINATION IN ECONOMIC LIFE. Lexington, Mass.: D.C. Heath and Company, 1972.

Pascal, Anthony H. THINKING ABOUT CITIES: NEW PERSPECTIVES ON URBAN PROBLEMS. Belmont, California: Dickenson Publishing Company, 1970.

Williams, John D. THE COMPLEAT STRATEGYST: BEING A PRIMER ON THE THEORY OF GAMES OF STRATEGY. New York: McGraw-Hill Book Co., Inc., 1954.